Eleanora's Kitchen

Eleanora's Kitchen

125 Fabulous Authentic Italian-American Recipes

Eleanora Russo Scarpetta

WITH SARAH BELK KING

BROADWAY BOOKS

NEW YORK

BROADWAY

ELEANORA'S KITCHEN. Copyright © 2004 by Eleanora Russo Scarpetta. All rights reserved. No part of this book may be reproduced or transmitted in any form or by any means, electronic or mechanical, including photocopying, recording, or by any information storage and retrieval system, without written permission from the publisher. For information, address Broadway Books, a division of Random House, Inc.

PRINTED IN THE UNITED STATES OF AMERICA

BROADWAY BOOKS and its logo, a letter B bisected on the diagonal, are trademarks of Random House, Inc.

Visit our website at www.broadwaybooks.com

Book design by Elizabeth Rendfleisch
Photographs by Mark Thomas

First edition published 2004

Library of Congress Cataloging-in-Publication Data
Scarpetta, Eleanora Russo.
Eleanora's kitchen : 125 fabulous authentic Italian-American recipes /
Eleanora Russo Scarpetta with Sarah Belk King.
p. cm.
Includes index.
1. Cookery, American. 2. Cookery, Italian. I. King, Sarah Belk. II. Title.

TX715.S288 2004
641.5945—dc21
2003051800

ISBN 0-7679-1221-7

1 3 5 7 9 10 8 6 4 2

This book is dedicated to my beloved mother,
Rosina Falzarano Russo, whose lifetime of knowledge and
expertise as a dedicated homemaker instilled in me a sense
of the beauty and importance of traditional cooking.

CONTENTS

ACKNOWLEDGMENTS

My gratitude and appreciation to Martha Stewart for giving me the opportunity to share my traditional recipes and for encouraging me to write my first cookbook.

Special thanks to my loving husband, Michael, who has shown his never-ending support, thus allowing me to follow my dreams; to my precious daughters, Juliet and Danielle, for having patience while I worked on my cookbook; and to my adorable son, Steven, who always gave me "thumbs up" after each meal.

Grazie tanto to my sister Maria Domenica Vairo (another marvelous cook), for sharing with me memorable family anecdotes along with her knowledge of our traditional Neapolitan foods.

Ciao to my *cara cugina* Maria Domenica Barbato—from my hometown, Cervinara, and a dedicated "home cook" like myself—to whom I give sincere thanks for both enlightening and inspiring me to stretch my cooking imagination. *"Until we meet again in Italy . . ."*

Respectful thanks to my godfather, Guerrino Lupetin, "a splendid chef," and to my godmother, Nicolina, for all their advice in my new ventures.

Tante grazie to my old friends and neighbors, Maria and Giustino Pagano, for sharing with me their warm hospitality, their canning tips, and their homemade wine. I will always treasure their friendship. (This calls for more homemade Champagne.)

Warmest thanks to my splendid writer, Sarah Belk King, for putting her heart and soul into helping me share the recipes and anecdotes of my beloved Neapolitan cuisine. I thank her especially for joining me on a visit to my hometown and family in Italy.

A huge thank-you to my fine and gracious editor, Jennifer Josephy, for recognizing my cooking talents, loving my food, and truly believing in my potential.

A big thanks to a wonderful man, Al Roker, for his professional guidance and his great sense of humor.

Thanks to my business consultants, Kathy Yacovelli and Michael Stone, for their keen direction with my website and for all their constant encouragement and praise.

Many thanks to Terry Barnes from Smithfield for helping me to rediscover the delicious taste of pork. Ribs will never be the same again.

Buon appetito! to Emanuelle and the Bariani family for their generosity in providing me with California's finest virgin olive oil and sharing a common love for the flavors of great Italian food.

Thank you to my good friend Margaret Lee for peeling all the garlic and never saying no to my food.

Much appreciation to my agent, Janis Donnaud, for her professionalism, support, and expert advice on writing my first cookbook.

Thanks to David Nussbaum for his role as a consultant in the editing of my recipes.

Bravo to photographer extraordinaire Mark Thomas, who brilliantly used his amazing artistic abilities to capture the essence of my southern Italian cuisine.

—Eleanora Scarpetta

Dear Eleanora, thank you for introducing me to your beautiful home-town, Cervinara. I have always been an Italophile, but now, because of your book, I'm even more so. Your Turkey Wing Broth, Taralli con Finocchetti, and other delicious dishes will always be staples in my home. Thank you for trusting me to work on your beloved culinary heirlooms; I know they hold a very special place in your heart. Thanks, too, to my ace editor, Jennifer Josephy, and to my agent, Janis Donnaud, who introduced me to Eleanora. *Grazie mille.*

—Sarah Belk King

INTRODUCTION

*F*ood is a beautiful thing in an Italian family. Neapolitans, especially, live for food and enjoy it with passion; they consider it fuel for life and look forward to every meal. After all, what is life without good food? I come from the very heart of Italy, so my love for Italian food is in my blood. Although I moved to America as a young child, I have vivid memories of the sights, sounds, aromas, and flavors of those early years in Cervinara, a province of Avellino, near Naples. The sun-kissed valleys in my hometown are blessed with rich, dark volcanic soil, which nourishes vegetable gardens and fruit orchards for some of the best-tasting produce imaginable. The woods are replete with wild mushrooms, pheasant, quail, and rabbit; the countryside is filled with the beauty of hazelnut, cherry, fig, and chestnut trees and the fragrant aroma of wild oregano.

Every time I return to Cervinara for a visit, I realize how fortunate I am to have such a rich culinary heritage. Not only is there a wealth of indigenous ingredients, but mealtime is of central importance, especially during the holidays and for family gatherings. The combination of this legacy, my down-to-earth cooking style, and my uncompromising *sfiziosa* personality has resulted in a collection of delicious dishes for everyday meals and festive entertaining. *Sfiziosa* means "whim or fancy"—my cooking style has often been described as *sfiziosa* since I frequently take classic dishes and traditional methods a step or two further for added flavor. But the changes I've made to some old-fashioned dishes never detract from their fresh, authentic, unpretentious style.

My love for food began at an early age. (I was the youngest of seven children, with four older sisters and two brothers: Maria Domenica, Luigia, Rocco, Giuseppe, Natalina, and Anna.) Weighing twelve and a half pounds at birth, I was, needless to say, a big baby. They called me *Bambolona,* which means "large baby doll." From the very beginning, my family noticed that I had a healthy appetite, but even so, I was very particular about the foods I enjoyed. It seems as though my passion for food and cooking was destined from the very beginning!

When I was three, my family moved to the United States to make a new home. We lived on 118th Street in Harlem for a little over a year before moving to Belmont Avenue in the Bronx, where we would live for seventeen years. When I was twenty-one, we moved to the northeast section of the Bronx, where I would eventually meet my husband, Michael, get married, and start a family. After enjoying our many years of the excitement and stresses of the city, my husband and I yearned for a change; we wanted a taste of the country life and decided to move north to Connecticut with our three children, Juliet, Danielle, and Steven.

Even with a healthy appetite and a craving for delicious food, I still would not have mastered the art of Italian cooking had it not been for my mother's teachings. She was my true inspiration. A perfectionist, she never settled for anything less than the best, always insisting that everything be as fresh as possible and of the finest quality. Mamma taught me all her little secrets for selecting the best produce, meat, and fish. I can still hear her voice: "An eggplant should be light in weight; if it is heavy, it is full of seeds and will be bitter. . . . If broccoli rabe stems are curled, it is past its prime. . . . A few creases around the top of a salad tomato is a sign that it's sweet, juicy, and ready to enjoy. . . ." She was always right. Selecting the best ingredients meant the resulting dish was not only more delicious but healthier, too.

My mother cooked every day of her life. Even though she prepared three meals a day, she never used measuring spoons, scales, or fancy appliances. Nor did she ever need to write down a single recipe. She taught her children the fundamentals of home cooking and instilled in us the belief that cooking was an important part of life.

Many of my mother's traditional Italian recipes have been passed down through the generations. Growing up, I was always by her side in the kitchen, watching her take great care making homemade noodles, preparing delicious sauces, and taking pride in her rustic pies. The aromas from her kitchen were unforgettable. Because I spent so much time observing and tasting, I've not only mastered many of my mother's traditional recipes but also enhanced some of the classics, making them even more appealing, I think.

I have been fortunate to be able to stay at home and raise my three children, which has allowed me to direct my energy toward my favorite room in the house: the kitchen. As a self-taught cook, my cooking style has been influenced by my many life experiences, my passion for food, and my innate curiosity. My dishes have evolved from a determination to achieve certain flavors, an uncompromising devotion to quality, and my need and desire to experiment.

Neighbors, relatives, and old friends—many who have numerous years of cooking experience—have also shared their culinary memories and stories with me. Like my mother, they have been a source of inspiration. I have found myself always mesmerized and fascinated by their many helpful cooking tips.

But it's not just day-to-day cooking that fascinates me; I'm also a die-hard devotee of the art of canning. For almost two decades I have continued to improve upon traditional techniques as year after year I put up tomatoes, eggplant, artichokes, peppers, and more. Because of my dedication to this and many other classic, old-fashioned cooking methods, Martha Stewart called me an "old-world cook."

Since I love to cook and eat, it is vital that exercise be a part of my lifestyle and I find it no coincidence that the gym was where my husband and I first met twenty years ago. To this day, we are both still very much dedicated to exercise and it has contributed to an overall healthier balance of mind and body.

Exercise is my fountain of youth. When I feel good inside, my overall outside appearance automatically reflects that feeling of contentment. Having a well-balanced lifestyle between enjoying good food and working out regularly keeps me looking and feeling young.

How I got from "there" to "here" is a story I also love to tell. One summer afternoon not long ago, after completing my annual canning project (including the usual three hundred jars of home-canned tomatoes), a neighbor encouraged me to write a letter to Martha Stewart asking if I could demonstrate my canning techniques on her show. Not long after I mailed the letter, Martha's office contacted me, asking if they could come over for an interview. They seemed impressed with my canning techniques and knowledge of cooking. The rest, as they say, is history. Not only did the producers want me to demonstrate canning, but also my chicken cacciatore—from market to table. Without hesitation, I took them to Arthur Avenue—New York's *real* Little Italy—in the Bronx. I showed them how to select tomatoes for canning and how to choose ingredients for making "hunter's chicken." The show was successful, and I was asked to come back again and again.

But the thrill of meeting an icon such as Martha Stewart and being on her show is only part of this Cinderella story. It was Martha who suggested that I write a cookbook. I knew I was a good cook, but had it not been for Martha's belief in me, I might not have had the confidence to follow my dream.

I began to reorganize all my recipes. I measured, weighed, and set the kitchen timer to compose precise formulas and to perfect the recipes. After a few segments on *Martha Stewart Living* and offers to do my own cooking show, I started a website to share my recipes with the television viewers. The website grew in popularity and I became a regular guest on *Martha Stewart Living*. Television personality Al Roker contacted me to appear on some network specials as well as work with him on a television project, which is now under way.

Who would have thought that a little girl from the Bronx would debut her first cooking segment on *Martha Stewart Living,* work with Al Roker on the Food Network, and then write her first cookbook? It has all been a dream come true. And the best part is that I am able to share my dream with so many other food lovers. My cuisine is straightforward and uncomplicated; it embraces the flavors, aromas, and textures associated with the best Neapolitan fare. The recipes in this book are not just variations of standard Italian recipes; they represent years of evolution, from the basic comfort foods on my mother's table in the Bronx to a more opulent and flavorful cuisine served on my table in Connecticut. My genuine love for the art of cooking has captivated me and I hope you and your family will share the same experience. *Buon appetito a tutti!*

PANTRY

ANCHOVIES

Anchovies are enjoyed fresh, salt-cured, or marinated in oil (a real delicacy) throughout southern Italy. I prefer unprocessed, salt-cured anchovies to canned anchovies because they have a milder, less fishy taste and are less salty than commercially canned anchovies. Salt-cured anchovies still have their bone intact and will keep for up to six months in the refrigerator. I add anchovies to pizza, breads, pasta dishes (such as Spaghetti Puttanesca, page 87), and they are an integral ingredient in Calzone with Spinach and Anchovies (page 211). Salt-cured anchovies are usually sold by the pound in large tins. Processed or store-bought anchovies packed in oil are sold in cans and in small jars. If you can't find salt-cured anchovies, opt for a good brand of canned anchovies, preferably those imported from Italy.

Oil-Packed Anchovies

If you can find salt-cured anchovies sold by the pound—that is, anchovies that are not processed—you can pack them in olive oil yourself. The oil helps preserve the anchovies, and if you use a very flavorful extra virgin olive oil, the oil will flavor the anchovies, and vice versa.

To Preserve Salt-packed Anchovies

Remove the excess salt by running a little cold water over the anchovies. Place them in a clean, wide jar and fill until the jar is about a third full. Add enough olive oil to cover the anchovies by an inch. Store at room temperature up to eight months, making sure that the anchovies are always submerged under the olive oil. (Note: You can store the anchovies in the refrigerator, but if you have used extra virgin olive oil, it will congeal when chilled.) When you're ready to use the anchovies, remove them from the jar and rinse them quickly under cold water. Split the fillet open with your fingers. Lift up the thin spine, peel it off, and discard. Use anchovies whole, chopped, or diced, as your recipe directs.

BASKET CHEESE

Basket cheese—sometimes called *formagetto*—is available in two forms, fresh and dry. Fresh basket cheese is moist with no salt added and is an excellent addition to an antipasto platter. Dry basket cheese is mild and slightly salty. Dry basket cheese is delicious as is, or can be added to savory pies and pasta dishes. Both fresh and dry basket cheeses are made from cow's milk and are formed in a basket, hence the name. If you can't find basket cheese, you can substitute dry mozzarella (see page 10).

BLACK PEPPER

Use a pepper mill to grind your own black pepper; it will taste so much fresher than purchased ground pepper.

BREAD CRUMBS

Homemade bread crumbs taste infinitely better than store-bought, which are usually filled with additives, preservatives, and unnecessary seasonings. I urge you to make your own. My recipes call for unseasoned dry bread crumbs. To make them, start with good-quality Italian bread that is at least one day old. (The bread can be up to one week old.) Break the bread into chunks (include the crust) that are small enough to fit inside a blender. Process two or three chunks at a time for two to four seconds or until fine crumbs form. (If crumbs don't form, then the bread chunks may be too large; remove them from the blender and crumble into smaller pieces.) Use as a recipe directs, or make plenty and store in a resealable plastic bag in your kitchen pantry.

BUTTER

Neapolitan fare doesn't call for butter very often, although we do use it in some desserts. Unless otherwise specified, use unsalted butter.

CALAMARI

Calamari—squid, in English—are available fresh, frozen, cleaned, and uncleaned. There are numerous species of squid, including seppia, or cuttlefish. Seppia—which is imported—has a thicker skin and has a sweeter, more pronounced flavor than calamari. It is also more expensive. Both seppia and calamari have ink sacs near the heart (the word *calamari* means "inkwell"). Although it is not to my taste, some cooks like to use the ink in sauces.

Cleaning Squid

Although you can buy cleaned squid, it's not hard to do it yourself. Rinse the squid under cold running water. Working with one squid at a time, hold the body in one hand and the head with the tentacles in the other. Pull the tentacles away from the body. Cut off the head behind the eyes and discard. Squeeze the body and remove the thin plastic-like bone from the inside. Rinse the inside and outside of the squid. Remove all the black ink, most of which is located behind the eyes, but is sometimes in the body of the squid, combined with sand and grit. Rinse the tentacle head and cut the remaining body into rings, or as a recipe directs.

CAPERS

Most capers are sold packed in a vinegar-brine mixture, although salt-packed capers are becoming easier to find in supermarkets across the country. The brine-packed capers are fine, but do opt for the salt-packed capers if possible—they are plumper in texture and much tastier than the brine-cured kind. Using salt-packed capers will make your dish taste more authentically Italian. Rinse salt-packed capers briefly before using. (Note: Only rinse off the excess salt; over-rinsing will dilute the flavor of the capers.) I like to pack capers in olive oil, to have on hand for seasoning fish, meats, greens, and more. The capers absorb some of the flavors of the oil, and vice versa. To pack them in oil, after briefly rinsing off the excess salt, drain the capers, then put them in a jar. Add enough extra virgin olive oil to cover the capers.

CITRON

Citron is a citrus fruit that is grown commercially in parts of the Mediterranean, Israel, and Puerto Rico. The most important part of the citron is its peel, which is processed (salted, rinsed, boiled, dried) then candied. Most of the candying process takes place in England, France, and the United States. The candied peel is popular in making Italian desserts. I use citron in several of my Neapolitan recipes including Pizza Gran (wheat pie, page 234), Migliaccio di Cervinara (page 230), and sometimes Sweet Lemon-Ricotta Pie with Brandied Cherries (page 232) and panettone.

I prefer to use fresh candied citron that is sold by the pound without preservatives (see Mail-Order Sources, page 283). Or, you can purchase candied citron at the supermarket during the holiday season, but it usually contains preservatives, which give it its long shelf life. If you prefer, candied orange, lemon, lime, or grapefruit peel can be substituted for candied citron.

DRIED HERBS

There are many recipes in which dried herbs are preferable to fresh. I strongly suggest that you dry your own herbs (see page 251); they're more aromatic and more flavorful than purchased dried herbs. My method for drying can even be done in the microwave oven (see page 253).

EGGPLANT

Eggplant comes in several sizes, but the smaller ones are tastier, firmer, and have fewer seeds. Eggplants have some natural bitterness, which is what makes them different from other vegetables. I love the inherent bitterness in fresh baby eggplant, and I don't believe in covering it up or hiding it. Baby eggplants are more expensive than medium-size eggplants, but they're worth it; use medium eggplants for dishes such as Eggplant Parmigiana (page 187). When choosing eggplants, look for those with tight, shiny skin; they should be blemish-free and light in weight. (A heavier eggplant means it has more seeds, which add to the bitterness.)

EGGS

I always use large eggs for desserts, sweet and savory rustic pies, and some pasta dishes. Look for eggs from organically fed chickens; they taste better and are better for you, too.

ESCAROLE

This nutritious vegetable, a member of the endive family, is available all year round but is at its peak summer through fall. When shopping for escarole, look for heads that are white at the stem end with no signs of discoloration, which ensures that the escarole is fresh. The tips of the leaves should look fresh and tender. Escarole leaves should be crisp, not wilted, and a heavy head is a better choice than one that is lighter. Baby escarole and the yellow inner leaves of a mature head of escarole (the heart) are very tender and are a delicious addition to salads.

FLOUR

For bread-baking, and for some desserts, I use bread flour, which is high in gluten. Otherwise, use unbleached all-purpose flour.

FRESH CHEESE

This mild, unsalted cheese is often used in savory pies and baked pasta dishes. If fresh cheese is unavailable, substitute basket cheese (page 6).

LEMON, LIME, AND ORANGE JUICE AND ZEST

Always use freshly squeezed citrus juices. Grated citrus zest should always be grated just before using for the best flavor and aroma.

LITTLENECK CLAMS

These small clams are preferable to larger clams (sometimes called chowder clams) for eating raw, for stuffing whole, and for adding to many fish and pasta dishes.

Cleaning Clams

To Clean Clams for Soups and Stews: Rinse each clam individually under cold running water until you feel no remaining residue on the shell. Discard any open or cracked clams. The shell should feel smooth and clean. Submerge the clams in a large pot or bowl of cold water for three to five minutes to expel additional sand or grit.

To Clean Clams for Baking: Rinse and soak clams as directed above. Place the clean clams in a large, wide pot and let them stand at room temperature until they open, up to two hours (up to six hours, if the clams are frozen). The juices that the clams release should be clear and free of grit. If there is any grit in the juices, strain the liquid through a coffee filter, repeating until the clam juice is clear and free from grit and sand.

MOZZARELLA

This mild, white fresh cheese is made with cow's milk in this country but imported *mozzarella di bufala* from southern Italy is also frequently available here. Made from the milk of the water buffalo, *mozzarella di bufala* has a different flavor and texture from that of regular mozzarella because it has a higher fat content. Both fresh cow's milk and buffalo mozzarella are usually sold submerged in whey or water and have a soft texture and a delicate flavor. Because of its high moisture content, fresh mozzarella doesn't melt well, and is best enjoyed as is. Fresh dry cow's milk mozzarella is also freshly made but has been dried for a short amount of time; it melts well and is excellent for pizza toppings, Eggplant Parmigiana, or in any recipe that you want the mozzarella to "pull." The plastic-wrapped mozzarella found in supermarkets is not as delicate in flavor as fresh mozzarella or fresh dry mozzarella, but it melts beautifully and is a good substitute if you can't find fresh dry mozzarella. Dry-aged (cow's milk) mozzarella has dried for a longer period of time than fresh dry mozzarella. It is ideal for savory pies such as Pizza Rustica (page 215). *Bocconcini* are small balls of mozzarella that are sometimes marinated in olive oil and herbs. Smoked mozzarella is delicious, as is *manteca,* mozzarella surrounding a lump of butter (see Mail-Order Sources, page 283). To crumble mozzarella: Cut the mozzarella into two-inch chunks. Place one or two chunks in a blender or food processor and process for two to three seconds or until crumbled. Repeat with the remaining mozzarella and use as a recipe directs.

OLIVE OIL

When extra virgin olive oil is called for, use the best cold-pressed kind that you can afford (I use Bariani brand; see Mail-Order Sources, page 283). For frying, use an olive oil that is light in color and in flavor.

OREGANO

Oregano grows prolifically near Naples, where I was born. As a very young child, I remember my Nonna Cristina picking fresh oregano with their little white flowers. She would tie branches together and dry them in the sun until they turned olive green. My grandmother would then press the dried herbs through a fine sieve, and the aroma of oregano would linger in the house all day. Bunches of imported dried Italian oregano are available in specialty foods stores and Italian markets. Look for the Marinella brand (see Mail-Order Sources, page 283), which is one of my favorites. Although I enjoy the flavor of imported dried oregano, too much of it—or of domestic oregano, for that matter—can be hard on the stomach. I suggest that you pass the dried leaves through a fine mesh sieve before using.

PANCETTA

This cured pork product is available smoked and unsmoked. You'll find it in the deli section of many supermarkets nationwide. In Italian markets, you can often find seasoned pancetta, which is spiced with black pepper, sweet paprika, and rubbed with red pepper flakes. Neapolitans love using it to flavor soups, beans, sauces, pasta dishes, breads, and greens. Although it is sometimes called Italian bacon, it is leaner and less salty than American bacon. Pancetta can be tightly wrapped and refrigerated up to three weeks or frozen up to six months. If you can't find pancetta, substitute Canadian bacon.

PARMIGIANO-REGGIANO

Never use anything but genuine Parmigiano-Reggiano; the words are stamped right on the wheel.

PECORINO ROMANO

When it comes to grated cheese, I prefer Pecorino Romano and use it far more often than Parmigiano-Reggiano in my Neapolitan cooking.

Pecorino Romano cheese is made from sheep's milk (the word *pecorino* means "sheep") and has a sharper, more pronounced flavor than Parmigiano-Reggiano.

HOT RED PEPPERS

The word *peperoncino* means chile pepper, but the word is often used to refer to small, hot red peppers. Bunches of fresh, hot green and red peppers can be found in Italian markets and some specialty stores in early September. I always buy several bunches, then hang them in a cool, dry place to use throughout the year. As they ripen and dry, the peppers turn from green to red; they can be used fresh or dried. In our Neapolitan food culture, some dishes are meant to be a little spicy, but the spiciness never dominates. Hot spices are for background flavors only. How spicy you like your food is a personal preference and is always optional. If you don't like spicy food, omit the hot spices.

Preserving Fresh Hot Red Peppers

Remove the peppers from the stems; do not discard the seeds. Chop the peppers into small pieces and place them in a small jelly jar or Mason jar. Add enough olive oil to cover the peppers by at least a half inch. Store in the refrigerator and use as needed. Kept in this manner, the peppers will keep up to six months or longer.

PERGONÉ LIQUEUR

Flavored with roasted cocoa seeds, roasted coffee beans, caramel, vanilla bean, and fruit rinds, this liqueur is said to date back to Marco Polo. Not only is it delicious for after-dinner sipping, it's a tasty and unusual addition to dessert recipes. Pergoné is available at wine and spirits stores.

SOPPRESSATA

Soppressata—dried, cured pork sausage—is a type of *salumi*, a general Italian term meaning cured meats. Soppressata is sausage casing stuffed with coarsely ground meat and diced fat and flavored with sweet or hot spices, including black peppercorns. It is dry-cured for six to eight weeks. Soppressata is often sliced and eaten just as it is, or it can be added to dishes like Pizza Rustica (page 215). To remove the casing from soppressata, slit the casing with the tip of a sharp knife, then place the sausage under cold water and you should be able to peel off the casing.

STREGA LIQUEUR

This Italian liqueur is made with more than seventy spices and herbs, including *zafferano* (saffron), which gives Strega its lovely golden color. It is said to have been used as a love potion by an ancient coven of witches (*strega* means "witch" in Italian). Strega liqueur originated in Benevento, near my hometown, where it is enjoyed as an after-dinner drink and used to flavor desserts such as Zeppole di Ferrara (page 237), Struffoli (page 244), and Migliaccio di Cervinara (page 230). Strega is always offered to guests and is enjoyed on special occasions, particularly during the holidays.

SUN-DRIED TOMATOES

Sun-dried tomatoes are available packed in oil or by the pound. I prefer to buy them by the pound, then submerge them in extra virgin olive oil when I get home from the market. To do so, pack the tomatoes in small Mason jars, then press them down lightly with a wooden spoon. Add enough olive oil to cover the tomatoes by a half inch and store in a cool, dry place for up to a year. (I don't recommend refrigerating them; the cold will cause the oil to congeal.) To use, drain off the flavored oil (reserve it to add to salad dressings, pasta, Sun-Dried Tomato Bread [page 201]; to marinate meat or poultry; or to sauté greens) and use the tomatoes as a recipe directs. If you prefer to store sun-dried tomatoes without oil, simply place them in a Ziploc bag, seal tightly, and refrigerate until ready to use.

TOMATOES

Fresh tomatoes are plum (Roma) variety unless otherwise specified. Canned tomatoes are preferably homemade (page 275), or purchased whole plum (Roma) tomatoes with their juices. Throughout the book I call for 32-ounce jars of my homemade canned tomatoes and tomato puree or the closest store-bought equivalents, which are 35-ounce cans. For half-jars of my homemade tomatoes and puree I suggest using 14^{1}/2-ounce store-bought cans.

TOMATO PUREE

Do try making your own homemade puree (page 275) for the best fla-vor and texture. Otherwise, substitute canned whole plum tomatoes with juice that have been processed in a blender or food processor. I never use commercially canned tomato puree.

VANILLA POWDER

This lovely ingredient is wonderful for baking. Unsweetened powdered vanilla is white in color, so when added to cream-based recipes—such as Tiramisù (page 236) or Vanilla Pastry Cream (page 241)—the mixture is not discolored as it would be by vanilla extract. It is extremely fra-grant and adds a perfumed aroma to desserts. Vanilla powder is avail-able at specialty stores or by mail order (see Mail-Order Sources, page 283).

VEGETABLE OIL

For frying, I usually call for light olive oil. However, if you don't have light olive oil on hand, use vegetable oil—such as canola or safflower oil—instead.

YEAST

I much prefer compressed fresh yeast to packaged active dry yeast. It is available at bakeries and at specialty foods stores.

**Tomato Bruschetta,
page 40**

Grilled Eggplant and
Bell Peppers, page 42;
Eggplant Rollatini,
page 44

Fried Zucchini Blossoms,
page 47

Baked Littlenecks Oreganata,
page 52

**Stuffed Mushrooms,
page 58**

Nonna's Homemade Minestrone,
page 62; Prosciutto Bread with
Pancetta and Basil, page 200

Linguine with White Clam Sauce,
page 102

Rigatoni with Broccoli Rabe, Sausage,
and Spicy Tomato Sauce, page 105

Classic Lasagna,
page 128

Striped Bass alla Pizzaiola,
page 139

Shrimp Marachiara,
page 142

**Veal Sorrentino,
page 156**

Braised Pork Chops with Marinated
Artichoke Hearts and Vinegar Peppers,
page 161

Stuffed Escarole with Sun-Dried Tomatoes and Capers, page 192; Zucchini with Fresh Mint, page 173

Mamma's Stuffed Italian
Peppers, page 189

Clockwise from top: Prosciutto Bread with Pancetta and Basil, page 200; Sun-Dried Tomato Bread, page 201; Olive Bread, page 201; Garlic Focaccia and Tomato Focaccia, page 202; Pizza Rustica, page 215; Onion Focaccia (center), page 202

Pignoli Cookies, page 218

Biscotti with Almonds and
Hazelnuts, page 220

Sweet Lemon-Ricotta Pie with Brandied Cherries, page 232

Struffoli, page 244

**Canning and
Preserving,
page 249**

ANTIPASTI

*A*ntipasti are little appetizers enjoyed with wine or an aperitivo before lunch or dinner. They may be cold or hot, light and simple, or rich and opulent—the delectable assortment ranges from cool summer salads to hot and spicy savories right from the oven. In fact, antipasti are so varied that some can be served as a first course, or as a light lunch or supper. This chapter includes dishes that fit into all of those categories—appetizer, first course, and small meal—and for each recipe I explain how the dish is traditionally served. However, you may want to bend the rules according to your own taste and appetite. Baked Littlenecks Oreganata (page 52), for example, is classically served as a hot appetizer, but there's no reason why it can't also be served as a first course or as a light lunch accompanied by a green salad and wedge of Italian bread.

Despite the apparent simplicity of some antipasto platters (it's not unusual to be offered a combination of roasted red peppers drizzled with olive oil, a mound of olives, and a wedge of local cheese) the concept of the antipasto is not an afterthought, nor is it simply a haphazard mix of whatever is in the refrigerator. Each offering of antipasto misto is thoughtfully considered, with seasonality, texture, and taste in mind.

When planning your antipasto platter, do as the Italians do: consider the season. Take a look at what's in the garden and what's in the farmers' market. If artichokes are at their peak (which often coincides with the first fresh mint), by all means try Old-fashioned Roasted Artichoke Hearts with Mint (page 51). Is your garden overflowing with flowering zucchini? To me, nothing celebrates the end of summer better—or more deliciously—than my delicate Fried Zucchini Blossoms (page 47). In winter, reach for home-preserved Caponatina Spread (see page 270), artichokes vinaigrette, Marinated Eggplant (see page 259), or pickled peppers, cured meats, plus one or more warm items like Stuffed Mushrooms (page 58) or Hot and Spicy Eggplant Frittelle (page 48).

Once you've checked out what's freshest at the market, plan your antipasto platter with a focus on variety of flavors and textures. For example, consider offering something tangy (Cured Green Olives, page 272), something smoked (razor-thin slices of prosciutto or sliced soppressata), something rich (two or three types of cheese), and something crunchy (Eggplant Bruschetta, page 39). But no matter what the season or what you serve, I encourage you to seek out the best ingredients possible: imported prosciutto (preferably prosciutto di Parma), Italian cheeses, and extra virgin olive oil. The results will be worth it.

Eggplant Bruschetta

The firm texture of leftover Italian bread is perfect for making bruschetta. Top it with eggplant, or with chopped fresh tomatoes and herbs (see Variations, below). I enjoy making this quick appetizer all year round but especially when baby eggplants are in season.

2 small Italian eggplants (about ¹⁄₂ pound total), with skin, cut lengthwise into ¹⁄₈-inch-thick slices

1 tablespoon salt

One 18- to 20-inch loaf of Italian bread, store-bought or homemade (page 198), preferably 1 day old

¹⁄₂ cup extra virgin olive oil

¹⁄₂ teaspoon dried oregano, preferably imported Italian

¹⁄₂ teaspoon dried parsley, preferably homemade (page 251)

¹⁄₂ teaspoon dried basil, preferably homemade (page 251)

¹⁄₂ pound fresh dry or processed whole-milk mozzarella cheese, thinly sliced (see page 10)

Serving Suggestions

It's nice to serve an assortment of bruschetta: The eggplant, tomato, and olive make an attractive presentation together on a platter. (See the variations on the following pages.)

1. Season both sides of the eggplant slices with salt and place them in a large bowl. Set aside for 1 hour.

2. Cut off about 4 inches from each end of the loaf of bread and reserve for another use, such as making bread crumbs. Cut the remaining loaf into 1-inch-thick slices and place them on a baking sheet.

3. Place the salted eggplant slices on a baking sheet and set aside. Preheat a grill or a grill pan to medium-high.

4. Whisk the olive oil, oregano, parsley, and basil in a small bowl. Brush the eggplant slices on both sides lightly with some of the herb oil and grill until golden brown on both sides, turning once, 4 to 5 minutes total.

5. Preheat the oven broiler. Broil the bread for 1 to 2 minutes, until slightly toasted, and remove from the broiler. Lower the oven temperature to 350°F.

6. Turn the bread slices over and lightly brush the untoasted side of each slice with the remaining herb oil. Place the eggplant on top of the bread, dividing the eggplant evenly among the bread slices. Arrange the mozzarella slices over the eggplant.

7. Bake at 350°F until the cheese melts and the toast is warmed through, 4 to 6 minutes total. Serve hot.

SUNDAY NIGHT
SPUNTINO

An Italian-English dictionary will tell you that *spuntino* means "snack." But really, the word means much more than that. In Italian households, it is used to describe the light evening meal that follows a heavier, midday meal. When I was growing up, an assortment of different foods—such as marinated eggplant, a variety of cheeses, breads, quickly prepared dishes, and wine, of course—were all part of our evening *spuntino*. It's a delicious and pleasurable tradition, and it's often as much fun to eat as the elaborate Sunday meal itself.

VARIATIONS

Tomato Bruschetta Combine 6 to 8 cored, diced plum tomatoes $1^1/4$ to $1^1/2$ pounds, 2 tablespoons extra virgin olive oil, 1 teaspoon dried imported Italian oregano, 3 chopped fresh basil leaves, and $1/2$ teaspoon salt in a bowl and mix well. Prepare the bread as directed above in steps 2 and 5. Top the untoasted side of the bread with 2 tablespoons of the tomato mixture and broil for an additional 3 to 4 minutes.

Green Olive Pesto Bruschetta Prepare the bread as directed above in steps 2 and 5. Top the untoasted side of the bread with 2 tablespoons of Green Olive Pesto (page 92) and broil for an additional 3 to 4 minutes.

Roasted Red Bell Peppers with Olive Oil and Garlic

Serves 4 to 6

Roasted peppers seasoned with olive oil and garlic are an easy but tasty antipasto. Serve them with olives, grilled eggplant, fresh mozzarella, and sliced tomatoes plus crusty Italian bread for a traditional antipasto platter. They're also wonderful as a sandwich filling or a topping for bruschetta. For a slightly different dish, use orange or yellow bell peppers instead. For a milder taste, use elephant garlic.

6 to 8 large red bell peppers
(3 to $3\frac{1}{2}$ pounds)
$\frac{1}{4}$ cup extra virgin olive oil
2 garlic cloves, pressed or finely chopped

$\frac{1}{2}$ teaspoon salt
Finely chopped fresh basil to taste

1. Roast the peppers over a gas flame until the peppers are soft and charred on all sides. Transfer to a brown paper bag and set aside for 15 minutes or until cool. Peel, core, and seed the peppers. Cut each pepper into quarters or 1-inch strips.

2. Place the peppers on a serving dish and top with the olive oil, garlic, and salt. Garnish with the basil. Serve immediately or at room temperature.

Eleanora's Tips

■ Placing the peppers in a brown paper bag after roasting reduces their moisture. The charred skin becomes dry and therefore easier to peel.

■ When seeding the peppers, do not run them under water because this will dilute their natural flavor.

Grilled Eggplant and Bell Peppers

Serves 6 to 8 as part of an antipasto platter or as a side dish

This is a dish that my godfather—*compare*—Guerrino introduced to his wife, my godmother—*comare*—Nicolina. She later passed it on to me. Although Guerrino is Milanese, this appetizer has a Neapolitan flair that I just can't resist. It's an easy and delicious beginning to a meal. The combination of grilled eggplant, bell peppers, salty capers, plus fragrant basil and mint, all splashed with balsamic vinegar, is cool and refreshing—perfect for warm-weather entertaining. It's colorful, too, so it looks great as part of a buffet.

Serving Suggestions

Serve as an antipasto, as a side dish, or as a main course for a light lunch. Let your guests help themselves to a few pieces of eggplant and some of the peppers and enjoy with a wedge of Sun-Dried Tomato Bread (page 201), Tomato Focaccia (page 202), or any good-quality Italian bread. This also makes the perfect late-night snack when accompanied with a crusty bread and a slice of cheese.

4 small Italian eggplants (about 1 pound total), with skin, cut into 1/8-inch lengthwise slices

1/2 cup plus 2 tablespoons extra virgin olive oil

Freshly ground black pepper

2 roasted red bell peppers (as on page 267, step 1) or one 16-ounce jar homemade Canned Roasted Red Peppers (page 267)

4 garlic cloves, pressed or finely chopped

1/2 teaspoon salt

4 fresh basil leaves, chopped

6 fresh mint leaves, chopped

1 tablespoon capers, drained

1/4 cup balsamic vinegar

1/4 cup Calabrese or Gaeta olives, optional

1. Preheat the broiler or preheat a grill or grill pan to medium-high.

2. Brush both sides of the eggplant slices with 1/2 cup of the olive oil and season with black pepper. Place the eggplant slices directly on the grill, or if broiling, place a baking sheet in the broiler. Grill or broil for about 2 minutes per side, until golden brown. Set aside until cool enough to handle.

3. On a large platter, arrange half the eggplant slices (8 to 10 slices) in a circle around the outside of the platter. Start a second layer overlapping the eggplant slices, forming a smaller circle. Drizzle with the 2 tablespoons olive oil. Mound the red peppers in the center of the platter. Top with the garlic, salt, basil, mint, and capers. Drizzle with the balsamic vinegar and garnish with the olives, if desired.

4. Cover the platter with plastic wrap and refrigerate for at least 1 hour or up to 3 days. Serve cold. (Note: If the olive oil has congealed in the refrigerator, let the dish stand at room temperature for 5 to 10 minutes before serving.)

Eleanora's Tips Freezing Grilled Eggplant

When you have an abundance of eggplant—from the garden or from the market—you can preserve grilled slices to enjoy all winter long. Simply slice the eggplant, skin and all, lengthwise into $\frac{1}{8}$-inch slices. Sprinkle with salt and set aside for 30 minutes. Brush the slices on both sides with olive oil and sprinkle with dried herbs to taste (basil, parsley, oregano, or a combination). Grill or broil for about 2 minutes on each side, until there are grill marks; the total cooking time will be about 4 minutes. Remove from the grill or broiler and let cool to room temperature on a platter. Wrap with plastic wrap and place in an airtight plastic container. Freeze until ready to use. Preserved in this manner, eggplant can be used for Grilled Eggplant and Bell Peppers (page 42), Veal Sorrentino (page 156), Grilled Eggplant with Portobello Pizzaiola (page 180), or Eggplant Bruschetta (page 39). You can also add thawed eggplant to pasta or use it to top crusty Italian bread for a sandwich. It's such a pleasure to have grilled eggplant on hand when you're unable to cook outside during the winter.

Eggplant Rollatini

Serves 6 to 8

Stuffed with ricotta, mozzarella, and prosciutto, this hot eggplant appetizer is like a savory cannoli. It can be made partially in advance, so it's great for parties.

3 large eggs

1 teaspoon salt

1 teaspoon freshly ground black pepper

2 tablespoons grated Pecorino Romano cheese

2 medium-small eggplants (about 1 1/2 pounds total), peeled and sliced lengthwise into 1/8-inch-thick slices

1/4 cup all-purpose flour

1 cup light olive oil or vegetable oil

1 pound fresh or processed whole-milk ricotta cheese (if using processed ricotta, drain overnight as directed on page 45)

1 tablespoon chopped fresh flat-leaf (Italian) parsley

1 cup shredded whole-milk mozzarella cheese, preferably fresh dry mozzarella (see page 10)

1/4 pound sliced prosciutto or smoked prosciutto (see Mail-Order Sources, page 283, for smoked prosciutto)

1/2 recipe of Quick Neapolitan Marinara Sauce (page 90)

1. Place 2 of the eggs, the salt, 1/2 teaspoon of the pepper, and the Pecorino Romano in a bowl and mix with a fork or a whisk until blended.

2. Dip the eggplant slices in the flour, then into the egg mixture.

3. Heat the olive oil in a large, deep skillet until hot but not smoking. Place the eggplant slices in the hot oil and fry for 2 minutes on each side, until golden. Remove from the skillet and place on paper-towel-lined baking sheets to drain until cool enough to handle.

4. Preheat the oven to 350°F.

5. Place the ricotta in a bowl and mash it with a fork. Add the remaining egg, the parsley, mozzarella, and the remaining 1/2 teaspoon black pepper and mix well. Set aside.

TO DRAIN RICOTTA

Place the fresh or processed ricotta in a fine sieve, and place the sieve over a bowl. Cover the ricotta with plastic wrap, sealing it over the sieve and around the sides of the bowl. Refrigerate for 6 to 8 hours, or overnight. (If you expose the ricotta to the open air of the refrigerator, it will absorb odors.) Discard the whey.

6. To stuff the eggplant: Place one slice of eggplant on a clean work surface. Place one slice of prosciutto on top of the eggplant. Spread 1 rounded tablespoon of the ricotta mixture on top of the prosciutto. Beginning from the wider end of the eggplant slice, roll up, from top to bottom. Repeat with the remaining eggplant, prosciutto, and ricotta mixture.

7. Pour 1 cup of the marinara sauce and $1/2$ cup of water into an 8 X 12-inch baking dish. Place the eggplant rolls side by side on top of the marinara sauce. Pour the remaining sauce over the eggplant. Cover the baking dish with foil and bake for 25 minutes or until bubbly around the edges. Remove from the oven and let cool for 2 to 3 minutes before serving. Serve hot.

Figs, Prosciutto, and Fennel

My family loves fresh figs, and back in Italy, we always had a fig tree in the garden. Figs are a beautiful and traditional addition to the antipasto platter especially when accompanied with prosciutto.

Serving Suggestions
Serve with antipasto, or as a starter or salad with just about any meat, fish, or poultry dish.

½ pound thinly sliced prosciutto

1 large fennel bulb, trimmed and cut into eighths

1 pint fresh figs (you will need 2 whole figs per serving), cut in half

2 tablespoons extra virgin olive oil

½ teaspoon salt

½ teaspoon freshly ground black pepper

Wrap the prosciutto slices around half of the fennel pieces. Arrange the figs (cut side up) and the prosciutto-wrapped fennel on a serving platter. Place the remaining fennel pieces on the platter and drizzle the fennel (not the fennel with prosciutto) with extra virgin olive oil and season with salt and pepper. Serve at room temperature.

Fried Zucchini Blossoms

Serves 6 to 8

My mother made these as a young girl in Italy as well as when we moved to America. As soon as she picked the blossoms, they were battered, fried, and enjoyed right away; they were truly a seasonal treat. Although she didn't stuff them with cheese, I prefer them that way. If using Gorgonzola, which is sharp and salty, combine it with Fiore di Sardegna cheese instead of Pecorino Romano, which is also sharp. If using goat cheese, which is milder than Gorgonzola, make sure to get a creamy, soft variety, and it's fine to combine with Pecorino Romano. I always look forward to seeing zucchini blossoms in the market; they're a delicious farewell to summer.

14 to 16 large zucchini blossoms, squash blossoms, or pumpkin blossoms

1 cup crumbled Gorgonzola or goat cheese

2 large eggs

1 teaspoon extra virgin olive oil

1 tablespoon baking powder

4 heaping tablespoons grated Fiore di Sardegna or Pecorino Romano cheese

1 cup bread flour or all-purpose flour, or more as needed

1 cup light olive oil or vegetable oil

1. Gently wash and dry the blossoms. Use a small, sharp knife to carefully remove the stem, the green base, and the pistil, leaving the blossom intact.

2. Crumble the Gorgonzola in a small bowl. Carefully stuff each blossom with the crumbled cheese, dividing the mixture evenly among the blossoms (about 1 teaspoon in each).

3. Lightly beat the eggs in a medium bowl. Add $^3/4$ cup of water. Whisk in the extra virgin olive oil, baking powder, and grated cheese. Gradually add 1 cup of flour to the egg mixture. The mixture should be slightly thicker than pancake batter; add a little more flour or water if necessary.

4. Heat the olive oil in a large, deep skillet until hot but not smoking. Working in batches, dip the blossoms into the batter, coating them evenly. Carefully transfer the batter-coated flowers, along with some of the batter, to the skillet. Cook, turning once, until golden brown, 5 to 6 minutes. Transfer to paper towels to drain. Serve warm.

VARIATION

Instead of battering and frying the whole blossom, you can also cut or tear the blossoms into small pieces and blend them into the batter. To do so, proceed as the recipe directs in step 3. Pour the batter into the hot oil by quarter cupfuls and fry as directed.

Hot and Spicy Eggplant Frittelle

Serves 8

These tasty little croquettes can be served as a side dish, an appetizer, or a snack. Whenever my niece Pasqualina comes to visit, she always asks me to make these.

4 small Italian eggplants (about 1 pound total), with skin, cut into small cubes

2 teaspoons salt

$1/4$ cup plus 2 tablespoons extra virgin olive oil

4 garlic cloves, 2 cracked and 2 pressed or finely chopped

1 dried hot red pepper, diced, or $1/2$ teaspoon red pepper flakes, or to taste

1 large portobello mushroom, coarsely chopped

2 large eggs

3 tablespoons grated Pecorino Romano cheese

$1/4$ teaspoon freshly ground black pepper

3 to 4 fresh basil leaves, finely chopped

1 tablespoon finely chopped fresh flat-leaf (Italian) parsley

$1 1/4$ cups unseasoned dry bread crumbs, preferably homemade (page 6)

$1 1/2$ cups vegetable oil or light olive oil

1. Place the eggplant in a small, deep bowl and sprinkle with the salt. Place a plate on top of the eggplant, then place a heavy object—such as a can of tomatoes—on top of the plate. Set aside for 45 minutes to an hour. Drain, then use your hands to squeeze the excess juices from the eggplant. Set aside.

2. Warm $1/4$ cup of the extra virgin olive oil in a medium skillet over medium heat. Add the cracked garlic, half the red pepper, the eggplant, and the mushroom and cook, stirring for about 3 minutes, or until the eggplant and mushroom are slightly crisp. Discard the garlic. Set aside.

3. Lightly beat the eggs in a large bowl. Add the Pecorino Romano, black pepper, the remaining red pepper, the remaining 2 tablespoons extra virgin olive oil, the fresh basil, and the parsley and stir to mix. Add the eggplant, mushroom, pressed garlic, and bread crumbs and mix thoroughly. Set aside.

4. Heat the vegetable oil in a large, nonstick skillet until hot but not smoking. Wet your hands and shape the mixture into $1/2$-cup patties that are about $1/2$ inch thick. Cook in the hot oil for 4 minutes on each side or until golden brown. Drain on paper towels and serve immediately.

VARIATION

Asparagus Frittelle Cook $3/4$ pound thin asparagus chopped into 1-inch pieces in boiling water for 4 to 5 minutes or until tender. Beat 2 eggs in a medium bowl and mix in 3 tablespoons Pecorino Romano cheese, $1/2$ teaspoon red pepper flakes, $1/4$ teaspoon freshly ground black pepper, the asparagus, 2 tablespoons extra virgin olive oil, 1 tablespoon chopped fresh flat-leaf (Italian) parsley, 3 to 4 chopped fresh basil leaves, $1/2$ teaspoon salt, and 1 cup unseasoned dry bread crumbs, preferably homemade (page 6). Shape and cook the patties according to step 4, above.

Fried Artichoke Hearts

Tender baby artichokes don't need much cooking, so they're delicious fried. Whenever I'm canning artichokes (page 254), I save a batch to make this side dish. They make great hot appetizers, too!

Serving Suggestions

Pass a platter of these around to serve with aperitivi. Or serve as a side dish to accompany Chicken Cacciatore (page 167) or Veal Francese (page 152).

16 baby artichokes (1$\frac{1}{2}$ to 2 pounds total), with stems

1 cup dry white wine

$\frac{1}{4}$ cup all-purpose flour

$\frac{1}{2}$ teaspoon salt

$\frac{1}{2}$ teaspoon freshly ground black pepper

3 large eggs

3 tablespoons grated Pecorino Romano cheese

1 cup unseasoned dry bread crumbs, preferably homemade (page 6)

$\frac{1}{2}$ teaspoon dried parsley, preferably homemade (page 251)

$\frac{1}{2}$ teaspoon dried basil, preferably homemade (page 251)

Three $\frac{3}{4}$-ounce packages Bel Paese cheese, optional

1 cup light olive oil

1. Wash, peel, and trim the artichokes. Cut the artichokes in half. (Note: There is no need to remove the chokes.)

2. Combine 3 cups of water with the wine in a large saucepan and bring to a boil over medium-high heat. Add the artichokes and cook until tender, 10 to 12 minutes. Drain well.

3. Mix the flour with the salt and pepper in a shallow bowl. Whisk the eggs with the Pecorino Romano in a large bowl. In another bowl, mix the bread crumbs with the parsley and basil.

4. Coat the artichokes with the flour mixture. If using, spread $\frac{1}{2}$ teaspoon of Bel Paese onto each artichoke. Dip the artichokes in the egg mixture, then into the bread crumb mixture. Turn to coat on all sides.

5. Heat the olive oil in a large skillet until hot but not smoking. Add the artichokes and cook until golden, about 3 minutes on each side. Drain on paper towels and let cool for 10 minutes before serving.

Old-fashioned Roasted Artichoke Hearts with Mint

Serves 6 to 8

Every fall when I can artichokes, I always make a batch of these lemon-and-mint-flavored roasted artichokes—they're so easy to prepare. They're delicious as an appetizer or tossed into salads. These roasted artichoke hearts are good warm or cold.

Serving Suggestions

For an appetizer, serve with provolone or fresh mozzarella, or add to an antipasto platter. This dish is also terrific served alongside grilled steak, veal, or chicken.

16 very small artichokes 1½ to 2
  pounds total, with stems
3 tablespoons extra virgin olive oil
1 teaspoon salt
3 garlic cloves, finely chopped

Juice of 1 large lemon
2 tablespoons coarsely chopped
  fresh mint leaves
6 fresh basil leaves, coarsely
  chopped

1. Preheat the oven to 375°F.

2. Place the artichokes on a baking sheet and bake for 45 to 50 minutes, until they have turned dark brown. Set aside to cool. Lower the oven temperature to 350°F. (Note: If you'll be serving the artichokes cold, just turn the oven off.)

3. Using a small, sharp paring knife, trim off ¼ inch from the artichoke stems. Remove the tough outer leaves and peel around the base of the artichoke, including the stem. Cut each artichoke in half and place the halves in a baking dish large enough to hold them in one layer. Season with the extra virgin olive oil, salt, garlic, lemon juice, mint, and basil. If serving the artichokes cold, let them cool to room temperature, then chill them in the refrigerator for 2 to 3 hours.

4. If serving the artichokes warm, cover the pan with foil and return them to the oven. Bake at 350°F for 10 minutes, then serve hot or at room temperature.

Baked Littlenecks Oreganata

Serves 6 to 8 as an hors d'oeuvre

Since it's quick, easy, and delicious, this dish is a terrific choice for dinner parties and holiday entertaining. The clams can be cleaned the morning of the party, and you can leave them to open up on their own while you set the table.

The topping can be made several hours ahead of time. So when my guests arrive, I just pop the clams in the oven and in almost no time, they're done. Everyone will think you slaved over this dish, and I guarantee that you won't have one left on the platter.

Serving Suggestions

I like to serve this as a hot appetizer with fresh lemon wedges and chilled, dry white wine. When I serve the clams with White Wine and Garlic Sauce (page 53), I always make sure to provide plenty of bread, which is delicious dipped into the sauce.

3 dozen fresh littleneck clams in their shells, cleaned (see pages 9–10)

1/4 cup extra virgin olive oil, or more to taste

4 to 5 garlic cloves, pressed or finely chopped

1 cup unseasoned dry bread crumbs, preferably homemade (page 6)

1 teaspoon dried oregano, preferably imported Italian

1/2 teaspoon dried basil, preferably homemade (page 251)

1/3 cup finely chopped fresh flat-leaf (Italian) parsley

2 tablespoons finely chopped fresh celery leaves, optional

2 tablespoons dry white wine

Juice of 1 large lemon

1/4 teaspoon paprika, optional

1/4 teaspoon salt

Lemon wedges

1. Place the clams in a large pot. Cover and leave at room temperature for 1 to 2 hours or until all the clams have opened. (Note: This way you won't have to open each clam with a knife.)

2. Pour the clam juice from the pot into a bowl, straining it through a coffee filter to remove grit. Strain it several times until the clam juice is clear and free from grit and sand. You should have about $1^{1}/2$ cups of clam juice.

3. Combine the strained clam juice, olive oil, garlic, bread crumbs, oregano, basil, parsley, celery (if using), wine, lemon juice, paprika (if using), and salt in a bowl. Mix well; you should have a moist mixture. If it seems dry, add a little more olive oil to moisten.

4. Preheat the oven to 350°F.

5. Working very carefully with one clam at a time (if possible, work over the bowl with the clams to reserve clam juices), use a sturdy paring knife and remove the clam meat from the shell to which it is attached and transfer it to the other shell. Discard the empty clam shell. Place the clams in their shells on a large baking sheet.

6. Top each clam with 1 teaspoon of the bread crumb mixture and gently pack the stuffing over the clam with a teaspoon. The clams can be made ahead up to this point and refrigerated for up to 24 hours, until you are ready to bake and serve.

7. Cover the clams with foil and bake for 15 to 20 minutes. (Note: If the clams have been refrigerated, let them warm to room temperature for 10 to 15 minutes before baking, or bake them for 20 to 22 minutes.) Do not overcook or the clams will be tough and chewy. Turn on the broiler and broil the clams for 2 to 3 minutes, until golden brown and crispy. With a serving spoon, transfer the clams to a serving platter garnished with lemon wedges and let guests serve themselves.

VARIATION

Littlenecks with White Wine and Garlic Sauce Prepare the clams as the recipe directs. While they are baking, prepare the sauce: Simmer 2 tablespoons extra virgin olive oil with 2 whole garlic cloves, $1/2$ cup reserved clam juice, 1 tablespoon butter, 1 teaspoon dried imported Italian oregano, 1 tablespoon minced celery leaves, $1/2$ teaspoon dried basil (page 251), $1/2$ teaspoon dried parsley (page 251), and $1/2$ cup dry white wine for 2 to 3 minutes. Pour or ladle the sauce over the clams and serve immediately.

Arancini con Tre Formaggi

Rice Balls with Three Cheeses

Makes about 14 rice balls; serves 6 to 8

If you love cheese, this is a great hot appetizer, and a delicious snack, too. My daughters, Juliet and Danielle, run to the kitchen whenever I make a batch! They can be made ahead of time and they reheat well so they're great for entertaining.

1 1/2 cups Arborio rice

1 cup crumbled Gorgonzola cheese

Two 3/4-ounce packages Bel Paese cheese, diced

1 large egg

1 egg yolk

1/2 cup grated Parmigiano-Reggiano cheese

1/2 cup unseasoned dry bread crumbs, preferably homemade (page 6)

1/2 teaspoon dried basil, preferably homemade (page 251), optional

1/2 teaspoon dried parsley, preferably homemade (page 251), optional

1 cup light olive oil

1. Bring 1 1/2 quarts of water to a boil in a medium skillet and add the rice. Stir to mix, then cover, reduce the heat, and cook at a low boil for 15 to 20 minutes. Drain.

2. Return the drained rice to the skillet and add the Gorgonzola. Cook over medium heat just until the Gorgonzola has melted, about 2 minutes. Remove from the heat and let cool for about 45 minutes. Add the Bel Paese, mix, and chill for 8 hours or overnight.

3. Lightly beat the egg and the egg yolk in a large bowl. Mix in the Parmigiano. Add the cooled rice mixture and stir with a fork until well blended.

4. When making the rice balls, wet your hands with water each time you form a ball. This will help keep the rice from sticking to your hands and help you make the balls as round as possible. Use about 1/3 cup of the rice mixture for each ball, rolling the mixture between your palms. Place all the rice balls on a baking sheet.

5. In a shallow bowl, combine the bread crumbs with the basil and parsley, if using. Roll the rice balls in the bread crumb mixture, coating them heavily.

6. Heat the olive oil in a large skillet until hot but not smoking. Place the rice balls in the skillet one by one and cook, turning gently, until golden brown on all sides, 8 to 10 minutes. Drain on paper towels, then serve hot.

VARIATION

Ricotta Balls with Pecorino Romano Beat 2 eggs in a large bowl with 1 pound drained fresh or processed whole-milk ricotta cheese, 1 cup unseasoned dried bread crumbs, preferably homemade (page 6), 3 heaping tablespoons Pecorino Romano cheese, $1/2$ teaspoon freshly ground black pepper, and $1/2$ teaspoon salt. Assemble the balls according to step 4, above, then fry as the recipe directs in step 6. Or simmer the balls in Quick Neapolitan Marinara Sauce (page 90) for 10 to 12 minutes, and serve with 1 pound of cooked pasta.

Mozzarella in Carrozza

Serves 6

My version of this Italian classic uses Pecorino Romano cheese instead of Parmigiano-Reggiano; Pecorino is sharper in taste. I also add herbs, panna (Italian heavy cream), and use Homemade Italian Bread (page 198) instead of sandwich bread. Mozzarella in Carrozza is excellent for lunch or with soup.

6 slices Homemade Italian Bread (page 198) sliced in half, or substitute white sandwich bread

1/2 pound thinly sliced prosciutto, preferably prosciutto di Parma

1/2 pound fresh dry or processed whole-milk mozzarella cheese, cut into 1/8-inch slices (see page 10)

Light olive oil

4 large eggs

2 tablespoons panna (see Mail-Order Sources, page 283), or 1/4 cup heavy cream or milk

2 heaping tablespoons grated Pecorino Romano cheese

Freshly ground black pepper to taste

1/2 teaspoon dried parsley, preferably homemade (page 251)

1/2 teaspoon dried basil, preferably homemade (page 251)

1. Place 6 slices of the bread on a work surface. Divide the prosciutto into 6 equal portions and place a portion on top of each of the bread slices. Top each with a slice of mozzarella, then cover with the remaining bread slices. Press each sandwich gently so that it binds slightly.

2. Lightly grease a large, nonstick griddle pan or skillet with about 1 teaspoon olive oil and heat over medium heat.

3. Beat the eggs, panna, Pecorino Romano, pepper, dried parsley, and dried basil in a wide, shallow bowl. One by one, dip the sandwiches into the egg mixture to coat lightly, letting any excess drip back into the bowl.

4. Immediately place three of the dipped sandwiches into the skillet and cook for 3 to 4 minutes on each side, until the mozzarella is melted and the bread is golden brown. Press down gently with a spatula as the sandwich cooks to bind the bread with the filling. Add a little more olive oil to the pan, if needed, and cook the remaining sandwiches. Serve hot.

Escarole Hearts with White Beans and Tuna

Serves 4 to 6

This easy salad is wonderful as a starter, lunch, or as part of a buffet in summer. For a slightly different flavor, substitute fava beans for the white beans and use salmon instead of tuna. When preparing this dish, save the outer escarole leaves to make Peasant-Style Escarole and White Bean Soup (page 70) or Baccalà with Escarole and Capers (page 147).

Serving Suggestions
Serve as a starter followed by Marinated Grilled Baby Lamb Chops with Fresh Mint (page 163).

2 cups cooked small white beans or Great Northern beans

1 garlic clove, pressed or finely chopped

1 teaspoon salt

2 large heads fresh escarole (1 1/2 to 2 pounds)

One 6-ounce can of tuna, packed in water, drained and flaked

1/2 cup diced scallions (white and light green parts)

1 cup cherry or grape tomatoes

1/2 teaspoon dried basil, preferably homemade (page 251)

1/2 teaspoon dried oregano, preferably imported Italian

1/4 cup extra virgin olive oil

1/4 cup red wine vinegar

Freshly ground black pepper to taste

1. Combine the beans, garlic, and 1/2 teaspoon of the salt in a medium bowl.

2. Remove all the dark outer leaves from the escarole (save them for another use), exposing the tender, light green inner leaves (the heart). Detach these tender leaves from the core and wash in several changes of cold water. You should end up with about 6 cups of tender leaves. Drain and spin-dry the leaves.

3. Arrange the leaves in the bottom of a large salad bowl. Top with the beans, tuna, scallions, tomatoes, basil, oregano, olive oil, vinegar, the remaining salt, and black pepper. Toss gently and serve.

Stuffed Mushrooms

Serves 8 to 10

This is a traditional Thanksgiving appetizer in my home. In fact, it's the first thing my sisters Natalina and Anna look for when they join us for the holiday feast. I also enjoy making these as a special weekend appetizer whenever button mushrooms look really fresh at the market.

2 pounds extra-large button mushrooms, wiped clean, stems reserved

6 tablespoons extra virgin olive oil

2 garlic cloves, finely chopped

3 ounces fresh shiitake mushrooms, caps and stems wiped clean and finely chopped (about 1 cup chopped shiitakes)

3 ounces baby portobello mushrooms, caps and stems wiped clean and finely chopped (about 1 cup chopped portobellos)

2 shallots, finely chopped (about ¼ cup)

½ teaspoon salt

½ teaspoon dried basil, preferably homemade (page 251)

½ teaspoon dried parsley, preferably homemade (page 251)

¼ cup dry red wine

1 large egg

2 heaping tablespoons grated Pecorino Romano cheese

2 tablespoons finely chopped fresh flat-leaf (Italian) parsley

¼ teaspoon freshly ground black pepper

1 cup unseasoned dry bread crumbs, preferably homemade (page 6)

1. Preheat the oven to 400°F.

2. Brush the button mushroom caps with half of the olive oil. Place the button mushrooms stem side down on a baking pan and bake until they are tender and have released their juices, 10 to 15 minutes. Transfer the caps to a bowl, reserving the juices in a separate dish. Cool completely. Finely chop the reserved mushroom stems and set aside. Lower the oven temperature to 350°F.

3. Warm the remaining 3 tablespoons of olive oil in a large skillet over medium-high heat. Add the garlic and cook for 1 minute. Add the finely chopped shiitakes and portobellos, the button mushroom stems, shallots, and salt and cook, stirring, until the mushrooms begin to release their juices, about 3 minutes. Add the dried basil and dried parsley, and cook, stirring for about 3 minutes. Add the wine and simmer until the liquid almost evaporates, about 6 minutes. Cool and set aside.

4. Whisk the egg, Pecorino Romano, fresh parsley, and pepper in a large bowl to blend. Add the cooled mushroom mixture, $1/4$ cup of the reserved mushroom juices, and the bread crumbs. Mix well.

5. Brush a large baking pan with olive oil. Stuff the mushroom caps with some of the filling, generously mounding it slightly in the center. Arrange the mushrooms stuffing side up in the prepared pan. Cover with foil and bake for 30 to 35 minutes.

6. Turn on the broiler. Remove the foil and broil the mushrooms until the stuffing looks slightly toasted, 2 to 3 minutes. Serve hot.

SOUPS AND STEWS

*I*talian soups come in many guises. Some are thick with legumes and pasta; others are light and brothy. They can be simple and parsimonious, made with on-hand ingredients, or composed of indulgences like lobster tails, shrimp, and blue crabs. Some soups—like Peasan-Style Escarole and White Bean Soup (page 70)—are down-to-earth and healthy, and although they are delicious anytime, they're often made specifically to comfort and to nourish.

There are light soups—like Tomato Soup with Fresh Basil (page 64) and Turkey Wing Soup with Winter Vegetables (page 78)—that are usually served as starters. And there are some hearty enough to serve as a main course: Nonna's Homemade Minestrone (page 62) and Italian Beef Stew (page 82) only need bread, salad, cheese, and wine for a complete and satisfying dinner. Many hearty, protein-rich soups can be served either way: A small bowl of Pasta e Fagioli (page 68) or Pasta and Chickpea Soup with Tomatoes and Basil (page 74) makes a terrific first course, but a larger serving can be a substantial lunch or supper.

Some holiday meals in Italy begin with soup. Fish soups are traditional for Christmas Eve; in my family, Zuppa di Pesce (page 83) is an absolute must. Maria Domenica's Chicken and Veal Soup with Tiny Meatballs (page 80) is the *primo piatto* at our Thanksgiving feast.

If you enjoy making soup, do keep the kitchen pantry stocked with the essentials. My own list would include pancetta, dried and canned legumes, homemade tomato puree, homemade dried herbs, small pasta (such as orzo, tubettini, or baby shells), as well as fresh celery, carrots, onions, garlic, potatoes, basil, and parsley.

Some of the recipes here need time to simmer, but none of them require tricky techniques or hard-to-find equipment. And remember: Most soups freeze well, so be sure to make plenty.

Nonna's Homemade Minestrone

Makes about 4 quarts; serves 6 as a main course, 8 as a first course

I remember my father coming home one night after work with a huge sack thrown over his shoulder filled with some wonderful, just-picked vegetables given to him by a neighbor. The very next day my mother made minestrone—the perfect soup for showcasing fresh vegetables. I can still recall the mouthwatering aroma of the soup, which wafted through our apartment building. I also remember the neighbors coming to our door and asking my mother, "Rosinella, what are you cooking that smells so good?"

This minestrone—a variation on my grandmother Cristina's recipe—is replete with beans, pasta, and fresh vegetables. It's so hearty that I often serve it as a meal in itself just as my father used to enjoy it: with a wedge of sharp provolone and a hunk of good bread.

Serving Suggestions
If serving minestrone as a first course, try Pork Chops al Forno (page 160) as a main course. Or, make the minestrone without pasta and serve a wedge of Neapolitan Spaghetti Pie (page 133) as a main course.

½ pound dried red kidney beans, picked over and rinsed

½-pound piece of pancetta (preferably spicy, see page 11) or Canadian bacon

2 tablespoons extra virgin olive oil

1 large Vidalia or other sweet onion, finely chopped, or substitute yellow onion

6 carrots, peeled and chopped (about 3 cups)

4 large russet potatoes, peeled and diced into ½-inch cubes (about 4 cups)

4 celery stalks, with leaves, cut into ½-inch pieces and leaves finely chopped

2 cups homemade tomato puree (page 275), or 2 cups canned whole plum tomatoes with juice, pureed in a blender or food processor for 3 to 5 seconds

1 teaspoon salt, or to taste

¼ pound green beans, trimmed and cut into 1-inch lengths, or substitute asparagus tips or diced eggplant

2 small zucchini, cut into ½-inch pieces (about 1 cup)

1 small yellow squash, cut into ½-inch pieces (about 1 cup)

6 fresh basil leaves, coarsely chopped

2 tablespoons coarsely chopped fresh flat-leaf (Italian) parsley

1 teaspoon freshly ground black pepper, optional

1. Place 12 cups of cold water in a large pot and bring to a boil. Add the kidney beans and pancetta and cook, partially covered, over medium heat for 1 hour.

2. Add the olive oil, onion, carrots, potatoes, celery, tomato puree, and salt, and cook at a low boil, stirring occasionally, for 40 to 45 minutes, until the potatoes and carrots are tender but not mushy. (Note: If the soup seems too thick, add 1 to 2 cups of water to dilute to the desired consistency.)

3. Add the green beans, zucchini, squash, basil, and parsley, and simmer for 10 to 15 minutes longer or just until the newly added vegetables are al dente. Taste for seasoning, adding more salt and pepper, if desired. Discard the pancetta and serve immediately.

VARIATION

Pasta—such as tubettini or elbows—can be added to the minestrone for a more substantial dish. After adding the vegetables in step 3, bring a separate pot of lightly salted water to a boil and cook $^{1}/_{2}$ pound of pasta according to the package directions. Drain, reserving 2 to 3 cups of the pasta water. When the vegetables are cooked, add the pasta to the minestrone. Add just enough of the pasta water to reach the desired consistency.

Eleanora's Tips Using Fresh Plum Tomatoes in Place of Tomato Puree or Canned Whole Plum Tomatoes

I often call for homemade canned plum tomatoes, homemade tomato puree, or canned whole plum tomatoes in my recipes. However, for some recipes, if very ripe, fresh plum tomatoes are available, by all means use them instead. There is no need to remove the skins; simply halve the tomatoes crosswise and squeeze out the seeds. Drop the seeded, halved tomatoes into a blender or food processor and process for 2 to 3 seconds for crushed tomatoes or 3 to 5 seconds for pureed tomatoes.

Two and a quarter to two and a half pounds plum tomatoes processed this way yield 3 to 4 cups (one 32-ounce jar) tomato puree.

Tomato Soup with Fresh Basil

Makes 3 quarts; serves 4 as a main course, 6 as a first course

I especially enjoy making tomato soup in early September when I'm canning tomatoes and have lots of tomato puree on hand. Not only is it delicious, but it keeps in the refrigerator for up to five days and can be frozen for up to six months. Fresh plum tomatoes can be used, but be sure to buy ones that are extremely ripe—almost overripe. The riper the tomatoes are, the less acidic they will be. I always find it a pleasure to see a bowl of homemade tomato soup on the table, no matter what time of year.

Serving Suggestions

When serving this for lunch or a light supper, try it with Mozzarella in Carrozza (page 56), Calzone with Spinach and Anchovies (page 211), or Neapolitan Spaghetti Pie (page 133). When serving Tomato Soup as a first course, I usually pair it up with crunchy Easy Garlic Bread (page 101), focaccia (page 202), or Taralli con Finocchetti (page 206), followed by Braised Pork Chops with Marinated Artichoke Hearts and Vinegar Peppers (page 161).

¼ cup extra virgin olive oil

1 medium onion, finely chopped (about ½ cup)

1 teaspoon salt

3 garlic cloves, pressed or finely chopped

One 32-ounce jar homemade tomato puree (page 275), or one 35-ounce can whole plum tomatoes with juice, pureed in a blender or food processor for 3 to 5 seconds

2 carrots, peeled and finely diced

2 celery stalks, finely diced

6 fresh basil leaves, finely chopped

2 tablespoons chopped fresh flat-leaf (Italian) parsley

½ teaspoon dried basil, preferably homemade (page 251)

½ teaspoon dried parsley, preferably homemade (page 251)

Freshly ground black pepper, optional

1. Warm the olive oil in a medium saucepan over medium heat for 1 to 2 minutes. Add the onion, salt, and garlic, and cook, stirring, for 2 to 3 minutes, until the onion is softened.

2. Add the tomato puree and 6 cups of cold water, stir to mix, and bring to a boil over high heat. Add the carrots and celery, and cook, partially covered, at a low boil, for 30 to 40 minutes if you're using homemade puree. If you're using canned tomatoes or fresh tomatoes, cook for 1 hour and 15 minutes.

3. Add the fresh basil, fresh parsley, dried basil, and dried parsley. Continue to cook partially covered at a low boil for an additional 30 minutes. (Note: If the soup looks too thick, add an additional cup of water.) Sprinkle with black pepper, if desired. Serve immediately.

Cauliflower Soup with Green Beans, Zucchini, and Basil

Makes about 4 quarts; serves 4 to 6 as a main course; 6 to 8 as a first course

I have fond memories of early-morning trips with my next-door neighbors, Maria and Giustino, to the Long Island's farmers' market to pick tomatoes and to stock up on summer produce, including cauliflower. After a morning at the market, this cauliflower soup was often on my table that night for dinner. It's a tasty, nutritious dish that celebrates the freshness of summer. When shopping for cauliflower, look for the largest, whitest heads available. To save time, start cooking the pancetta, garlic, onion, and tomatoes before you trim, cut, and peel the potatoes, beans, and zucchini.

Serving Suggestions

Serve as a light lunch or supper dish with a piece of Tomato Focaccia (page 202), a wedge of provolone, and a glass of red or rosé wine. I've also enjoyed this soup with breadsticks and a wedge of Gorgonzola. If serving as a first course, try following it with Beef Amburg (page 166).

1 cauliflower head, trimmed and broken up into florets that are slightly larger than bite-size (Note: If florets are too small, they may crumble during the cooking process.)

¼ cup extra virgin olive oil

¼-pound piece of pancetta (preferably spicy, see page 11), or Canadian bacon

3 garlic cloves, pressed or finely chopped

1 medium onion, diced

Half a 32-ounce jar homemade tomato puree (page 275), or one 14½-ounce can whole plum tomatoes with juice, pureed in a blender or food processor for 3 to 5 seconds

4 large russet potatoes (about 1½ pounds), peeled and diced

2 celery stalks, chopped

½ pound fresh green beans, trimmed and cut into 1-inch pieces, or substitute 2 cups fresh or frozen shelled peas,

1 medium zucchini, diced (about 1¼ cups), or substitute 1¼ cups asparagus tips

¼ cup coarsely chopped fresh celery leaves

4 to 5 fresh basil leaves, coarsely chopped

½ teaspoon salt

½ teaspoon freshly ground black pepper

1. Bring a large pot of water to a boil. Add the cauliflower and cook for 10 to 12 minutes or until tender. Drain and set aside.

2. Warm the olive oil in a large pot over medium heat. Add the pancetta, garlic, and onion, and cook, stirring occasionally, for 2 minutes, or until the onion has softened. Add the tomato puree and cook for 5 to 10 minutes longer. Add 4½ cups of water and bring to a boil.

3. Add the potatoes and celery and cook, stirring occasionally, for 25 to 30 minutes, until the potatoes are tender.

4. Add the cooked cauliflower, the green beans, zucchini, celery leaves, basil, salt, and pepper, and simmer, partially covered, for 8 to 10 minutes, until the beans and zucchini are tender. If the soup is too thick, add a little more water. Discard the pancetta. Serve immediately.

Lentil Soup with Carrots, Potatoes, and Pancetta

Makes 3½ to 4 quarts; serves 4 to 6 as a main course; 6 to 8 as a first course

This simple, peasant-style soup is considered by many to be a "poor man's dish," because it requires only the most basic pantry ingredients. But it is because of its simplicity that lentil soup was popular on Italian tables after World War II. Fifty-some years later, this soup—filled with protein-rich lentils and healthful vegetables—continues to be a favorite. It's seasoned with pancetta, tomato puree, and—my personal addition—sweet, roasted garlic, which takes this old-timey dish to new heights.

Serving Suggestions

Serve lentil soup as a main course with a wedge of Home-made Italian Bread (page 198) or seeded Italian bread and a glass of Chianti. Or serve as a first course followed by Pork Chops al Forno (page 160), Neapolitan Spaghetti Pie (page 133), Stuffed Chicken Breast with Mozzarella (page 168), or Pork Loin Roast (page 159).

¼-pound piece of pancetta (preferably spicy, see page 11) or Canadian bacon

1 teaspoon salt

2 cups lentils, rinsed and picked over

4 large boiling potatoes or russet potatoes (1¼ to 1½ pounds), peeled and cut into ½-inch dice

3 carrots, cut into ½-inch dice

2 celery stalks with leaves, cut into ½-inch dice

1 Vidalia onion or yellow onion, diced

Half a 32-ounce jar homemade tomato puree (page 275), or one 14½-ounce can whole plum tomatoes with juice, pureed in a blender or food processor for 3 to 5 seconds

2 tablespoons finely chopped fresh flat-leaf (Italian) parsley

6 fresh basil leaves, finely chopped

3 garlic cloves, peeled and sliced lengthwise

3 tablespoons extra virgin olive oil

1. Place 12 cups of cold water in a deep pot. Add the pancetta, ½ teaspoon of the salt, and the lentils. Bring to a boil over high heat, then add the potatoes, carrots, celery, onion, tomato puree, parsley, and basil, and return to a boil.

2. Reduce the heat so that the liquid is at a low boil. Cook, partially covered, stirring occasionally, for 1 to 1¼ hours or until the vegetables are tender.

3. While the soup simmers, roast the garlic: Preheat the oven to 350°F.

4. Place the garlic in a ramekin or small baking dish. Add the olive oil and sprinkle with the remaining ½ teaspoon salt. Bake uncovered for 15 to 20 minutes, until the garlic turns slightly golden. (Note: To roast garlic in the microwave, see page 67.)

5. Add the roasted garlic oil to the soup. (Note: Add the garlic itself, too, if you like.) Discard the pancetta, ladle the soup into warm bowls, and serve immediately.

ROASTING GARLIC

When garlic is roasted in extra virgin olive oil, it loses its pungency and becomes sweet and tender. An added plus: The oil becomes flavored with the garlic. I often add roasted garlic—and the oil that results—to soups, stews, and other dishes when I want a milder garlic flavor.

To Roast Garlic in the Oven

Preheat the oven to 350°F. Peel 3 garlic cloves and slice them lengthwise. Place the garlic in a ramekin or small baking dish with 3 tablespoons extra virgin olive oil and $1/2$ teaspoon salt. Roast uncovered in the oven for 15 to 20 minutes or until golden. Reserve the garlic and the oil and use as the recipe directs.

To Roast Garlic in the Microwave Oven

I do not use a microwave oven for roasting garlic; I prefer to do so in a standard oven. However, to save time—or to keep the kitchen cool—a microwave oven can be used for this purpose.

Peel 3 garlic cloves and slice them lengthwise. Place the garlic in a microwave-proof ramekin or small baking dish with 3 tablespoons extra virgin olive oil and $1/2$ teaspoon salt. Cook uncovered on medium-high for 2 to $2^1/2$ minutes, until slightly golden. (Note: Since microwave ovens vary in power, it is difficult to provide exact timing and temperature. Depending on the type of microwave oven, you may need to cook the garlic on high.)

Pasta e Fagioli

*Makes 2^1/2 to 3 quarts; serves 4 as a main course,
6 as a first course*

One of my fondest memories of this dish goes back to my childhood days in Italy. Whenever my mother made Pasta e Fagioli, my brother Giuseppe would take his bowl to the window and open up the wooden shutters so the cold outside air would cool the dish. When it was just the right temperature, he would savor each bite. I enjoy this old-fashioned dish with its light, vegetable-flavored broth just as much as Giuseppe did, and I prepare it frequently. It's often referred to as "pasta fazool" (considered a pasta dish by some, a soup by others) and was a staple in just about every Italian home following the war. It was—and still is—an affordable source of protein. Thrifty and nourishing, Pasta e Fagioli can be made from basic pantry ingredients.

Serving Suggestions
When serving Pasta e Fagioli as a first course, try a healthy wedge of Toma Pie (page 213) or serve Marinated Grilled Baby Lamb Chops with Fresh Mint (page 163) or Calzone with Spinach and Anchovies (page 211) for the second course.

2 cups dried cannellini beans, rinsed and picked over, or 4 cups canned cannellini beans, rinsed and drained

^{1}/2-pound piece of pancetta (preferably spicy, see page 11) or Canadian bacon

^{1}/4 cup plus 3 tablespoons extra virgin olive oil

1 medium yellow onion, diced

^{1}/2 teaspoon red pepper flakes, optional

2 teaspoons salt

1 celery stalk with leaves, chopped

Half a 32-ounce jar homemade tomato puree (page 275), or one 14^1/2-ounce can whole plum tomatoes with juice, pureed in a blender or food processor for 3 to 5 seconds

6 fresh basil leaves, left whole or coarsely chopped

3 garlic cloves, peeled and sliced lengthwise

1 pound tubettini, or substitute other small pasta such as small shells, ditali, or homemade Polenta Noodles (page 122)

1. If you're using dried beans: Bring 8 cups of cold water to a boil in a large saucepan over high heat. Add the beans and the pancetta, reduce the heat, and simmer, tightly covered, stirring the beans from time to time, for about 2 hours or until tender. (Note: If you're using canned beans, add them to the sauce in step 3.) Except when turning over the beans, make sure the saucepan is tightly covered to prevent evaporation. (Note: For presoaked beans—see page 69—cook the beans for only 45 minutes to 1 hour, until tender.) The beans will turn slightly pink as they cook. Drain, reserving the cooking liquid and the pancetta.

2. Warm ^{1}/4 cup of the olive oil in a medium saucepan over medium heat. Add the onion, the reserved pancetta, red pepper flakes (if using), and ^{1}/2 teaspoon of the salt, and cook, stirring, for 2 to 3 minutes, until the onion has softened.

3. Add the reserved bean cooking liquid and 2^1/2 cups of water and bring to a boil. (Note: If using canned beans, substitute 1 cup of water for the bean cooking liquid.) Add the celery, and cook for 10 minutes longer. Add the tomato puree and basil, reduce the heat, and cook, partially covered, for 20 minutes. Add the beans and stir to mix. Discard the pancetta.

4. While the soup simmers, roast the garlic: Preheat the oven to 350°F.

SOAKING BEANS

I'm a real stickler for old-fashioned methods when it comes to beans. I prefer to cook them slowly and gently, without any presoaking at all. I find that soaking causes the skins to shrivel, tear and become separated from the bean. However, soaking dried beans does partially reconstitute them, so that cooking time is somewhat reduced. Quick-soaking saves time, but some quality is compromised.

To Presoak Beans:

Rinse and pick over the beans. Place the beans in a large bowl and add enough water to cover the beans by 4 inches. Let stand 8 hours or overnight. Drain, and proceed as the recipe directs.

5. Place the sliced garlic in a ramekin or small baking dish. Add the remaining 3 tablespoons olive oil and sprinkle with $1/2$ teaspoon of the salt. Roast uncovered for 15 to 20 minutes, until the garlic turns slightly golden. Set aside, reserving the oil and the garlic. (Note: To roast garlic in the microwave, see page 67.)

6. Combine $4^{1}/2$ to 5 quarts of water and the remaining teaspoon of salt in a large pot and bring to a boil. Add the pasta and cook according to the package directions. Drain, reserving 1 cup of the pasta water. Toss the pasta in a bowl with the roasted garlic and its oil, then add the pasta to the soup. Add some of the reserved pasta water, if desired. Reheat if necessary, and serve immediately.

Peasant-Style Escarole and White Bean Soup

Makes 4 quarts; serves 6 to 8 as a first course, 4 to 6 as a main course

In my beautiful hometown, Cervinara, and in the surrounding region, hearty greens are often combined with white beans in soups and stews. Escarole is widely used, but so is *cardille,* which is similar to escarole, as well as *catalogna,* which is in the chicory family. We also use dandelion greens quite often. My escarole and bean soup is easy to make and freezes beautifully.

Serving Suggestions

This healthy, substantial dish need only be accompanied by a crusty wedge of Prosciutto Bread with Pancetta and Basil (page 200), some provolone, and a glass of dry red wine. It can also be served as a first course; I like to follow it with one of these main dishes: Grilled Steak Pizzaiola (page 164), Pork Loin Roast (page 159), or Marinated Grilled Baby Lamb Chops with Fresh Mint (page 163).

2 cups dried navy beans or cannellini beans, rinsed and picked over

1/4-pound piece of pancetta (preferably spicy, see page 11) or Canadian bacon

7 garlic cloves, 3 peeled and sliced lengthwise and 4 pressed or finely chopped

1/4 cup plus 3 tablespoons extra virgin olive oil

1 1/2 teaspoons salt, plus more to taste

2 large heads (1 1/2 to 2 pounds) fresh escarole or dandelion greens

1 tablespoon finely chopped fresh celery leaves or 1 teaspoon dried celery flakes, preferably homemade (page 251)

Half a 32-ounce jar homemade tomato puree (page 275), or one 14 1/2-ounce can whole plum tomatoes with juice, pureed in a blender or food processor for 3 to 5 seconds, or 6 to 8 (1 1/4 to 1 1/2 pounds) very ripe, fresh plum tomatoes, halved, seeded, and pureed in a blender or food processor for 3 to 5 seconds

6 fresh basil leaves, coarsely chopped

Red pepper flakes to taste, optional

1. Place the beans and the pancetta in a large pot. Add 8 cups of cold water and bring to a boil. Reduce the heat, cover tightly, and simmer for 2 hours (or 1 hour, if beans have been soaked overnight) or until the beans are tender but not mushy.

2. While the beans are cooking, roast the garlic: Preheat the oven to 350°F.

3. Place the sliced garlic in a ramekin or small baking dish. Add 3 tablespoons of the olive oil and sprinkle with 1/2 teaspoon of the salt. Roast uncovered for 15 to 20 minutes, until the garlic turns slightly golden. Set aside, reserving the oil and the garlic. (Note: To roast garlic in the microwave, see page 67.)

4. Drain the beans, reserving 2 cups of the cooking water. Set aside the beans and the cooking water. Discard the pancetta.

5. Trim the tough stem end of the escarole and discard any tough or discolored leaves. Place the escarole in a large pot of cold water and set aside for 3 to 5 minutes. Drain and repeat until all the grit has been removed. Drain thoroughly.

6. Combine 8 cups of water and $1/2$ teaspoon of the salt in a large pot and bring to a boil. Add the escarole and cook for 5 to 6 minutes, until just tender.

7. Set a colander over a large bowl and drain the escarole into it, reserving 2 cups of the cooking liquid. Set aside the escarole and the reserved cooking liquid.

8. Warm the remaining olive oil in a large saucepan over medium heat. Add the pressed garlic, the remaining $1/2$ teaspoon of the salt, and the celery leaves. Cook, stirring, until the garlic turns slightly golden, about 2 minutes.

9. Add the reserved bean cooking liquid and 2 cups of the escarole cooking liquid and simmer for 2 to 3 minutes. Add the tomato puree, salt to taste, and the basil, and simmer for 10 minutes, stirring occasionally. (Note: If using canned tomatoes, simmer for 15 to 20 minutes longer.)

10. Add the escarole and simmer for 2 minutes more. Add the beans and the roasted garlic, toss gently to mix, and cook for 8 minutes more or until hot. Taste for seasoning; if you have used plain pancetta instead of seasoned pancetta—or if you prefer a spicier soup—add the red pepper flakes. Ladle into bowls and serve immediately.

Creamy Split Pea Soup with Potatoes

*Makes about 3 quarts; serves 4 to 6 as a main course,
6 to 8 as a first course*

I created this comforting soup about the time I got married and have been making it ever since. The combination of split peas with smoky pancetta is a delicious one. This soup is easy and nutritious, and especially satisfying with freselles (small, crunchy doughnut-taralli-shaped Italian bread) or any good-quality, crusty Italian bread.

Serving Suggestions

This soup is delicious on its own for lunch or supper, or serve as a first course followed by Beef Amburg (page 166) or Pork Chops al Forno (page 160).

- 1/4 cup plus 3 tablespoons extra virgin olive oil
- 1 medium yellow onion, finely chopped
- 1/2-pound piece of pancetta (preferably smoked, see page 11) or Canadian bacon
- 1 teaspoon salt
- 2 cups split peas, rinsed and picked over
- 5 russet or boiling potatoes, cut into 1/2-inch dice (about 4 cups)
- 8 to 10 sprigs of fresh flat-leaf (Italian) parsley
- 1 chicken bouillon cube
- 1/2 teaspoon dried basil, preferably homemade (page 251)
- 1/2 teaspoon dried parsley, preferably homemade (page 251)
- 3 garlic cloves, peeled and sliced lengthwise

1. Warm 1/4 cup of the olive oil in a medium pot over medium heat. Add the onion, pancetta, and 1/2 teaspoon of the salt, and cook, stirring, for 2 to 3 minutes or until the onion has softened.

2. Add 8 cups of cold water and the split peas. Bring to a boil, then add the potatoes, fresh parsley, bouillon cube, dried basil, and dried parsley, and return to a boil. Cook, partially covered, at a low, steady boil, stirring occasionally, for 45 minutes to 1 hour, until thick and creamy. (If the soup is too thick, add 1 cup of water or more.)

3. Preheat the oven to 350°F.

4. Place the sliced garlic in a ramekin or small baking dish. Add the remaining 3 tablespoons olive oil and the remaining 1/2 teaspoon salt. Roast uncovered for 15 to 20 minutes, until the garlic turns slightly golden. Set aside, reserving the oil and the garlic. (Note: To roast garlic in the microwave, see page 67.)

5. Discard the fresh parsley and pancetta. Add the roasted garlic with the oil. Ladle into bowls and serve immediately.

VARIATION

For an even heartier dish, cooked pasta—such as baby shells—can be added to the soup. To add pasta, bring a large pot of lightly salted water to a boil. Add $^1/_2$ pound pasta and cook according to the package directions. Drain, reserving 1 to 2 cups of the pasta water; add just enough pasta water to the soup to reach the desired consistency.

Pasta and Chickpea Soup with Tomatoes and Basil

Makes 4 quarts; serves 6 to 8

Back in Italy, my family used to dry their own chickpeas in late summer to preserve them for the long winter ahead. After harvesting, the fresh-picked chickpeas were carefully laid out on white linen or cotton tablecloths until they were completely dry, at which point they could be stored in the pantry for use in nutritious dishes all year long.

Made from a very old recipe, this soup is simple, robust, and incredibly satisfying particularly in winter. It's guaranteed to warm you up and make you feel good.

Serving Suggestions

The combination of pasta, nutty chickpeas, and vegetables is a meal in itself and need only be accompanied by Tomato Focaccia (page 202) and a glass of red wine.

1 cup dried chickpeas or fava beans, rinsed and picked over, or one 19-ounce can chickpeas

3 garlic cloves, peeled and sliced lengthwise

1/4 cup plus 3 tablespoons extra virgin olive oil

2 teaspoons salt

1/4-pound piece of pancetta (preferably spicy, see page 11) or Canadian bacon

1 medium Vidalia or yellow onion, chopped (about 1 cup)

One 32-ounce jar homemade tomato puree (page 275), or one 35-ounce can whole plum tomatoes with juice, pureed in a blender or food processor for 3 to 5 seconds

2 celery stalks with leaves, chopped (about 1 cup)

3 to 4 russet or boiling potatoes, peeled and cut into 1/2-inch dice (about 2 cups)

6 fresh basil leaves, coarsely chopped

1 pound uncooked short, flat noodles, small shells, orecchiette, tubettini, ditali, or other small pasta

Freshly ground black pepper to taste

Grated Pecorino Romano cheese

1. If you are using dried chickpeas: Place the chickpeas in a large pot with enough water to cover by 4 inches and soak at room temperature for 1 hour. Drain and rinse under cold water.

2. In the large pot, bring 8 cups of cold water to a boil. Add the chickpeas and cover tightly. Adjust the heat so that the liquid is at a low boil, then cook for $1\frac{1}{2}$ hours or longer, until the chickpeas are tender. (Note: If you have soaked the chickpeas overnight—see page 69—the chickpeas will only need to cook for 1 hour at this point.) Drain, reserving 2 cups of the cooking liquid.

3. While the chickpeas are cooking, roast the garlic: Preheat the oven to 350°F.

4. Place the sliced garlic in a ramekin or small baking dish. Add 3 tablespoons of the olive oil and sprinkle with $^1/2$ teaspoon of the salt. Roast uncovered for 15 to 20 minutes, until the garlic turns slightly golden. Set aside, reserving the oil and the garlic. (Note: To roast garlic in the microwave, see page 67.)

5. Warm the remaining olive oil in a medium saucepan over medium heat. Add the pancetta, onion, and $^1/2$ teaspoon salt, and cook, stirring occasionally, for 2 to 3 minutes, until onion has softened.

6. Add the reserved chickpea cooking liquid, tomato puree, and 2 cups of water, and bring to a boil over high heat. (Note: If using canned chickpeas, add the liquid from the can plus 4 cups of water.)

7. Add the celery, potatoes, and basil, and cook for 35 to 40 minutes. Check the soup occasionally, adding 1 to 2 cups of additional water if desired. Add the chickpeas.

8. Combine $4^1/2$ to 5 quarts of water with the remaining 1 teaspoon salt in a large pot and bring to a boil. Add the pasta and cook according to the package directions. Drain, then toss the pasta with the roasted garlic oil, and the roasted garlic, if desired. Add the pasta to the soup and stir to mix. Reheat if necessary, garnish with black pepper and Pecorino Romano, and serve immediately.

Eleanora's Tips **Adding Fresh Basil and Parsley**

If both tomatoes and fresh basil or fresh parsley are called for in a recipe, and you're using canned tomatoes to make a puree, you can add the fresh herbs to the blender after processing the tomatoes. It saves a step, and in seconds, you'll have chopped herbs without ever touching a knife. Just be sure to process the tomatoes first, then add the herbs and process again for 2 to 3 seconds more. This will keep the herbs from being overprocessed and turning the mixture green.

Pasta with Peas

*Makes 2 1/2 to 3 quarts; serves 4 to 6 as a main course,
6 to 8 as a first course*

Except for the Vidalia onion—which is my addition—this real old-world, peasant-style dish is known as *pasta e piselli*. It's not exactly a soup (some consider it a pasta dish), but since it's eaten *like* a soup—in a bowl with a spoon—and is often very liquidy, I've included it in this chapter. My mother considered this dish a staple, because it's easy and requires very few ingredients, most of which are already in freezer or the pantry. Everyone in our family loved it; my husband and children love it, too. It's delicious all year round, but do try it in spring when fresh peas and Vidalias are at their peak.

Serving Suggestions
I usually serve Pasta with Peas as a first course followed by Stuffed Chicken Breast with Mozzarella (page 168) or Pork Loin Roast (page 159), but it's also delicious on its own for lunch or for a light supper.

3 garlic cloves, peeled and sliced

1/4 cup plus 3 tablespoons extra virgin olive oil

2 teaspoons salt

2 cups shelled fresh peas, or one 10-ounce package frozen peas

1 medium Vidalia onion or yellow onion, diced

1/4-pound piece of pancetta (preferably spicy, see page 11) or Canadian bacon

One 32-ounce jar homemade tomato puree (page 275), or one 35-ounce can whole plum tomatoes with juice, pureed in a blender or food processor for 3 to 5 seconds

6 fresh basil leaves, coarsely chopped

1 pound tubettini or baby shells

Freshly ground black pepper to taste, optional

Grated Pecorino Romano cheese, optional

1. Preheat the oven to 350°F.

2. Place the sliced garlic in a ramekin or small baking dish. Add 3 tablespoons of the olive oil and sprinkle with 1/2 teaspoon of the salt. Roast uncovered for 15 to 20 minutes, until the garlic turns slightly golden. Set aside, reserving the oil and the garlic. (Note: To roast garlic in the microwave, see page 67.)

3. Bring 4 cups of water to a boil in a medium saucepan. Add the peas, cover, and reduce the heat so that the liquid is at a simmer. Cook until just tender, about 20 minutes for fresh peas. If using frozen peas, follow the package directions. Drain and set aside.

4. Warm the remaining 1/4 of cup olive oil in a medium saucepan over medium heat. Add the onion and pancetta, and cook, stirring, for 2 to 3 minutes, until the onion has softened. Add the tomato puree and 1/2 teaspoon of the salt and simmer, partially covered, stirring occasionally, until the mixture has thickened slightly. (Note: If the sauce is too thick or has condensed too much, add 1 cup of water.)

5. Add the basil and simmer for 5 minutes longer. Add the peas and stir to mix. Remove from the heat and set aside.

6. Combine $4^1/2$ to 5 quarts of water and the remaining teaspoon of salt in a large pot and bring to a boil. Add the pasta and cook according to the package directions. Drain, reserving 1 cup of the cooking liquid. Add the roasted garlic and its oil to the pasta and toss gently to mix. Discard the garlic cloves, if desired.

7. Add the pasta to the tomato sauce with peas and stir to mix. Add the reserved 1 cup pasta water, if needed. Heat through if necessary. Sprinkle with pepper and Pecorino Romano, if desired, and serve immediately.

Turkey Wing Soup with Winter Vegetables

*Makes about 4 quarts; serves 4 as a main course,
6 as a first course*

My light, brothy soup is redolent with the earthy flavors of carrots, parsnips, and basil with just a bit of tomato puree for a hint of color and sweetness. This soup is particularly welcome in autumn, when root vegetables abound at the farmers' market and turkey is plentiful. This is a terrific soup to have on hand in the freezer all winter long, just in case someone in the family gets a cold or the flu; it's soothing and healthy. An added plus: It's so simple to make. The vegetables can be prepared and the garlic can roast while the turkey broth is coming to a boil. It's really that easy.

Serving Suggestions

When tortellini is added to this soup, it becomes more substantial and is delicious for lunch or supper with Tomato Focaccia (page 202) or Onion Focaccia (page 202), or Sun-Dried Tomato Bread (page 201).

1 teaspoon salt

3 large turkey wings with skin, about 2½ pounds, rinsed, or 1 whole chicken

3 garlic cloves, peeled and sliced lengthwise

3 tablespoons extra virgin olive oil

1 large yellow onion, cut in half or in quarters

1 leek, trimmed, cleaned, and cut in half

3 celery stalks with leaves, cut in half

5 carrots, peeled and cut in half

2 parsnips, peeled and cut in half

1 turnip, peeled and cut in half

8 to 10 sprigs fresh flat-leaf (Italian) parsley

6 fresh basil leaves

2 very ripe, fresh plum tomatoes (6 to 8 ounces), or home-frozen (see page 79), or 2 whole canned plum tomatoes

1 cup homemade tomato puree (page 275), or 1 cup canned whole plum tomatoes with juice, pureed in a blender or food processor for 3 to 5 seconds

1 chicken bouillion cube

½ teaspoon dried parsley, preferably homemade (see page 251)

½ teaspoon dried basil, preferably homemade (see page 251)

1 pound cheese tortellini or ½ pound angel hair pasta, baby shells, orzo, baby bow ties, or other small pasta, cooked according to the package directions, or 5 cups cooked white or brown rice, optional

1. Preheat the oven to 350°F.

2. Fill a stockpot or soup pot with 3½ quarts (14 cups) of cold water. Add ½ teaspoon of the salt and the turkey and bring to a boil.

3. While the water is coming to a boil, roast the garlic: Place the sliced garlic in a ramekin or small baking dish. Add the olive oil and sprinkle with the remaining ½ teaspoon salt. Roast uncovered for 15 to 20 minutes, until the garlic turns slightly golden. Set aside, reserving the oil and the garlic. (Note: To roast garlic in the microwave, see page 67.)

FREEZING TOMATOES FOR WINTER

When plum tomatoes are at their peak, make sure to buy plenty. Select those that are the most perfect— they should be extremely ripe, very meaty, and free of blemishes. Set those aside for freezing. Here's how: Wash them thoroughly, and dry well with paper towels or a kitchen towel. Place the whole tomatoes in freezer bags and seal tightly. Freeze the tomatoes, and use them for soups, stews, and sauces in winter when finding ripe plum tomatoes can be difficult. When added to a hot liquid, the frozen tomatoes add flavor and color; the skin breaks down slightly, so there is no need to peel the tomatoes before freezing them. Frozen plum tomatoes will remain as vivid in color as on the day you froze them.

4. Remove the foam from the top of the liquid with a ladle or skimming spoon and discard. Add the onion, leek, celery, carrots, parsnips, turnip, fresh parsley, fresh basil, tomatoes, tomato puree, bouillon cube, dried parsley, dried basil, and roasted garlic. Cover and adjust the heat so that the mixture cooks at a low boil for $1^1/2$ hours.

5. Place a large colander over a large saucepan and pour the soup into the colander. Let the solids stand until they're cool enough to handle. Cut the carrots into $^1/2$-inch dice and set aside. Shred the meat from the turkey wings and chop into bite-size pieces. Discard the remaining vegetables, herbs, and turkey bones.

6. Return the carrots and the turkey meat to the strained broth, heat through, and serve immediately. For a more substantial soup, place about 1 cup cooked pasta or rice into each serving bowl. Ladle the hot soup over it and serve immediately.

Maria Domenica's Chicken and Veal Soup with Tiny Meatballs

Makes 5¹/2 quarts; serves 6 to 8 as a main course, 8 to 10 as a first course

After my sister Maria Domenica got married, she frequently dined with her in-laws, who introduced her to this soup from Salerno. Similar to a classic Italian favorite known as "Wedding Soup," this dish is a great choice for family gatherings because it appeals to all ages. (Children, in particular, are fond of this soup because the tiny meatballs are just their size.) My sister introduced this soup to my mother, who liked it so much that it became a staple in our home as well. It even became a tradition: We enjoyed it as a first course every Thanksgiving. But don't wait until the holidays to enjoy this dish. Try it any time of year, serving the chicken and veal as a main course, immediately following the soup. It's delicious with a glass of rosé wine and crusty Italian bread.

FOR THE SOUP

1 whole 3¹/2-pound chicken

1 large chicken neck or 4 chicken wings

2 teaspoons salt

One 1-pound veal osso buco or veal shoulder with bone, or beef bones or turkey wings

4 carrots, trimmed and peeled

3 celery stalks with leaves

1 medium onion, halved

3 fresh, ripe plum tomatoes or 3 canned whole plum tomatoes

8 to 10 sprigs fresh flat-leaf (Italian) parsley, tied together with kitchen twine

FOR THE MEATBALLS

1 large egg, beaten

2 tablespoons unseasoned dry bread crumbs, preferably homemade (page 6)

1 tablespoon grated Pecorino Romano cheese

¹/2 teaspoon freshly ground black pepper

1 teaspoon extra virgin olive oil

¹/2 teaspoon salt

³/4 pound ground beef

FOR SERVING

Lemon slices, optional

Freshly ground black pepper, optional

1¹/4 pounds Mamma Rosina's Homemade Tagliatelle (page 121) or fresh angel hair pasta, or 3 cups cooked white rice, or 2 cups chopped uncooked escarole (about 1 large head escarole)

Grated Pecorino Romano cheese, optional

To make the soup

1. Bring 16 cups of water to a boil in a large pot. Add the chicken, chicken neck, and 1 teaspoon of the salt to the boiling water. Cook until foam comes to the surface, then remove the foam with a ladle or skimming spoon and discard.

2. Add the veal, carrots, celery, onion, tomatoes, and parsley. Lower the heat, cover tightly, and cook at a low boil for 1¹/4 hours.

MAKING MEATBALLS FOR SOUPS

When making meatballs, be careful not to stack them on top of one another as you make them; stacking will cause them to lose their shape. When adding meatballs to a soup or sauce, be sure there is enough liquid, and add more if necessary. Wetting your hands will help you form the meatballs with ease. Ground pork or ground veal can be added to the ground beef in most meatball recipes. If using only veal or pork—which are more tender than beef— make sure to add enough bread crumbs so that the mixture binds.

When adding meatballs to soup, do not brown them before adding to the soup. Browning makes the meatballs crunchy; un-cooked meatballs are more tender, and they will exude more of their meaty flavor into the broth.

To make the meatballs

3. Combine the egg, bread crumbs, cheese, pepper, olive oil, and salt and mix well. Add the beef and mix thoroughly. Using $1/2$ teaspoon of meat at a time, use your hands to form the mixture into tiny meatballs. Place the meatballs on a baking sheet in one layer and set aside. (Note: Do not stack the meatballs.)

4. When the soup has cooked for 1 hour, set a colander over a large pot and pour the soup through the colander. Set aside the solids until they are cool enough to handle. Bring the drained broth to a low boil. Add the tiny meatballs and cook for 10 minutes more.

5. When the chicken is cool enough to handle, arrange it—along with the veal osso buco—on a platter. If desired, garnish with lemon slices and sprinkle with black pepper to serve as a second course.

6. If using fresh pasta: Combine $4^1/2$ quarts of water and the remaining teaspoon of salt in a large pot and bring to a boil. Add the pasta and cook for 6 to 7 minutes or until tender. Drain, then add to the soup. If using rice: Place about 1 cup cooked rice in each bowl, then ladle the soup over the rice. If using escarole, proceed with the recipe through step 4. Bring the drained broth to a low boil, add the escarole, and cook for 15 minutes. Sprinkle with Pecorino Romano, if desired, and serve immediately.

Italian Beef Stew

Makes about 4 quarts; serves 6 to 8

I often turn to this recipe for old-fashioned comfort in cold weather. This robust stew gets its Italian flair from the addition of red wine, portobello mushrooms, herbs, sweet Italian onions, and my homemade tomato puree. My version is easier than the one I grew up with: My mother often made beef stew with homemade beef stock, which is delicious but time-consuming. My father—a hard-working building contractor—usually came home with a big appetite, and he was always pleased when he smelled beef stew simmering on the stove. In my own home, this dish is a savior when there's only one shell steak in the freezer and several hungry people to feed. Adding potatoes and other vegetables stretches the meal, so that one steak serves many.

Serving Suggestions
I serve this stew as a main course with bread, a mixed green salad, and hearty Italian red wine.

½ cup extra virgin olive oil

3 garlic cloves, cracked

1 medium Vidalia onion or yellow onion, diced, or 1 leek, trimmed, cleaned, and cut into 1-inch pieces

1 teaspoon salt

¼ cup all-purpose flour

½ teaspoon freshly ground black pepper

1½ pounds boneless sirloin shell steak, porterhouse steak, London broil, or veal cut from the neck or shoulder, cut into 1-inch cubes

½ cup dry red wine

2 cups homemade tomato puree (page 275), or 2 cups canned whole plum tomatoes with juice, pureed in a blender or food processor for 3 to 5 seconds

5 large russet or boiling potatoes, peeled and cut into 1-inch dice (2 to 2½ cups)

3 carrots, peeled and cut into ½-inch dice, or ¼ pound string beans, cut into 1-inch lengths

2 cups diced portobello mushrooms, or ½ pound broccoli florets

4 celery stalks with leaves, finely chopped (about 2 cups)

1 beef boullion cube

One 10-ounce box frozen peas

1. Warm the olive oil in a large pot over medium heat. Add the garlic, onion, and ½ teaspoon of the salt, and cook, stirring, for 2 to 3 minutes.

2. Combine the flour with the pepper in a large bowl and stir to mix. Dredge the beef chunks in the flour mixture to coat thoroughly.

3. Add the floured beef to the onion mixture, and cook, stirring, over medium-high heat for 2 minutes, or until the beef is browned all over. Add the wine and simmer for 2 minutes more, until some of the liquid has evaporated. Discard the garlic, if desired.

4. Add the tomato puree, 4 cups of cold water, and the remaining ½ teaspoon salt. Bring to a boil and add the potatoes, carrots, mushrooms, celery, and bouillon cube. Reduce the heat and cook, partially covered, at a low boil for 45 to 50 minutes, stirring occasionally. (Note: If the stew has condensed too much, add up to 1 cup of water.)

5. Cook the frozen peas in a separate saucepan according to the package directions and drain thoroughly. Add the peas to the stew and cook for an additional 2 to 3 minutes. Serve immediately.

Zuppa di Pesce

Makes about 4 1/2 quarts, serves 8 to 10

This festive, elaborate soup is absolute heaven for fish lovers. And for Italians, it is a must for Christmas Eve and Good Friday, two holidays on which meat is forbidden. However, one will hardly feel deprived when eating this spectacular dish, which is filled with aromas of the sea. Serve the soup with a wedge of crusty Homemade Italian Bread (page 198) or Easy Garlic Bread (page 101) on the side. Or place a piece of toasted Italian bread on the bottom of the bowl before adding the soup.

Zuppa di Pesce is traditionally served as a first course, followed by a variety of fish and shellfish, such as fried calamari, shrimp, and baccalà, as well as calamari salad. In our family the meal also included *capitone*—marinated saltwater eel—a true southern Italian Christmas Eve tradition. Since there is so much to be done at holiday time, it is a blessing that the fish stock can be made up to two to three days in advance. For a more substantial dish, cooked spaghetti or linguine can be placed in individual bowls before the soup is added.

FOR THE FISH STOCK

1 medium onion, quartered

2 garlic cloves, sliced

2 celery stalks, quartered

10 sprigs fresh parsley

4 fresh basil leaves

3 cups dry white wine

1 1/2 to 2 pounds whole cleaned fish with bones, such as tile fish, sting ray, or shark

FOR THE SOUP

1/2 cup extra virgin olive oil

9 garlic cloves: 3 cracked and 6 pressed or finely chopped

1 teaspoon red pepper flakes, optional

2 large blue crabs (about 1 pound total weight), cleaned and split in half

2 medium langostini (prawns; about 1/2 pound total weight), heads discarded, shell and tail intact and belly split

1 large yellow onion, finely chopped

One 32-ounce jar homemade canned plum tomatoes (page 275), or one 35-ounce can whole plum tomatoes with juice, crushed in a blender or food processor for 2 to 3 seconds

One 32-ounce jar homemade tomato puree (page 275), or one 35-ounce can whole plum tomatoes with juice pureed in a blender or food processor for 3 to 5 seconds

1 teaspoon salt

1 cup Calabrese olives

12 littleneck or Vongole clams (about 1 pound), scrubbed

12 small mussels, scrubbed and debearded

1/2 pound medium shrimp, peeled and deveined with tails intact

1/2 pound cleaned calamari or octopus, cut into 1/4-inch rings (Note: Include the tentacles if you like; some cooks find this the most delicious part of the calamari.)

3 to 4 lobster tails, cooked and shells removed

1 1/2 cups dry white wine

1/4 cup drained small capers

8 to 10 fresh basil leaves, finely chopped

2 tablespoons finely chopped fresh flat-leaf (Italian) parsley

To make the fish stock

1. Place the onion, garlic, celery, parsley, basil, wine, 4 cups of water, and the fish in a large saucepan. *(continued)*

2. Bring to a boil, lower the heat, and cook, partially covered, at a low boil for 20 minutes. Strain, reserving the liquid and discarding the solids.

To make the soup

3. Warm the olive oil in a very large, wide pot over medium heat. Add the cracked garlic and the red pepper flakes, if using, and cook, stirring, for 1 to 2 minutes, until the garlic releases its fragrance.

4. Add the crabs and langostini and cook over medium to high heat until the crabs turn a deep orange color, 3 to 4 minutes on each side. Remove the cracked garlic and discard. Add the pressed garlic and the finely chopped onion.

5. Add the crushed plum tomatoes, the tomato puree, and the salt, and stir to mix. Add the fish stock and the olives, cover partially, and cook, stirring occasionally, for 25 to 30 minutes, until the sauce has condensed and thickened.

6. Add the clams, mussels, shrimp, calamari, lobster, wine, capers, basil, and parsley. Cook, partially covered, for 7 to 10 minutes, stirring occasionally, until the clams and mussels open and the meat is just cooked through. (Note: Do not overcook or the clams, mussels, and calamari will be tough and chewy.) Serve immediately.

PASTA

*F*rom a simple plate of spaghetti marinara to an elaborate dish of homemade cavatelli served with *braciole,* osso buco, and Italian sausages, pasta is, without a doubt, one of the most versatile foods. It can be economical or extravagant, quick and easy or—as in the case of homemade noodles—best reserved as a project for an entire Sunday morning. And, like soups, many pasta dishes can be served as a first course or as a main dish, depending on the rest of the menu or the size of your appetite.

Despite its humble ingredients—water, flour, and sometimes eggs— pasta is not only one of the most versatile foods in Italian cooking, but some dishes are considered almost sacred: They play an integral role in our culinary traditions. In my home, for example, Traditional Sunday Sauce alla Russo (page 109) is a must-have dish once a week. And I can't imagine a special occasion—holidays, christenings, graduations, or family gatherings—without my Classic Lasagna (page 128), an opulent dish layered with four kinds of cheese, homemade tiny meatballs, and a rich tomato sauce.

In this chapter, I share regional specialties, family favorites, and some creations of my very own. And I wouldn't dream of writing a cookbook without my mother's recipes for cavatelli, tagliatelle, and potato gnocchi. I've grouped the recipes according to how the pasta is sauced. There is pasta with simple sauces and vegetables; pasta with shellfish; meaty pastas, which are hearty and filling and excellent choices for cool temperatures and big appetites; and baked pasta dishes, which, by the way, are terrific for buffets, tailgating, and potluck suppers.

Spaghetti with Garlic and Oil

Serves 4 to 6

This simple dish known as *aglio e olio* was one that Italians depended upon during World War II, when produce and meat were scarce. Olive oil was considered a treasured ingredient, one that helped stave off hunger. During that time, a meal was often no more than olive oil and bread or—as in the dish here—olive oil tossed with garlic and spaghetti. My relatives in Salerno harvested their own olives and made their own olive oil, which they hid from the German soldiers by burying crates containing the bottled oil deep underground, where the cool earth also kept it from spoiling. In this simple dish, the flavor of extra virgin olive oil comes through. It's a quick, easy dish that is almost as popular in the States as it is in Italy. I hope you enjoy it as much as I do!

Serving Suggestions
Serve as a first course followed by Braised Pork Chops with Marinated Artichoke Hearts and Vinegar Peppers (page 161) or Calzone with Spinach and Anchovies (page 211).

¼ cup extra virgin olive oil

4 garlic cloves, pressed or finely chopped

2 dried hot red peppers, finely chopped, or ½ teaspoon red pepper flakes, optional

¼-pound piece of pancetta, (preferably spicy, see page 11) or Canadian bacon

1 teaspoon dried parsley, preferably homemade (page 251)

1½ teaspoons salt

1 pound spaghetti, linguine, or vermicelli

1. Warm the olive oil in a saucepan over medium-low heat. Add the garlic, red pepper (if using), pancetta, parsley, and ½ teaspoon of the salt, and cook, stirring, for 1 to 2 minutes. Do not overcook or the garlic may burn and taste bitter. Discard the pancetta.

2. Combine $4\frac{1}{2}$ to 5 quarts of water and the remaining salt in a large pot and bring to a boil. Add the pasta and cook according to the package directions, until al dente. Drain thoroughly, toss with the oil and garlic mixture, and serve immediately.

VARIATIONS

My mother sprinkled this dish with crumbled bits of Italian bread. It's delicious served that way, or you can sprinkle the dish with toasted bread crumbs. Use a paper towel to smear 1 tablespoon of olive oil inside a small skillet. Place the skillet over medium heat. Add ¼ cup unseasoned homemade fresh bread crumbs (page 6) and cook, stirring, for 2 minutes, or until lightly toasted. If you like anchovies, add 6 diced anchovies to the garlic mixture in the skillet and toss with the pasta. Or, for Spaghetti with Garlic, Oil, and Wild Mushrooms, heat ¼ cup extra virgin olive oil and ½ teaspoon salt in a skillet (add ½ teaspoon red pepper flakes, if desired). Add 2 cups diced wild mushrooms (such as fresh porcini, shiitake, or oyster mushrooms), 2 tablespoons finely chopped fresh parsley, and 6 finely chopped fresh basil leaves, and cook, stirring frequently, for 3 to 5 minutes, until the mushrooms are slightly golden. Proceed as the recipe directs. (Note: When I combine spaghetti with wild mushrooms, I do not use pancetta.)

Spaghetti Puttanesca

There's an old tale about this recipe that goes something like this: There was a certain married woman who was unfaithful to her husband and found that she had little time to prepare dinner when she returned home from her trysts. She was clever, though: She made a quick sauce from olives, anchovies, and herbs and served it over pasta. Her husband enjoyed the dish, and figured that since it was so delicious, it must have taken her hours to prepare, never suspecting that she hadn't been in the kitchen cooking all day!

Serving Suggestions

Serve as a first course with red table wine followed by Veal Sorrentino (page 156) or Stuffed Chicken Breast with Mozzarella (page 168). A mixed green salad is also a good addition to either of these second course suggestions.

¼ cup extra virgin olive oil

4 garlic cloves, pressed or finely diced

1 small onion, or 2 shallots, finely diced

1 teaspoon plus 1 pinch salt

One 32-ounce jar homemade canned plum tomatoes (page 275), crushed in a blender or food processor for 2 to 3 seconds, or 1¾ to 2 pounds very ripe, fresh plum tomatoes, cored and chopped

1 cup Gaeta, black oil-cured Sicilian, or Kalamata olives, pitted

2 tablespoons drained capers

6 anchovy fillets packed in salt

6 fresh basil leaves, finely chopped

2 tablespoons finely chopped fresh flat-leaf (Italian) parsley

1 pound thin spaghetti or thin linguine

1. Warm the olive oil in a large skillet over medium heat. Add the garlic, the onion, and the pinch of salt, and cook, stirring, until the onion has softened, 2 to 3 minutes.

2. Add the tomatoes, olives, capers, and anchovies, and cook, stirring occasionally, for 15 minutes. Add the basil and parsley and cook for 5 minutes more.

3. Combine $4\frac{1}{2}$ to 5 quarts of water and the remaining teaspoon of salt in a large pot and bring to a boil. Add the pasta and cook according to the package directions, until al dente. Drain, pour the spaghetti into the skillet, and toss to mix. Serve immediately.

Penne alla Vodka

Serves 4 to 6

This quick, easy dish is a real life-saver when you don't have much time to cook. The smooth, creamy tomato sauce has the added "bang" of vodka—although the alcohol content cooks away, the flavor remains. My mother never made this dish, so I created my own version, as well as an even more robust variation using pancetta. Either way, the dish takes only minutes to prepare.

1 ½ teaspoons salt

¼ cup extra virgin olive oil

1 pound penne

1 medium onion, peeled and cut in half

One 32-ounce jar homemade tomato puree (page 275), or one 35-ounce can whole plum tomatoes with juice, pureed in a blender or food processor for 3 to 5 seconds

1 cup half-and-half, 1 cup heavy cream, or ½ cup panna (see Mail-Order Sources, page 283), or 2 tablespoons mascarpone

½ cup finely grated Pecorino Romano cheese, plus extra for garnish

¼ cup vodka

4 fresh basil leaves, coarsely chopped

1. Combine $4^{1}/2$ to 5 quarts of water with 1 teaspoon of the salt and 1 tablespoon of the olive oil in a large pot and bring to a boil. Add the pasta, stir several times, then cook according to the package directions, or until tender.

2. Warm the remaining olive oil in a medium saucepan over medium heat. Add the onion halves, cut sides down. Add the remaining $^{1}/2$ teaspoon salt and cook for 2 minutes.

3. Add the tomato puree, half-and-half, and cheese, and stir to combine. Add the vodka and basil, increase the heat to high, and boil for 10 minutes (so that the alcohol will evaporate).

4. Drain the pasta and set aside. Remove the onion halves from the tomato sauce and discard. Add the pasta to the sauce and toss until the pasta is well coated. Top with Pecorino Romano, if desired, and serve immediately.

VARIATION

Penne alla Vodka with Pancetta Cook the pasta with salt and olive oil as the recipe directs in step 1. Omit step 2. Instead, proceed as follows: Heat 3 tablespoons of olive oil in a skillet and add $^{1}/4$ pound diced pancetta and 1 finely diced onion. Cook, stirring, for 2 to 3 minutes, then proceed as the recipe directs, beginning at step 3.

Fettuccine Alfredo

Serves 4

My Fettuccine Alfredo is quick and easy. I've been making it for over twenty-five years and my family and friends never say no to it. My version is different from the classic dish in several ways. First, I add chopped wild mushrooms, prosciutto, and fresh parsley to the finished dish. And second, I use Pecorino Romano cheese instead of Parmigiano-Reggiano. Pecorino Romano—made from sheep's milk—is sharper than Parmigiano and results in a more assertive-tasting dish.

Serving Suggestions
I like to serve this as a first course with Veal Marsala (page 151) or Veal Scarpetta (page 154) as a main course.

1 teaspoon salt

1 tablespoon extra virgin olive oil

¼ pound thinly sliced prosciutto, coarsely chopped

2 ounces shiitake mushrooms, stems removed, caps thinly sliced

2 tablespoons coarsely chopped fresh flat-leaf (Italian) parsley

4 tablespoons unsalted butter

1 cup heavy cream or half-and-half

1 cup grated Pecorino Romano cheese

1 large egg yolk, lightly beaten

1 pound Mamma Rosina's Homemade Tagliatelle (page 121), cut into fettuccine noodles, or best-quality fresh or dried fettuccine

1. Combine $4^{1}/_{2}$ to 5 quarts of water and the salt in a large pot and bring to a boil.

2. While the water is coming to a boil, warm the olive oil over medium heat in a small skillet. Add the prosciutto, mushrooms, and parsley. Cook, stirring, for 8 to 10 minutes, until light golden brown. Set aside.

3. Melt the butter in a small saucepan over medium-low heat. Add the heavy cream and the Pecorino Romano. When the cheese has melted, gradually add the egg yolk. Cook, stirring constantly, until the mixture thickens enough to coat the back of a spoon. Remove from the heat.

4. Add the fettuccine to the boiling water and cook for 6 to 8 minutes for fresh fettuccine. If using dried fettuccine, cook according to the package directions. Drain, and transfer pasta to a large platter. Pour the sauce over the fettuccine. Sprinkle with the mushroom-prosciutto mixture and serve immediately.

Spaghetti with Quick Neapolitan Marinara Sauce

Makes about 1 quart sauce, enough for 1 pound of pasta; serves 4 to 6

This easy sauce is said to have gotten its name from *marinaio,* the Italian word for sailor. After being at sea, a sailor returning home would want a delicious, homemade meal but would be too hungry to wait for something that took hours to prepare. Marinara sauce was the perfect solution: It was ready in twenty minutes or less, could be used to sauce a variety of pasta dishes, and it made the house smell of garlic, basil, and sweet tomatoes. After World War II, when meat was scarce, my mother improvised and sometimes served Marinara al Purgatorio for my father's supper. Mamma would poach one or two eggs in simmering marinara sauce, then serve the eggs and sauce on top of spaghetti. The red sauce represents fire; the yellow yolk represents the sun (or life). The two colors together symbolize the in-between state of purgatory. Marinara sauce is easy to make and can be frozen for up to three months.

¼ cup extra virgin olive oil

1 small onion, finely chopped (about 1 cup)

3 garlic cloves, pressed or finely chopped

1½ teaspoons salt

One 32-ounce jar homemade tomato puree (page 275), or one 35-ounce can whole plum tomatoes with juice, pureed in a blender or food processor for 3 to 5 seconds

2 tablespoons fresh flat-leaf (Italian) parsley, finely chopped (see page 75)

4 to 6 fresh basil leaves, coarsely chopped (see page 75)

1 pound spaghetti, vermicelli, fedelini, or linguine

Grated Pecorino Romano cheese, optional

1. Warm the olive oil in a medium saucepan over medium heat. Add the onion, garlic, and ½ teaspoon of the salt and cook, stirring, for 2 to 3 minutes, until the onion has softened.

2. Add the tomato puree, parsley, and basil, cover partially, and cook at a low boil, stirring occasionally, for 20 to 25 minutes. (Note: If the tomatoes condense too much, add a little water.)

3. Meanwhile, combine 4½ to 5 quarts of water with the remaining 1 teaspoon of salt in a large pot and bring to a boil. Add the pasta and cook according to the package directions, until al dente. Drain thoroughly, and place the pasta in a bowl or serving dish and ladle with the sauce. Top with cheese, if desired, and serve immediately.

TO TOSS OR NOT TO TOSS?

Some pasta sauces are meant to be tossed with the pasta while others—like Quick Neapolitan Marinara Sauce—are best ladled on top of the cooked pasta and served as is, letting each diner toss his or her own serving right on the dinner plate. The sauce for Spaghetti alle Vongole (page 99), for example, is very flavorful, but rather thin in consistency. Therefore, it's important to saturate each strand of pasta thoroughly with the sauce and this is best done individually. However, some very thick sauces—like pesto—must be tossed with pasta before serving.

Fettuccine with Green Olive Pesto

Serves 4 to 6

I love olives, and every fall I look forward to curing and canning my own. Home-cured olives (see page 272) would be wonderful in this dish, but of course, purchased imported olives are terrific, too. A variety of olives—from Sicily and southern Italy—combined with garlic, cheese, and olive oil results in an unusual pesto that is easy to make and keeps well, too.

Serving Suggestions

If serving this as a first course, I like to follow with Veal Marsala (page 151), Veal Scarpetta (page 154), or Veal Francese (page 152).

4 garlic cloves, peeled and sliced, plus 2 garlic cloves, cracked

$1/4$ cup plus 2 tablespoons extra virgin olive oil

$1^1/2$ teaspoons salt

1 pound fettuccine

2 cups Cured Green Olives (page 272), Sicilian olives, Castelvetrano olives, or Cerignola olives, pitted

6 fresh basil leaves

$3/4$ cup grated Parmigiano-Reggiano or Pecorino Romano cheese

Freshly ground black pepper to taste

1. Preheat the oven to 350°F.

2. Place the sliced garlic in a ramekin or small baking dish. Add $1/4$ cup of the olive oil and sprinkle with $1/2$ teaspoon of the salt. Roast uncovered for 15 to 20 minutes, until the garlic turns slightly golden. Set aside, reserving the oil and the garlic. (Note: To roast garlic in the microwave, see page 67.)

3. Combine $4^1/2$ to 5 quarts of water and the remaining 1 teaspoon salt in a large pot and bring to a boil. Add the pasta and cook according to the package directions, until al dente.

4. Warm the remaining 2 tablespoons of olive oil in a large skillet and add the cracked garlic. Cook over low heat just until the oil is warm. Discard the cracked garlic, but reserve the flavored oil in the skillet.

5. Combine the oven-roasted garlic and its oil, the olives, basil, and Parmigiano in a blender or food processor. Add $1/2$ cup of water (or more if the mixture is too thick) and blend for 2 seconds, until the olives are crushed.

6. Drain the pasta, then add it to the garlic-flavored oil in the skillet and toss to coat. Add the olive paste and toss again. Top with black pepper and serve immediately.

Eleanora's Tips **Cracked Garlic Cloves**

If I'm cooking a sauce, meat, fish, or skinless chicken over high or medium-high heat and I want the final dish to have garlic flavor—but no garlic—I often call for cracked garlic instead of pressed garlic. Cracked garlic cloves provide a lot of garlic flavor but don't burn as quickly as pressed garlic. (Note: This technique does not apply to chicken with skin, since the fat in chicken skin keeps pressed garlic from burning.)

Here's how I do it: Place a whole, peeled garlic clove in a kitchen towel on a sturdy work surface. Press down on the garlic with the palm of your hand, using enough pressure to crack the garlic clove. Or you can place the garlic clove directly on a work surface, place the flat side of a chef's knife on the garlic clove, then press down on the knife quickly to crack the garlic.

Rigatoni with Baby Eggplant, Tomatoes, and Basil

Serves 4 to 6

I find the tangy flavor of fresh eggplant utterly irresistible. It marries beautifully with two other southern Italian ingredients: tomatoes and basil. I make this dish often in summer, particularly when I have only two eggplants in the refrigerator and a garden full of tomatoes and basil. My family loves this as a first course, followed by a charcoal-broiled steak, hot from the grill. What a feast!

Serving Suggestions

Serve as a first course followed by Veal Scarpetta (page 154), Grilled Halibut with Green Olive–Basil Pesto (page 140), or a simply grilled steak.

¼ cup extra virgin olive oil

1 small onion, diced

4 garlic cloves, pressed or finely chopped

2 teaspoons salt

One 32-ounce jar homemade tomato puree (page 275), or one 35-ounce can whole plum tomatoes with juice, pureed in a blender or food processor for 3 to 5 seconds

6 fresh basil leaves, finely chopped

2 baby Italian eggplants (about ¾ pound total), with skin, trimmed and cut into 1-inch dice

1 pound small rigatoni or campanelle

Grated Pecorino Romano cheese to taste

1. Warm the olive oil in a large skillet over medium heat. Add the onion, garlic, and $1/2$ teaspoon of the salt, and cook, stirring, for 1 to 2 minutes, until the garlic is golden, taking care not to burn the garlic. Add the tomato puree, basil, and $1/2$ teaspoon of the salt, and cook, partially covered, for 10 to 15 minutes, stirring occasionally. (Note: If using a puree of homemade plum tomatoes or canned plum tomatoes, increase the cooking time to 20 to 25 minutes.) Add the eggplant and simmer uncovered for 10 minutes, or until the eggplant is tender. (Note: Do not overcook or the eggplant will become soft and mushy.)

2. While the sauce cooks, combine $4^1/2$ to 5 quarts of water with the remaining teaspoon of salt in a large pot and bring to a boil. Add the pasta and cook according to the package directions, until al dente. Drain, toss with the sauce, and serve immediately with the cheese.

Eleanora's Tips

To rid eggplant of its bitter flavor, proceed as follows: Slice the eggplant into 1-inch cubes. Place the cubes in a bowl and toss with 1 teaspoon of salt. Place a dish on top of the eggplant—the dish should cover all of the eggplant—then place a heavy object on top of the plate. A large can will do. This will compress the eggplant and release the juices. Let the mixture stand for 1 hour, then discard the juices. Squeeze the eggplant with your hands and add to the sauce as the recipe directs.

Gemelli with Pesto Napoletano

Makes 1 cup sauce, enough for 1 pound of pasta; serves 4 to 6

I like to use toasted pine nuts and cooked garlic—instead of raw garlic and uncooked pine nuts—for a rounder, more richly flavored pesto. When the pine nuts roast, their natural oils are released; when garlic cooks, it becomes sweeter; and both these measures make the basil less assertive—which is what makes my pesto different from classic Genovese-style pesto sauce. I love making this dish in late summer, when I've finished canning my tomatoes and I still have enough fresh basil on hand to make a big batch of pesto. It's quick and easy and the aroma of just-picked basil is irresistible. This is a wonderful dish for large gatherings since it reheats beautifully. The pesto is actually better made in advance (up to five days) because the flavors have a chance to develop.

Serving Suggestions
Try it as a first course for lunch or supper followed by Old-fashioned Tuna Loaf (page 141) or Veal Francese (page 152).

½ cup pine nuts

¼ cup extra virgin olive oil

5 garlic cloves, peeled and sliced

1½ teaspoons salt

8 to 10 large fresh basil leaves

½ cup finely grated Pecorino Romano cheese

¼ cup finely grated Parmigiano-Reggiano cheese

1 pound gemelli or Gnocchi (page 118), campanelle, rotelle, small rigatoni, penne, or medium shells

1. Preheat the oven to 350°F. Spread the pine nuts on a baking sheet and roast for 4 to 6 minutes. Turn on the broiler and broil on high for 1 to 2 minutes, until lightly golden brown. Remove from the broiler and cool to room temperature.

2. Warm the olive oil in a medium skillet over medium heat. Add the garlic and ½ teaspoon of the salt and cook, stirring, for 1 to 2 minutes, making sure the garlic does not burn. Remove from the heat and let cool for at least 1 minute.

3. Place the garlic and oil, pine nuts, basil, Pecorino Romano, and Parmigiano in a blender and process until smooth.

4. Bring 4½ to 5 quarts of water and the remaining salt to a boil in a large pot. Add the pasta and cook for 9 to 10 minutes. Drain, reserving ½ cup of the cooking water. Add the water to the blender and process until smooth. Pour the sauce over the pasta, toss to blend, and serve immediately.

Spaghetti with Cherry Tomatoes and Porcini

Serves 4 to 6

Quick, easy, and flavorful, this aromatic dish is delicious any time of year since the ingredients are always available. My hometown, Cervinara, is noted for its wild mushrooms, so my passion for them is in my blood. When I was growing up there, wild mushrooms were not only consumed fresh but also preserved in oil to enjoy all winter long. When I was a child, my cousins Luigi and Cicillo were the members of the family who were the most enthusiastic about gathering wild mushrooms for the evening meal. As an adult, I've spent many weekends in upstate New York mushroom hunting with friends. After finding gorgeous, golden specimens of wild fungi—often clustered around old trees—we would come home and prepare a quick "spaghetatta" with wild mushrooms, garlic, and oil. It's such a simple dish, but so earthy, so special.

1½ teaspoons salt

¼ cup extra virgin olive oil

4 to 6 garlic cloves, pressed or finely chopped

2 large fresh porcini mushrooms, wiped clean and chopped (about 1½ cups chopped porcini), or 1 cup (about 1 ounce) dried porcini mushrooms, reconstituted in water (see Note)

6 fresh basil leaves, finely chopped, or ½ teaspoon dried basil, preferably homemade (page 251)

1 teaspoon finely chopped fresh parsley, or ½ teaspoon dried parsley, preferably homemade (page 251)

¼ cup dry red wine

1 pint cherry tomatoes

1 cup homemade tomato puree (page 275), or 1 cup canned whole plum tomatoes with juice, pureed in a blender or food processor for 3 to 5 seconds, optional

1 pound spaghetti or linguine

1. Combine 4½ to 5 quarts of water and 1 teaspoon of the salt in a large pot and bring to a boil.

2. While the water is coming to a boil, prepare the sauce: Warm the olive oil in a large skillet over medium heat. Add the garlic and the remaining salt and cook, stirring, for 1 to 2 minutes, until the garlic is light golden in color.

3. Add the mushrooms, basil, and parsley and cook, stirring, for 2 to 3 minutes. Add the wine and cook until most of the liquid has evaporated. Add the cherry tomatoes and cook for 4 to 5 minutes. (Note: Mash the tomatoes with a potato masher or with a fork, if desired.) Add the tomato puree (if using) and cook for 5 to 7 minutes.

4. When the water comes to a boil, add the pasta and cook according to the package directions, until al dente. Drain, toss with the sauce, and serve immediately.

Note: To reconstitute dried mushrooms, place 1 cup of dried mushrooms in a small bowl with 1¼ cups of warm water. Let stand for 15 to 20 minutes or until softened. Drain (reserving the liquid if the recipe calls for it) and squeeze the mushrooms with your hands to extract as much liquid as possible.

Fusilli with Zucchini, Eggplant, and Mushrooms

Serves 4 to 6

This fast, easy dish is a variation of one that my mother used to make with sardines. Anchovies, herbs, and garlic combine in an intensely flavored sauce that marries beautifully with the eggplant, zucchini, and mushrooms. This dish is heaven for anchovy lovers. The twisted shape of the fusilli is perfect for holding the sauce. Light, and full of flavor, this dish is wonderful all year round, but I particularly enjoy it in autumn, when the days become cooler, but the garden is still producing eggplant and zucchini.

Serving Suggestions

Serve as a first course followed by Pork Loin Roast (page 159), Veal Osso Buco (page 158), or Italian-Style Sausage and Peppers (page 162).

1 1/2 teaspoons salt

1/4 cup plus 1 teaspoon extra virgin olive oil, for optional breadcrumbs

4 garlic cloves, pressed or finely chopped

1 zucchini, cut into 1/2-inch dice

1 small Italian eggplant (6 to 8 ounces) with skin, cut into 1/2-inch dice

10 anchovies packed in olive oil, diced into 1/4-inch pieces

1/4 pound fresh shiitake, porcini, or cremini mushrooms (caps and stems), wiped clean and diced

1/2 teaspoon dried oregano, preferably imported Italian

1/2 teaspoon dried parsley, preferably homemade (page 251)

1/2 teaspoon dried basil, preferably homemade (page 251)

1 pound fusilli, trenette, or bucatini

2 tablespoons unseasoned dry bread crumbs, preferably homemade (page 6), optional

Freshly ground black pepper to taste

1. Combine $4 1/2$ to 5 quarts of water and 1 teaspoon of salt in a large pot and bring to a boil for the pasta.

2. Meanwhile, make the sauce: Warm $1/4$ cup of the olive oil in a large skillet over medium heat. Add the garlic and cook, stirring, for 1 to 2 minutes, until slightly golden. Add the zucchini, eggplant, anchovies, mushrooms, oregano, parsley, basil, and $1/2$ teaspoon of the salt. Cook, stirring, for 3 to 5 minutes, until the zucchini, eggplant, and mushrooms are tender.

3. Add the pasta to the boiling water and cook according to the package directions, until al dente.

4. While the pasta cooks, toast the bread crumbs, if desired: Use a paper towel to smear the remaining teaspoon of the olive oil inside a small skillet. Add the bread crumbs and cook, stirring, over medium heat for 1 to 2 minutes, until golden. Set aside.

5. Combine the pasta with the sauce and toss to mix. Sprinkle with the toasted bread crumbs, if using, and serve immediately. Garnish with freshly ground black pepper to taste.

Spaghetti alle Vongole

I adore this classic Neapolitan dish! It's one of the most popular offerings in *ristoranti* along the Amalfi Coast, and it's easy to see why: It's light, elegant, and as fresh and as pleasant as an ocean breeze. Vongole are a delicate treat: tiny but very flavorful clams that are widely available in Naples and surrounding areas. Vongole imported from Italy are available in some of our fish markets, but if you can't find Vongole, opt for small, tasty Manila clams instead.

Serving Suggestions
Spaghetti alle Vongole is usually served as a first course. I like to follow it with Striped Bass alla Pizzaiola (page 139) or Shrimp Marachiara (page 142).

1½ pounds Vongole or Manila clams

¼ cup extra virgin olive oil

6 garlic cloves, pressed or finely chopped

2 teaspoons salt

2 dried hot red peppers, finely chopped, or ½ teaspoon red pepper flakes, optional

One 32-ounce jar homemade canned plum tomatoes (page 275) or one 35-ounce can whole plum tomatoes with juice, crushed in a blender or food processor for 2 to 3 seconds

1 pound thin spaghetti

½ cup dry white wine

6 fresh basil leaves, finely chopped

2 tablespoons finely chopped fresh flat-leaf (Italian) parsley

1. Rinse the clams under cold running water. Clean the clams (see page 9). Drain, and set aside.

2. Warm the olive oil in a medium saucepan over medium heat. Add the garlic, 1 teaspoon of the salt, and the red pepper, if using, and cook for 2 to 3 minutes. Add the tomatoes and cook, stirring occasionally, for 20 minutes, or until somewhat condensed.

3. While the sauce cooks for about 10 minutes, combine 4½ to 5 quarts of water and the remaining salt in a large pot and bring to a boil. Add the pasta to the boiling water and cook according to the package directions, until al dente.

4. While the pasta cooks, finish the sauce: Add the Vongole, wine, basil, and parsley to the sauce, cover, and cook for 5 to 7 minutes, until the clams have opened.

5. Drain the pasta and toss it with the sauce. Serve immediately.

Linguine with Shrimp, Clams, and Arugula

Serves 4 to 6

Without a doubt, this is one of my favorite pasta dishes.

Fresh shellfish, pungent capers, and the fresh "bite" of arugula combine to make a dish that's special enough for a dinner party but quick enough for busy cooks.

Start the water for the pasta, simmer the sauce, and *eccola!* Your dish is finished in almost no time at all. It's simply splendid!

Serving Suggestions
Serve with Easy Garlic Bread (page 101) as a first course followed by Striped Bass Oreganata (page 138).

¼ cup extra virgin olive oil

6 garlic cloves, pressed or finely chopped

1½ teaspoons salt

One 32-ounce jar homemade canned plum tomatoes (page 275), crushed in a blender or food processor for 2 to 3 seconds, or 1¾ to 2 pounds very ripe, fresh plum tomatoes, cored and diced

¼ cup Calabrese, Gaeta, Kalamata, or black, oil-cured Sicilian olives

¼ cup drained capers

6 fresh basil leaves, finely chopped

2 tablespoons finely chopped fresh flat-leaf (Italian) parsley

½ pound large shrimp, deveined and peeled with tails intact

1 dozen littleneck clams, cleaned (see page 9)

1 dozen Vongole or Manila clams, cleaned

1 cup coarsely chopped arugula leaves

¼ cup dry white wine

1 pound thin linguine, vermicelli, or thin spaghetti

1. Warm the olive oil in a large skillet over medium heat. Add the garlic and ¹⁄₂ teaspoon of the salt and cook for 2 to 3 minutes or until the garlic is golden in color. Do not overcook or the garlic will burn. Add the tomatoes, olives, capers, basil, and parsley, and cook for 10 minutes, stirring occasionally.

2. Add the shrimp, littlenecks, Vongole, arugula, and wine, cover, and simmer for 10 minutes more.

3. Combine $4^1/2$ to 5 quarts of water and the remaining teaspoon of salt in a large pot and bring to a boil. Add the pasta and cook according to the package directions, until al dente. Drain, and toss with the sauce. Serve immediately.

EASY GARLIC BREAD

Try this quick mix spread on purchased Italian bread:

Makes 4 to 8 slices of garlic bread, depending on the size of the slices

One 20- to 24-inch loaf of Italian bread

1 cup extra virgin olive oil

3 garlic cloves, finely chopped

**1/4 teaspoon dried basil, preferably
   homemade (page 251)**

**1/2 teaspoon dried parsley, preferably
   homemade (page 251)**

1/2 teaspoon salt

**1/2 teaspoon dried oregano, preferably
   imported Italian**

**1 teaspoon grated Pecorino Romano
   cheese, optional**

1. Preheat the oven to 350°F.

2. Slice the bread on the diagonal into 1-inch-thick slices.

3. Mix the olive oil, garlic, basil, parsley, salt, oregano, and cheese (if using) in a bowl until blended.

4. Spread the mixture onto one side of the bread slices. Place the bread, garlic side up, on a baking sheet and bake for 8 to 10 minutes. Turn on the broiler, and broil for 1 to 2 minutes until toasty and golden brown.

Linguine with White Clam Sauce

Serves 4 as a main course, 6 as a first course

Linguine bathed in fresh clam juices and white wine, and showered with garlic and parsley . . . it's no wonder that *linguine alle Vongole* is so popular in Naples and other seaside cities and towns along the Amalfi Coast. I have vivid memories of enjoying this dish in Positano, where it tasted as fresh as the sea. My family has made this for generations, and I continue to make it here, at home, for my husband and children. We all love it!

Serving Suggestions

Serve as a first course with Easy Garlic Bread (page 101), followed by Grilled Halibut with Green Olive–Basil Pesto (page 140), or serve as a meal in itself with Easy Garlic Bread and a mixed green salad.

1 1/2 teaspoons salt

1/4 cup extra virgin olive oil

6 garlic cloves, finely chopped

2 dried hot red peppers, finely chopped or crushed, or 1/2 teaspoon red pepper flakes, or to taste, optional

1 1/2 dozen littleneck clams, cleaned (see page 9)

1/4 cup dry white wine

2 tablespoons fresh flat-leaf (Italian) parsley, finely chopped

1 pound linguine or fedelini

1. Bring $4\frac{1}{2}$ to 5 quarts of water and 1 teaspoon of the salt to a boil in a large pot.

2. While the water is coming to a boil, make the sauce: Warm the olive oil in a large skillet over medium heat. Add the garlic, red pepper, if using, and the remaining salt, and cook for 1 to 2 minutes. Add the clams, cover, and cook for 5 minutes.

3. Add the wine and parsley, cover, and cook over medium heat until the clams have opened, 8 to 10 minutes. Do not overcook the clams or they will be tough and chewy.

4. While the clams simmer, add the pasta to the boiling water and cook according to the package directions, until al dente. Drain, then add the pasta to the skillet and toss to mix. Serve immediately.

VARIATION

Red Clam Sauce To make Red Clam Sauce, add half a 32-ounce jar homemade tomato puree (page 275), or one $14\frac{1}{2}$-ounce can whole plum tomatoes with juice that have been pureed in a blender for 3 to 5 seconds, after the garlic has cooked in step 2. Simmer for 10 minutes before adding the clams. (Note: If using puree from commercially canned tomatoes, simmer for 10 to 15 minutes.)

Spaghettini with Calamari Fra Diavolo

Spaghettini with Spicy Calamari Sauce

Serves 4 to 6

My mother would go to the fresh fish market every Wednesday at Montesarchio, a village in the mountains near Cervinara. She would return with an array of assorted fresh fish and calamari; the latter she would always cook on Friday.

Italian oregano is one of the dominant flavors in this pasta dish. My grandmother Cristina used to pick the stems with white bud flowers, tie them, and hang them upside down to dry in the sparkling sun until the oregano buds turned olive green. She would then sieve them to a fine powder. The aroma of fresh oregano would linger in the air all day. My town, Cervinara, is noted for having the best-tasting and most aromatic oregano of any place in Italy.

Serving Suggestions

Serve as a first course followed by Striped Bass Oreganata (page 138) or Fried Baccalà (page 146). Or serve as a meal in itself with bread, salad, and wine.

1 1/4 pounds calamari, cleaned, and body cut into 1/4-inch-thick rings (see page 7)

1/4 cup extra virgin olive oil

6 garlic cloves, pressed or finely chopped

2 teaspoons salt

3 dried hot red peppers, finely chopped or crushed, or 1 teaspoon red pepper flakes

1/2 teaspoon freshly ground black pepper

1 teaspoon dried oregano, preferably imported Italian

1/2 teaspoon dried basil, preferably homemade (page 251)

1/2 cup dry white wine

One 32-ounce jar homemade canned plum tomatoes (page 275) or one 35-ounce can whole plum tomatoes, with juice, crushed in a blender or food processor for 2 to 3 seconds

1 tablespoon finely chopped fresh flat-leaf (Italian) parsley

6 fresh basil leaves, finely chopped

1 pound spaghettini or thin linguine

1. Place the calamari rings and the head with the tentacles flat on paper towels and dry well. (Note: It is important that the calamari be very dry before you cook them in oil, or the moisture will make the oil spatter.)

2. Warm the olive oil, garlic, 1/2 teaspoon of the salt, the red pepper, black pepper, oregano, and dried basil in a large skillet over medium heat and cook, stirring, for 2 minutes.

3. Add the calamari and cook on medium to medium-high heat, stirring frequently, for 2 to 3 minutes, until the calamari has absorbed all the oil.

4. Add the wine and cook on medium heat for 2 minutes more, or until the wine has evaporated.

5. Add the tomatoes, 1/2 teaspoon of the salt, the parsley, and the fresh basil, and cook, stirring, for 6 to 8 minutes.

6. Combine 4 1/2 to 5 quarts of water and the remaining teaspoon of salt in a large pot and bring to a boil. Add the pasta and cook according to the package directions, until al dente. Drain thoroughly.

7. Distribute the pasta among the serving plates, then top with some of the calamari sauce. Let each diner toss his or her own pasta and sauce.

Pasta Mare e Monte

Pasta with Shrimp and Mushrooms

The combination of shrimp fresh from the sea and mushrooms from the earth is a splendid one. (*Mare* means "sea," and *monte* means mountain, the source of many varieties of wild mushrooms). I created this dish using home-cured green olives and marinara sauce made with crushed tomatoes. It's fast, easy, and special enough for a dinner party. I think you'll love it as much as I do.

Serving Suggestions
Serve as a first course followed by Veal Scarpetta (page 154), Veal Francese (page 152), or Stuffed Chicken Breast with Mozzarella (page 168).

1/2 cup extra virgin olive oil

1/2 teaspoon dried basil, preferably homemade (page 251)

1/2 teaspoon dried parsley, preferably homemade (page 251)

6 garlic cloves, pressed or finely chopped

3/4 pound large fresh shrimp, deveined, with tails intact

1 1/2 teaspoons salt

1 large portobello mushroom, wiped clean, stem end trimmed, diced

1 cup (about 3 ounces) dried porcini mushrooms, reconstituted in 1 cup of water and drained, or 2 cups sliced fresh shiitake mushrooms

1 cup Cured Green Olives (page 272) or imported green Sicilian olives, pitted and halved

One 32-ounce jar homemade canned plum tomatoes (page 275), or one 35-ounce can whole plum tomatoes with juice, or 1 3/4 to 2 pounds ripe, fresh plum tomatoes, cored, crushed in a blender or food processor for 2 to 3 seconds

6 fresh basil leaves, coarsely chopped

2 tablespoons fresh flat-leaf (Italian) parsley, coarsely chopped

1 pound fedelini, thin linguine, or spaghettini

1. Combine 2 tablespoons of the olive oil, the dried basil, dried parsley, and one of the pressed garlic cloves in a large bowl. Add the shrimp, toss to mix, cover, and marinate in the refrigerator for at least 2 hours or up to 12.

2. Warm the remaining olive oil in a large skillet over medium heat. Add the remaining 5 pressed garlic cloves, 1/2 teaspoon of the salt, and the portobello and porcini mushrooms, and cook, stirring, for 2 minutes. Add the olives and cook, stirring, for 2 minutes more. Add the tomatoes, fresh basil, and fresh parsley, and cook for 10 minutes. Add the shrimp, cover, and cook for 6 to 8 minutes more, until the shrimp are tender and cooked through.

3. Meanwhile, combine 4 1/2 to 5 quarts of water and the remaining teaspoon of salt in a large pot and bring to a boil. Add the pasta and cook according to the package directions, until al dente. Drain and transfer to a platter. Pour the sauce over the pasta and serve immediately.

Rigatoni with Broccoli Rabe, Sausage, and Spicy Tomato Sauce

Serves 4 to 6

Broccoli rabe is, without a doubt, one of my favorite vegetables. It was one of my mother's favorites, too; she could eat broccoli rabe every day and never tire of it. And no wonder: It's available year round, it's healthy, and it has an addictive bitter taste. Broccoli rabe is versatile, too: Try it sautéed with garlic and oil, blanched and served with a vinaigrette dressing, and, of course, with pasta. Broccoli rabe's natural bitterness is delicious paired with sweet Italian sausages, fresh tomatoes, and pasta. Try this quick dish when you're craving fresh greens.

3 garlic cloves, peeled and sliced lengthwise, plus 4 garlic cloves, pressed or finely chopped

1/4 cup plus 3 tablespoons extra virgin olive oil

2 teaspoons salt

1 medium bunch broccoli rabe (about 1 pound), trimmed

1/2 cup sun-dried tomatoes packed in olive oil

One 32-ounce jar homemade canned plum tomatoes (page 275), crushed in a blender or food processor for 2 to 3 seconds, or 1 3/4 to 2 pounds very ripe, fresh plum tomatoes, cored, seeded, and crushed in a blender or food processor for 3 to 5 seconds

2 dried hot red peppers, finely chopped or crushed, or 1/2 teaspoon red pepper flakes, optional

1 pound sweet Italian sausage, chopped into 1/2-inch pieces

1 pound rigatoni, penne, rotelli, gemelli, or campanelle

1. Preheat the oven to 350°F.

2. Place the sliced garlic, 3 tablespoons of the olive oil, and 1/2 teaspoon of the salt in a ramekin or small baking dish. Roast uncovered for 15 to 20 minutes, until the garlic turns slightly golden. Set aside, reserving the oil and the garlic. (Note: To roast garlic in the microwave, see page 67.)

3. Bring a large pot of water and 1/4 teaspoon of the salt to a boil. Add the broccoli rabe and cook until it is bright green, 1 to 2 minutes. Drain and set aside until cool enough to handle. Cut the broccoli rabe into 1-inch pieces and set aside.

4. Crush the sun-dried tomatoes in a blender and transfer to a small bowl and set aside.

5. Combine the remaining olive oil, pressed garlic, red pepper (if using), and 1/4 teaspoon of the salt in a large skillet over medium heat. Cook, stirring, for 1 to 2 minutes. Add the sausage and cook, stirring frequently, until the sausage is brown, about 10 minutes.

(continued)

6. Combine $4\frac{1}{2}$ to 5 quarts of water and the remaining salt in a large pot and bring to a boil. Add the rigatoni and cook according to the package directions, until al dente. Drain and toss with the roasted garlic and oil.

7. While the pasta cooks, finish the sauce: Add the pureed sun-dried tomatoes, plum tomatoes, and broccoli rabe to the skillet and cook uncovered until the liquid is reduced, 10 to 12 minutes. Toss the pasta with the sauce. Stir to combine, and serve immediately.

Eleanora's Tips Trimming and Cooking Broccoli Rabe

Always trim fresh broccoli rabe stems half an inch to 1 inch from the bottom. If the stems are really big, you will need to trim the stems and slit them lengthwise, which will allow the broccoli rabe to cook more evenly. Be careful not to overcook broccoli rabe; this will result in a bland-tasting, limp vegetable lacking in nutrients. Blanching broccoli rabe before adding it to a recipe helps reduce the bitter taste and tenderize the stalks.

Spaghetti Carbonara with Soppressata and Pancetta

Serves 4 as a main course, 6 as a first course

"Old hens make good soup and their eggs make good carbonara." That's what my mom used to say when she lived in Italy and had a chicken coop. You don't have to raise your own chickens to make this easy, satisfying dish; in fact, it's one of my favorite recipes for hurried nights. My family loves Spaghetti Carbonara; after all, ham and eggs are a classic combination that appeals to just about everyone. Although I call for soppressata and pancetta, you can use prosciutto or just about any smoked or cured pork for this quick dish.

Serving Suggestions
If serving as a first course, follow by Veal Scarpetta (page 154) or Stuffed Chicken Breast with Mozzarella (page 168).

1/4 cup extra virgin olive oil

1/4 pound sliced pancetta (preferably spicy, see page 11) or Canadian bacon

1/4 pound hot or sweet soppressata or dry-cured Italian sausage

2 large eggs

2 tablespoons panna (see Mail-Order Sources, page 283) or heavy cream, optional

1/4 cup grated Pecorino Romano cheese

2 tablespoons finely chopped fresh flat-leaf (Italian) parsley

1 teaspoon salt

1 pound spaghetti, linguine, thin spaghetti, or vermicelli

1/2 teaspoon dried basil, preferably homemade (page 251), optional

1/2 teaspoon dried parsley, preferably homemade (page 251), optional

Freshly ground black pepper to taste, optional

1. Warm the olive oil in a large skillet over medium heat. Add the sliced pancetta and cook uncovered until the fat has been rendered, about 2 minutes. Add the soppressata and cook, stirring, for 3 to 5 minutes. (Note: Do not overcook the soppressata or it will be tough and dry.)

2. Beat the eggs, panna (if using), Pecorino Romano, and fresh parsley in a small bowl and set aside.

3. Combine $4\frac{1}{2}$ to 5 quarts of water and the salt in a large pot and bring to a boil. Add the pasta and cook according to the package directions, until al dente.

4. Drain the pasta, then pour it into the skillet. Garnish with dried basil and dried parsley, add the egg mixture, and toss quickly and completely. Add black pepper, if desired, and serve immediately.

VARIATIONS

Vegetable (Zucchini) Carbonara (My cousin Fausto says that this is his favorite pasta dish.) Wash and trim 4 to 5 zucchini and slice them into 1/4-inch rounds. Warm 1/4 cup extra virgin olive oil in a large skillet over medium heat. Add 3 pressed garlic cloves, 1/2 teaspoon salt, the zucchini, and 6 to 8 coarsely chopped fresh basil leaves. Cover, and cook over low heat for 20 to 25 minutes, until the zucchini is soft and tender. Meanwhile, in a large pot of lightly salted boiling water, cook 1 pound of pasta until tender and drain thoroughly. Add the drained pasta to the skillet. In a bowl, beat 2 eggs with $1/4$ cup grated Pecorino Romano cheese and 1 teaspoon freshly ground black pepper. Add it to the pasta and zucchini mixture and toss well to mix completely. Serve immediately.

Bread Crumb Topping Some cooks like to top this dish with bread crumbs instead of grated cheese. To do so, warm 1 teaspoon olive oil in a small skillet. Add 2 tablespoons unseasoned dry bread crumbs, preferably homemade (page 6), and cook uncovered for 1 to 2 minutes, until golden brown. Sprinkle on top of the pasta just before serving.

Traditional Sunday Sauce alla Russo

Serves 8 to 10

I have such sweet memories of Mamma's tomato sauce simmering on the stove and the aroma of *braciole* and *codina* browning on the back burner every Sunday. I wasn't surprised when I learned that this comforting, hearty dish, brimming with tradition (the recipe has been in our family for more than a hundred years), was what my father yearned for when he returned home after ten years in Africa, where he was a prisoner during World War II. These days, I serve Sunday dinner a bit later than my mother, but the tradition and the recipe remain basically unchanged. The sauce can be reheated later in the week and ladled over a different kind of pasta dish such as Spaghetti and Meatballs.

Serving Suggestions

I usually serve this sauce over pasta as a first course on Sundays, followed by the sausage, *braciole*, spareribs, and meatballs, plus salad, bread, wine, and fresh fruit. Ziti, penne, pennoni, stuffed shells, lasagna, fresh tagliatelle (page 121), ravioli, and manicotti are all very good with Sunday Sauce.

½ cup plus 2 teaspoons extra virgin olive oil

1 medium onion, halved

¼-pound piece of pancetta (preferably spicy, see page 11) or Canadian bacon

10 garlic cloves: 5 pressed, 2 finely chopped, and 3 cracked

Salt

Three 32-ounce jars homemade canned plum tomatoes (page 275) or three 35-ounce cans whole plum tomatoes with juice, pureed in a blender or food processor for 3 to 5 seconds

One 32-ounce jar homemade tomato puree (page 275), or one 35-ounce can whole plum tomatoes with juice, pureed in a blender or food processor for 3 to 5 seconds

6 large fresh basil leaves

2 medium beef cutlets (about 9 ounces each)

2 teaspoons finely chopped fresh flat-leaf (Italian) parsley

2 teaspoons freshly grated Pecorino Romano cheese, plus extra for serving

Freshly ground black pepper to taste

4 to 5 links sweet Italian pork sausage with fennel (about ¾ pound total)

4 pork spareribs (about ¾ pound total)

½ cup dry white wine

Meatballs (recipe follows)

1 pound pasta of your choice

1. Warm ¼ cup of the olive oil in a large saucepan over medium heat. Add the onion, pancetta, pressed garlic, and ½ teaspoon salt, and cook, stirring, for 2 minutes. Add the tomatoes, tomato puree, and basil, and simmer, partially covered, for 45 minutes, stirring occasionally. Discard the onion.

2. Place the beef cutlets on a work surface to make the *braciole*. Sprinkle each piece of meat with 1 teaspoon of the olive oil, 1 finely chopped garlic clove, 1 teaspoon of the parsley, and 1 teaspoon of the Pecorino Romano. Season to taste with salt and pepper. Working with one cutlet at a time, roll up into a log shape and tie with kitchen twine.

3. Heat the remaining ¼ cup of olive oil in a large cast-iron skillet over medium heat. Add the cracked garlic and cook for 2 minutes. Add the *braciole*, sausage, and spareribs to the skillet and cook uncovered until the meats are golden brown all over, 8 to 10 minutes. Add the wine, and cook for 2 minutes longer. Remove the browned meats from the pan and add them to the sauce along with the meatballs.

4. Add 2 cups of water to the sauce and return to a simmer. Cook, partially covered, stirring occasionally over medium heat for $1^{1}/4$ hours.

5. Just before the sauce is done, bring a large pot of lightly salted water to a boil. Add the pasta and cook according to the package directions, until al dente. Drain, then transfer to a large serving platter. Serve the pasta with additional meat sauce, sprinkle with Pecorino Romano, and serve immediately.

VARIATION

Other meats can be used instead of the *braciole*, spareribs, and sausages. Try a $^{3}/4$- to 1-pound piece of veal osso buco or veal shoulder, a $^{3}/4$- to 1-pound pork loin, or a $^{1}/2$-pound piece of pancetta or pork rib. My mother often added an old-fashioned ingredient called *codina*, which is a piece of fatty pork skin seasoned, rolled, and tied with string. I find *codina* a bit fatty, so I substitute pancetta instead.

Meatballs

3 large eggs, lightly beaten

$^{1}/2$ cup freshly grated Pecorino Romano cheese

2 tablespoons finely chopped fresh flat-leaf (Italian) parsley

$^{1}/4$ teaspoon freshly ground black pepper, or to taste

$1^{1}/2$ pounds ground top sirloin

$^{3}/4$ pound ground pork

$^{3}/4$ pound ground veal

2 garlic cloves, pressed or finely chopped

2 tablespoons extra virgin olive oil

$^{1}/2$ teaspoon salt

1 slice Italian bread, soaked in water (hold the bread
   under running water for 1 to 2 seconds)

¾ cup unseasoned dry bread crumbs, preferably homemade (page 6)

½ cup light olive oil

1. Line a baking sheet with paper towels and set aside.

2. Beat the eggs, cheese, parsley, and black pepper in a large bowl. Add the beef, pork, veal, garlic, extra virgin olive oil, and salt, and mix to combine.

3. Squeeze the water from the bread and tear it into small pieces. Add the bread and the bread crumbs to the meat mixture and mix well.

4. With damp hands, working with ¼ cup of the mixture at a time, form the mixture into balls. Set the meatballs aside on a plate or platter and repeat with the remaining mixture. (Note: Do not stack the meatballs or they will lose their shape.)

5. Warm the olive oil in a large nonstick skillet over medium-high heat. When the oil is very hot, add the meatballs in one layer but do not crowd the skillet. Cook, turning frequently, until the meatballs are golden brown all over, about 2 minutes per side. Transfer the meatballs to the paper-towel-lined baking sheet to drain.

VARIATION

Baked Meatballs To bake the meatballs instead of frying, preheat oven to 350°F, and follow steps 2, 3, and 4 in the Meatball recipe. Place the formed meatballs onto greased baking pans and bake for 20 minutes. Turn the meatballs over and bake for 20 minutes longer. Add the meatballs to the sauce along with the other meats at the end of step 3 in the sauce recipe.

Homemade Cavatelli

Serves 6 to 8

Cavatelli is a traditional, hand-shaped pasta that's formed with your fingers; it's delicious with an almost endless number of sauces and no pasta machine is needed. It was a staple in our home in the Bronx, just as it was a staple in my mother's home when she was growing up in Italy. My mother would buy wheat grain then take it to the grist mill—*il mulino*—to be ground. There, the flour would be packed into a large sack, which she would carry home on her shoulder. Procuring flour was a bit of an ordeal, but necessary for making pasta of all kinds, including cavatelli. As a child, I remember watching my older sisters help my mother make cavatelli. They would gather around the large, wooden board that my father had made for pastas and breads, and it seemed that in almost no time a mound of flour, water, and eggs was turned into pasta. Later, I, too, learned to shape cavatelli at that table. This recipe makes about two pounds of pasta, enough for a large gathering. For fewer people, halve the recipe or freeze the extra pasta.

2 large eggs

1 tablespoon olive oil

9 cups all-purpose flour or bread flour, or more, as needed

1/2 cup semolina (or use all-purpose flour if semolina is unavailable)

1. Beat the eggs, 3 cups of cold water, and the olive oil in a large bowl with a fork until well combined. Gradually begin to add 5 cups of the flour while mixing with a fork. Add the flour little by little while beating continuously, until the mixture comes together to form a dough.

2. Lightly flour a rubber scraper and use it to transfer the dough to a clean, lightly floured work surface. The dough will be sticky at this point. With lightly floured hands, begin to knead the dough, slowly incorporating the remaining 4 cups as you knead. Continue to knead for 10 to 12 minutes, until the dough is smooth and elastic and not sticky. (Note: To test for doneness, dip your thumb into the dough. If the dough sticks to your thumb, it is too sticky and more flour should be incorporated.)

3. With floured hands, pat the dough into a thick, elongated loaf and let it rest for 10 to 15 minutes. Slice off a piece of dough that is approximately 2 inches wide. Slice that piece into 3 or 4 pieces.

4. Working with one piece at a time on a lightly floured work surface, roll out the dough into a long rod, about 1/2 inch in diameter and 12 to 14 inches long. Use a sharp knife to cut each rod into 1/2-inch square pieces; they will look like tiny pillows. Sprinkle a baking sheet with semolina to hold the shaped cavatelli.

5. Working with one "pillow" at a time, form the cavatelli: If you are right-handed, dip the left side of your thumb into some of the flour to prevent the dough from sticking to your thumb. Then, using medium pressure, press the "pillow" of dough away from you toward the right. (Note: Instead of using your thumb, you can use your index finger and middle finger, pressed together, to shape the cavatelli.) You are actually smearing the dough slightly across the work surface. As you make the cavatelli, use a pressure that is consistent and rhythmical, with a slight flick of the thumb; release the thumb when the cavatelli has been formed into a slightly curled shape. If you are left-handed, use the right side of your thumb and smear

MAKING CAVATELLI WITHOUT EGGS

Basic cavatelli dough can be made without eggs. If omitting eggs, use boiling water instead of cold water. Since the hot water almost "cooks" the flour, there is no need to let the dough rest after mixing.

the "pillow" away from you toward the left. Place the cavatelli in one layer on the baking sheet.

6. If you're making the cavatelli in advance, cover the cavatelli on the baking sheet with plastic wrap and refrigerate for up to 3 days. To freeze, place the cavatelli on the baking sheet in the freezer for 25 minutes. Remove the cavatelli from the baking sheet and place them in a plastic bag. Seal tightly and freeze for up to 3 months.

Eleanora's Tips

I never add salt to the cavatelli dough; salt absorbs moisture and will cause the dough to sweat and become sticky. You can add salt to the cooking water, if desired. Whenever I make cavatelli, I like to add 2 cups of cold water to the cooked pasta just before draining to stop the cooking and to prevent the cavatelli from sticking together.

Cavatelli with Sausage, Spareribs, and Pork Shoulder in Tomato Sauce

Serves 6 to 8

One 2½-pound boneless pork shoulder

2 garlic cloves, peeled and cut into slivers

2 tablespoons fresh flat-leaf (Italian) parsley leaves

½ teaspoon red pepper flakes, optional

Salt

1 pork sparerib (about ¾ pound)

½ pound sweet Italian sausage

½ pound hot Italian sausage

¼ cup extra virgin olive oil

1 small onion, finely chopped (about ½ cup)

Three 32-ounce jars homemade canned plum tomatoes (page 275) or three 35-ounce cans whole plum tomatoes with juice, pureed in a blender or food processor for 3 to 5 seconds

6 fresh basil leaves

½ cup dry red wine

½ teaspoon freshly ground black pepper

2 pounds Homemade Cavatelli (page 112)

Grated Pecorino Romano cheese, for serving

1. Preheat the broiler to high. Use the tip of a sharp knife to make eight to ten ½-inch slits about ½ inch apart on the pork shoulder. Into each slit, place the following: a sliver of garlic, some of the parsley, some of the red pepper (if using), and a small pinch of salt.

2. Place the pork shoulder, the sparerib, and the sweet and hot sausages on a roasting rack in a roasting pan. Place the pan 6 to 8 inches from the broiler and broil for 35 to 40 minutes, until well browned, turning once after 15 or 20 minutes. Prick the sausages in several places to release excess fat, then continue to broil for 5 minutes longer. Discard the fat; set the meats aside. (Note: The meats can be browned in a skillet—a cast-iron skillet works quite well—on top of the stove instead of under the broiler, if you prefer.)

3. In a large pot, warm the olive oil over medium heat. Add the onion and cook, stirring, for 2 to 3 minutes, until softened. Add the tomatoes, basil, and ½ teaspoon salt, and simmer, partially covered, for 30 minutes. Add the browned meats and simmer for 45 minutes to 1 hour, until the sauce has thickened. Add the wine and simmer for 1 to 2 minutes. Add the black pepper and remove the meats from the sauce. (The meats can be covered to keep warm, and served as a second course, after the cavatelli.)

4. Bring a large pot of lightly salted water to a boil. Add the cavatelli and cook for 10 to 12 minutes or until tender. Drain, and transfer to a platter. Top with the sauce, sprinkle with the Pecorino Romano, and serve immediately.

VARIATION

Instead of sweet sausage, substitute 2 medium pork tenderloins (1 pound each), butterflied. Place the tenderloins on a work surface and sprinkle the opening of each with 2 teaspoons extra virgin olive oil, 1 finely chopped garlic clove, 1 tablespoon grated Pecorino Romano cheese, and 1 teaspoon finely chopped fresh flat-leaf (Italian) parsley. Roll up each tenderloin to close it; tie with kitchen twine.

Baked Cavatelli with Lamb-Tomato Sauce

Serves 6 as a main course, 8 as a first course

Whenever I make cavatelli, I always make plenty—so that we can enjoy it later in the week. I love serving cavatelli with Traditional Sunday Sauce alla Russo (page 109), but when time is limited, this meaty sauce is much faster and easier. (Incidentally, if you prefer, veal, pork, or beef can be substituted for the lamb.) If you have cavatelli on hand, you can have a hearty, homemade baked pasta main dish on the table in just a little over an hour. My family and friends love it! The presentation—individual baking dishes—is pretty fabulous, too. Of course, you can also make this in a larger, 9 X 13-inch baking pan if you prefer.

Serving Suggestions

If serving this as a first course, try following it with Veal Sorrentino (page 156). If serving this as a main course, serve with a tossed green salad, bread, and red wine.

$1/4$ cup plus 1 tablespoon extra virgin olive oil

6 garlic cloves, pressed or finely chopped

2 shallots, finely chopped

$1\frac{1}{2}$ teaspoons salt

$1\frac{1}{4}$ pounds ground lamb, veal, pork, or beef

$1/2$ teaspoon freshly ground black pepper

1 cup dry red wine

One 32-ounce jar homemade canned plum tomatoes (page 275) or one 35-ounce can whole plum tomatoes with juice, pureed in a blender or food processor for 3 to 5 seconds

One 32-ounce jar homemade tomato puree (page 275), or one 35-ounce can whole plum tomatoes with juice, pureed in a blender or food processor for 3 to 5 seconds

6 sprigs fresh flat-leaf (Italian) parsley

6 fresh basil leaves

$1\frac{1}{2}$ pounds Homemade Cavatelli (page 112)

$1/2$ pound smoked whole-milk mozzarella cheese, cut into $1/2$-inch dice

Grated Pecorino Romano cheese, optional

1. Warm $1/4$ cup of the olive oil in a large skillet over medium heat. Add the garlic, shallots, and $1/2$ teaspoon of the salt, and cook, stirring, until the garlic turns slightly golden, 1 to 2 minutes.

2. Mix the lamb with 1 tablespoon of the olive oil, $1/2$ teaspoon of the salt, and the pepper in a bowl until combined. Add the seasoned lamb to the skillet and immediately begin to stir, making sure the meat breaks into small pieces and browns completely. Cook, stirring, for 3 to 5 minutes, until the mixture almost begins to stick to the skillet.

3. Add the wine and cook for 2 to 3 minutes longer. Add the pureed plum tomatoes, tomato puree, parsley, basil, and the remaining $1/2$ teaspoon salt. Bring to a boil, lower the heat, and cook, partially covered, at a low boil for 1 hour.

4. Preheat the oven to 375°F.

5. Ten minutes before the sauce is done, cook the pasta: Bring $5^1/2$ to 6 quarts of water to a boil in a large pot. Add the cavatelli and cook for 10 to 12 minutes, until tender. Drain, and set aside.

6. Ladle $^1/2$ cup of the sauce into each of 6 to 8 individual baking dishes that are $6^1/2$ inches in diameter and 3 inches deep. Place about $1^1/2$ cups of the cooked, drained cavatelli into each baking dish on top of the sauce, dividing the cavatelli equally among the baking dishes. Top the cavatelli with the remaining sauce, dividing it equally among the baking dishes. Top with the mozzarella. Cover with foil and bake for 10 to 15 minutes, until the mozzarella has melted. Sprinkle with Pecorino Romano, if desired, and serve immediately.

Gnocchi

Made from flour, eggs, and potatoes, this homemade pasta is melt-in-the-mouth tender. My kids are crazy about potato gnocchi; they gather around the table—each with a fork in hand—eager to help shape and press the dough. This classic southern Italian dish can be served with Neapolitan ragù (Traditional Sunday Sauce alla Russo, page 109) or tossed with Green Olive Pesto (page 92), Rich Marinara Sauce (page 127), or cooked broccoli rabe. I also serve gnocchi with the quick Sun-Dried Tomato Sauce that follows this recipe.

Serving Suggestions
Serve as a first course followed by Veal Osso Buco (page 158) or Stuffed Chicken Breast with Mozzarella (page 168).

1 1/4 pounds baking potatoes (russet or Idaho), scrubbed

2 large eggs

1 tablespoon extra virgin olive oil

3 1/2 cups all-purpose flour, plus additional flour for rolling and shaping the gnocchi

1 teaspoon salt

Sun-Dried Tomato Sauce (recipe follows) or desired sauce

Grated Pecorino Romano or Parmigiano-Reggiano or crumbled Gorgonzola cheese, optional

1. To make the dough: Put the potatoes in a large saucepan and add enough water to cover by at least 4 inches. Bring to a boil and cook for 40 to 50 minutes, until tender. Drain, then set aside until cool enough to handle. Peel the potatoes.

2. Beat the eggs in a large bowl. Press the potatoes through a strainer into the egg mixture. Add the olive oil and mix well.

3. Gradually add 2 cups of the flour and mix until you have a smooth dough that is slightly sticky.

4. Place the dough on a lightly floured work surface and with lightly floured hands, knead for 4 to 5 minutes, incorporating up to 1 1/2 cups of additional flour into the dough as you knead. The dough should not adhere to your thumb or fingers when you press a small portion of it onto the work surface. (Note: Although I usually make gnocchi dough by hand, you can mix the dough with an electric mixer and knead it with a dough hook, if you prefer.)

5. Form the dough into a 12-inch-long loaf shape. Let the dough rest for 10 to 15 minutes. Cut the loaf into 4 equal pieces, and then cut each of those pieces into 4 more equal pieces. You will have 16 pieces of dough.

6. On a lightly floured surface, use your hands to roll out each piece into rods that are about 10 inches long and about 3/4 inch in diameter, adding

Eleanora's Tips **Boiling Potatoes**
When boiling potatoes, leave the skin on so that the potatoes absorb less water. This is particularly important when boiling potatoes for gnocchi, since watery potatoes will add too much water to the dough.

flour as needed to prevent sticking. Cut each rod into $3/4$-inch lengths; they will resemble square pillows. (Note: You can press the sides or top surface of the gnocchi with the tines of a fork for a ridged effect; the ridges help "capture" the sauce.) Place the gnocchi on a baking sheet that has been lined with lightly floured parchment paper. The gnocchi are ready to cook or freeze at this point.

7. To cook gnocchi: Combine $4^1/2$ to 5 quarts of water and the salt in a large pot of water and bring to a boil. Add the gnocchi and cook for about 6 to 8 minutes, until tender. Check for doneness by opening the gnocchi with a fork to see if there is any uncooked dough in the center. Use a large slotted spoon to remove the gnocchi from the boiling water and transfer them to the bowl. Add your sauce to the gnocchi, toss gently to mix, sprinkle with Pecorino Romano, if desired, and serve immediately.

VARIATION

Ricotta Gnocchi   Omit the potatoes and add 1 pound (2 cups) fresh or processed whole-milk ricotta. (If you can get *ricotta di bufala*—buffalo milk ricotta—by all means use it.)

Eleanora's Tips   Refrigerating or Freezing Gnocchi

To refrigerate gnocchi, place the gnocchi in one layer on a flat baking pan, cover with plastic wrap, and refrigerate for up to 3 days. To freeze gnocchi, place them in one layer on a flat baking pan (do not cover the pan) and place in the freezer for 20 to 25 minutes. Transfer the gnocchi from the pan to a plastic bag, seal tightly, and freeze for up to 3 months.

Sun-Dried Tomato Sauce

5 garlic cloves, peeled and sliced lengthwise

¼ cup extra virgin olive oil

1 teaspoon salt

1½ cups sun-dried tomatoes packed in oil

½ teaspoon dried basil, preferably homemade (page 251)

½ teaspoon dried parsley, preferably homemade (page 251)

1. Preheat the oven to 350°F.

2. Place the sliced garlic in a ramekin or small baking dish. Add the olive oil and sprinkle with the salt. Roast uncovered for 15 to 20 minutes, until the garlic turns slightly golden. (For roasting garlic in a microwave oven, see page 67.)

3. Place the sun-dried tomatoes, basil, parsley, and the roasted garlic and its oil into a blender and blend until coarsely chopped.

VARIATION

For a slightly different flavor, add 2 cups finely chopped fresh spinach to the sauce.

Mamma Rosina's Homemade Tagliatelle

Serves 4 to 6

2¼ cups all-purpose flour	5 large eggs
2¼ cups semolina, plus more for sprinkling	1 tablespoon olive oil
	1 teaspoon salt

Although there was a very good noodle shop up the street when I was growing up on Belmont Avenue, even their freshest homemade noodles couldn't hold a candle to my mother's homemade fettuccine and tagliatelle. She made noodles early in the morning, and then she'd lay the flat sheets of dough on a sheet of fresh linen on her bed. Everyone in the neighborhood agreed that there was no fresh pasta that could compare to those made with love by Mamma Rosina. Homemade noodles aren't difficult to make, and except for an extra-long rolling pin, they don't require any special equipment. And just wait until you taste them: They're heavenly. You'll no doubt see what all the fuss was about on Belmont Avenue in the Bronx.

Serving Suggestions
Serve these noodles with Sunday Sauce alla Russo (page 109), Rich Marinara Sauce (page 127), Alfredo sauce (page 89), or use instead of cavatelli in Baked Cavatelli with Lamb-Tomato Sauce (page 116).

1. Mix the flour and 2¼ cups of the semolina in a large bowl until combined. Mound the mixture onto a large work surface and make a well in the center. Add the eggs and ³/₄ cup of water to the well and beat them with a fork until combined. Gradually draw the flour-semolina mixture into the liquid, until all is incorporated into a smooth dough. Knead the dough on a lightly floured surface for 10 minutes, or until smooth and elastic. Cut the dough in half and cover it with an inverted ceramic bowl or with wax paper and let rest for 10 to 15 minutes.

2. Sprinkle the work surface with some semolina. Working with one piece of dough at a time, begin to roll out the dough with a rolling pin to flatten it as much as you can, turning the dough a quarter turn clockwise every time you start to stretch it out. When the dough circle has reached about 14 inches in diameter, place the rolling pin at the edge of the circle, then roll the dough around the rolling pin. Bring the rolling pin with the dough wrapped around it to the edge of the work surface and begin to roll it out halfway until the tail end of the dough "flops" onto the board. Bring it back again toward the end of the work surface and repeat 3 to 4 times, working your way around the rim of the dough circle. Roll out gently by turning the rolling pin in the opposite direction to release the dough, allowing the dough to lie flat on the work surface. Turn the dough a quarter turn so that you can begin again at a different edge of the dough. Repeat 3 to 4 times, working your way around the rim of the dough circle. Continue in this manner until the dough circle is 20 to 24 inches in diameter. Sprinkle some semolina on top of the dough, then let it dry uncovered at room temperature for 1 hour.

3. Fold the dough as follows: Bring both ends of the circle to meet in the center of the dough. Repeat, taking the folded ends and folding them toward the center. Finally, fold the dough in half—folding one entire side to sit on top of the other side—to make one long, layered piece of dough.

(continued)

4. Use a sharp knife to cut the folded dough crosswise into $1/4$-inch-wide strips. (Note: The noodles will swell as they cook.)

5. Unfold the noodle strands by picking them up with a fork and letting the noodles dangle. (If the noodles cling to one another, untangle them gently with your fingers.) Place the noodles on a sheet of wax paper that has been lightly sprinkled with some semolina. Do not let the noodles dry out at this point; if they sit at room temperature uncovered longer than 15 minutes, they will become brittle. (You can store the noodles for later use by wrapping them in plastic wrap and then placing them into an airtight freezer bag. Refrigerate until needed.)

6. Bring 7 quarts of water to a boil in a large pot. Add the salt. Add the tagliatelle and cook for 6 to 8 minutes, until tender but not too soft. (To check for doneness, use a long fork to remove one strand of tagliatelle from the pot. Place it in a small dish, let it cool slightly, then taste. If the strand is chewy and tough, the pasta needs to cook longer.) Drain thoroughly, and top with your desired sauce.

VARIATION

Polenta Noodles Substitute polenta or cornmeal for the semolina. Polenta noodles are somewhat heartier than regular noodles and are especially delicious when combined with beans, such as in Pasta e Fagioli (page 68). Sometimes I like to cut Polenta Noodles into small, ragged pieces about $1 1/2$ by $1/2$ inches—a short pappardelle shape. Or cut them slightly wider, if you prefer.

Homemade Ravioli
with Ricotta Stuffing

Makes about 60 ravioli; serves 8 to 10 as a
main course, 10 to 12 as a first course

At my house, ravioli are served on Sunday. That's when I have time to cook, and it's also when I want to serve something special. My ravioli are large, with plenty of creamy filling made with a combination of fresh ricotta and ricotta salata. I've been told that my homemade ravioli are absolutely irresistible; whenever I make them, my family is all smiles.

Serving Suggestions
Serve ravioli with Traditional Sunday Sauce alla Russo (page 109), or make a quick Rich Marinara Sauce (page 127).

2 pounds (4 cups) fresh or processed whole-milk ricotta cheese

1 large egg

1 teaspoon freshly ground black pepper

2 tablespoons finely chopped fresh flat-leaf (Italian) parsley

1 cup (4 ounces) grated ricotta salata or Pecorino Romano cheese

Mamma Rosina's Homemade Tagliatelle (page 121) prepared through step 1

Semolina, for dusting

1 teaspoon salt

1. Place the ricotta in a sieve set over a bowl to drain. Cover and place in the refrigerator for 2 to 3 hours (for fresh ricotta) or 8 hours (for processed ricotta). Discard the whey (or use it for baking bread) and keep the drained ricotta refrigerated until ready to use.

2. Beat the egg, pepper, and parsley in a large bowl with a fork. Add the grated cheese and mix well. Add the drained ricotta and mash the mixture with a fork to blend completely. Set aside.

3. Working with one piece of tagliatelle dough at a time on a lightly floured work surface, roll out the dough into a rectangle about 18 inches by 14 inches. (Note: The dough for ravioli needs to be thicker than that for tagliatelle.) Place the dough on the work surface vertically; one of the short sides of the rectangle should be right in front of you and the long sides on the left and the right.

4. Begin by making one row of ravioli at a time. Measure 4 inches from the bottom end of the dough (the short end that is nearest you). Working from left to right, begin to place little mounds of the ricotta filling (about

Eleanora's Tips **Cooking Homemade Pasta and Gnocchi**
When cooking homemade pasta and gnocchi, if the boiling water begins to overflow, do not reduce the heat. Instead, add 1 cup of cold water to the boiling water, which will keep the boiling water from overflowing.

2 teaspoons per mound) on the dough about 1 inch apart from each other and 4 inches away from the bottom end of the dough.

5. When you have completed the row, take the 2 corners of the dough that are closest to you and pull them up, gently stretching the dough to come up and over the row of ricotta mounds—like pulling up a blanket—to cover them. Be sure to leave about $1/8$ inch of dough away from the ricotta filling where the fold is, so that the fold is not directly on the filling.

6. Use a pizza cutter or a sharp knife to cut the dough horizontally from left to right, cutting off the entire row of ravioli. Then cut out each ravioli. You now have 6 to 7 ravioli. Continue in this manner, making one row of ravioli at a time, until all the dough is used. (Note: If you have excess dough around the ravioli, trim it off and reserve it to roll out and make additional ravioli.)

7. Seal the outer rims of the ravioli with a fork, as you would press the rim of pastry when making a pie, to bind the dough and to create an attractive look. Lightly dust a baking sheet with the semolina and arrange the sealed ravioli in one layer on the sheet. At this point, you can refrigerate or freeze the ravioli; see below.

8. To cook ravioli: Bring 7 quarts of water and the salt to a boil in a large pot. Add the ravioli and stir a few times to prevent them from sticking to one another. Cover the pot and return the water to a boil. Cook for about 8 minutes, or until the ravioli are cooked through. (To test, use a slotted spoon and remove one ravioli from the water and let it cool slightly. Cut into it—or taste it—to check for doneness.) Drain thoroughly.

9. Once you've drained the cooked ravioli, immediately place 1 cup of the desired sauce on a large serving platter (this will keep the ravioli from sticking to one another). Place the ravioli on the sauce, then top with 2 cups of sauce. Do not toss the ravioli. Serve immediately.

Eleanora's Tips **Refrigerating or Freezing Ravioli**

Proceed as the recipe directs through step 7.

To Refrigerate Ravioli

After placing the ravioli in one layer on the baking sheet, cover completely with plastic wrap (so that they won't dry out) and refrigerate for up to 5 days. Let the cold ravioli warm at room temperature for 10 to 15 minutes before cooking.

To Freeze Ravioli

Sprinkle some of the semolina onto a baking sheet or flat dish. Place the ravioli in one layer on the baking dish. Place in the freezer uncovered for 10 to 15 minutes. Remove from the baking sheet and place the ravioli one by one, side by side in one layer, in a flat plastic freezer container lined with parchment paper. Place another sheet of parchment paper on top of the ravioli, then repeat the process until all the ravioli are in the container. Cover tightly and freeze for up to 3 months. When ready to use, open the lid and let the ravioli thaw at room temperature for 10 minutes. Remove the ravioli from the container and place them in one layer on a large baking sheet for at least 1 hour before cooking.

Manicotti Stuffed with Ricotta and Mozzarella with Rich Marinara Sauce

Serves 8 to 10

I associate manicotti with special occasions, since my mother always made it for holidays, birthdays, anniversaries, and other festive gatherings. Sometimes she would make it just to ensure that every member of the family would be at the table; no one wanted to miss her manicotti. Mamma always served it with her famous ragù (Traditional Sunday Sauce alla Russo, page 109), but it is also delicious with this Rich Marinara Sauce. Leftovers reheat beautifully; you'll have a delicious dinner later in the week.

Serving Suggestions

Manicotti is traditionally served as a first course, followed by *braciole*, meatballs, and sausages (see Traditional Sunday Sauce alla Russo, page 109) or with Pork Loin Roast (page 159). For starters, I like to serve an antipasto platter.

Rich Marinara Sauce (recipe follows)

1 large egg

1 1/2 pounds (3 cups) fresh or processed whole-milk ricotta cheese, preferably fresh

2 cups (8 ounces) shredded whole-milk mozzarella cheese, preferably fresh dry mozzarella (see page 10)

2 tablespoons grated Pecorino Romano cheese

1 1/2 teaspoons salt

1/2 teaspoon freshly ground black pepper

1 tablespoon finely chopped fresh flat-leaf (Italian) parsley

1 teaspoon olive oil

1 pound manicotti

Grated Parmigiano-Reggiano or Pecorino Romano cheese, optional

1. Prepare the Rich Marinara Sauce as the recipe directs.

2. While the sauce cooks, prepare the stuffing: Break the egg into a large bowl and beat well. Add the ricotta and blend to mix. Add the mozzarella, Pecorino Romano, 1/2 teaspoon of salt, pepper, and parsley, and mix well.

3. Bring about 6 1/2 quarts of water with the remaining salt to a boil. Add the olive oil and the manicotti and cook for 12 to 14 minutes, until al dente. Drain, and set aside.

4. When the manicotti is cool enough to handle, stuff about 5 heaping tablespoons of the ricotta stuffing into each of the manicotti.

5. Ladle or pour 1 cup of Rich Marinara Sauce and 1/2 cup of water onto the bottom of a 9 X 13-inch baking dish. Place the manicotti in the baking dish in one layer. Pour half the remaining Rich Marinara Sauce (about 1 1/2 cups) over the manicotti. Cover with foil and bake for 35 to 40 minutes, until bubbling around the edges. Heat the remaining Rich Marinara Sauce. To serve, remove one or two manicotti from the baking dish, top with additional sauce, and sprinkle with grated Parmigiano, if desired.

Rich Marinara Sauce

Makes about 1½ quarts

This marinara sauce—flavored with pancetta—is thicker and more condensed than Quick Neapolitan Marinara Sauce (page 90). It can be made up to 5 days in advance or frozen for up to 3 months. I prefer to use fresh basil in this sauce, but you can use dried instead if fresh is not available.

¼ cup extra virgin olive oil

4 large garlic cloves, pressed or finely chopped

1 medium onion, halved

½-pound piece of pancetta (preferably spicy, see page 11) or
    Canadian bacon

½ teaspoon salt

One 32-ounce jar homemade canned plum tomatoes (page
    275) or one 35-ounce can whole plum tomatoes with
    juice, pureed in a blender or food processor for
    3 to 5 seconds

One 32-ounce jar homemade tomato puree (page 275), or
    one 35-ounce can whole plum tomatoes with juice,
    pureed in a blender or food processor for 3 to 5
    seconds

6 fresh basil leaves

1. Warm the olive oil, garlic, onion, pancetta, and salt in a medium saucepan over medium heat, until the garlic is pale golden.

2. Add the processed plum tomatoes and cook at a low boil, stirring occasionally, for 15 to 20 minutes.

3. Discard the onion, then add the tomato puree and cook at a low boil for 10 minutes more. (Note: If the sauce seems too condensed or too thick, add 1 cup of water.) Add the basil and simmer for 5 minutes longer.

Classic Lasagna

Serves 8 to 10

When I was growing up, lasagna was the ultimate pasta dish, made for special occasions and for festive events. My sisters and I remember some of my mother's earliest lasagna dinners at our home on 118th Street in Harlem. My mother frequently made it on Sundays and for events such as my nephew Vincenzo's baptismal celebration party. But no matter what the occasion, Mamma's lasagna always brought excitement to the table. Today, I also prepare lasagna on Sundays as well as for festive gatherings in my Connecticut home, including Easter, Christmas, and New Year's Day. The most crucial step in making lasagna is the first: draining the ricotta. If the ricotta is not drained, the mixture will not bind properly. Processed ricotta cheese has a higher water content than fresh ricotta, so it requires about twice as much time to drain.

3 pounds fresh or processed whole-milk ricotta cheese

2 large eggs

1 pound fresh dry or processed whole-milk mozzarella cheese, shredded or crumbled (see page 10)

½ pound fresh cheese or basket cheese (page 6), optional

2 teaspoons salt

1 teaspoon freshly ground black pepper

2 tablespoons finely chopped fresh flat-leaf (Italian) parsley

2 cups grated Pecorino Romano cheese, plus extra for serving

1 tablespoon olive oil

18 strips lasagna (1 to 1¼ pounds), preferably imported, or no-boil lasagna

Traditional Sunday Sauce alla Russo (page 109), omit meatballs

Lasagna Meatballs (recipe follows)

1. Place the ricotta cheese in a sieve set over a bowl to drain. Cover and place in the refrigerator for 2 to 3 hours (for fresh ricotta) or 8 hours (for processed ricotta). Discard the whey and keep the drained ricotta refrigerated until ready to use.

2. Prepare the ricotta mix: Combine the eggs, mozzarella, fresh cheese (if using), 1 teaspoon of the salt, the pepper, parsley, ricotta, and ½ cup Pecorino Romano in a bowl and stir gently to mix.

3. Cook the pasta (unless you are using no-boil): Combine 8 to 9 quarts of water, the olive oil, and the remaining teaspoon of salt in a large, wide pot and bring to a boil. Add the pasta and cook 11 to 12 minutes, until tender. (Note: Do not overcook; if you see the pasta beginning to tear, it is done and should be drained immediately.) Drain, and let cool briefly until easy to handle. Hang the strips one by one over the colander so that they cool without sticking to one another (or lay the strips flat on a sheet of parchment paper). Note: If the lasagna sits out for too long, the strips will stick to one another.

4. Preheat the oven to 350°F.

5. Ladle or pour 1 cup of the Sunday Sauce with 1 cup of water onto the bottom of a 9 X 13-inch baking dish. Spread the sauce-water mixture evenly on the bottom of the dish. (Note: You can use a smaller baking dish if you prefer a deeper lasagna with more layers. Adjust the cooking time accordingly.)

6. Lay the cooked pasta strips or dry no-boil noodles on the sauce to cover the bottom. You will need about 4 strips of lasagna for the length of the dish and 1 strip for the short ends of the dish. (Note: Some strips will fit perfectly; other brands may need to be trimmed to fit. Use a knife or kitchen scissors to trim the strips to fit the dish or simply break no-boil pieces.)

7. Spread half the ricotta mixture on top of the pasta. Arrange half of the Lasagna Meatballs in one layer on top of the ricotta mixture. Ladle or pour $1^{1}/2$ cups of Sunday Sauce over the cheese. Sprinkle evenly with $^{1}/2$ cup of Pecorino Romano.

8. Repeat the layers: Pasta, remaining ricotta mix, remaining meatballs, $1^{1}/2$ cups sauce, and $^{1}/2$ cup Pecorino Romano. For the final layer, place the remaining pasta on the Pecorino Romano, top it with $1^{1}/2$ cups sauce, then add the $^{1}/2$ cup Pecorino Romano.

9. Cover with foil and bake for 45 minutes to 1 hour, until bubbling around the edges. Remove from the oven and set aside for 15 minutes at room temperature before serving. Use a metal spatula to cut portions that are about 4 inches square. Serve immediately with additional tomato sauce and grated cheese.

Lasagna Meatballs

2 large eggs

3 tablespoons grated Pecorino Romano cheese

2 tablespoons finely chopped fresh flat-leaf (Italian) parsley

$\frac{1}{2}$ teaspoon salt

$\frac{1}{2}$ teaspoon freshly ground black pepper

$\frac{1}{2}$ pound ground veal

$\frac{1}{2}$ pound ground beef

$\frac{1}{2}$ pound ground pork

2 garlic cloves, pressed or finely chopped

1 tablespoon extra virgin olive oil

$\frac{1}{2}$ cup unseasoned dry bread crumbs, preferably homemade (page 6)

1 $\frac{1}{4}$ cups light olive oil

1. Beat the eggs, Pecorino Romano, parsley, salt, and pepper together in a large bowl.

2. Add the ground veal, ground beef, ground pork, garlic, extra virgin olive oil, and bread crumbs, and mix until just combined.

3. Wet your hands with water and make the meatballs, using about 1 teaspoon of the mixture for each meatball. Place them in one layer on a baking pan as you work. The meatballs can be made up to 1 day in advance; cover and refrigerate.

4. Heat the olive oil in a 10-inch nonstick skillet over medium heat. Working in batches, add the meatballs and cook for 3 to 4 minutes, turning frequently, or until the meatballs are nicely browned. Transfer the meatballs as they are done to a paper-towel-lined baking dish or baking sheet, use as the recipe directs, or cover and refrigerate for up to 4 days.

Baked Penne with Peas, Prosciutto, and Mozzarella

Serves 6 to 8

Combining onions and garlic in the same dish can be baffling to some Neapolitans, who believe that one cancels out the other. However, they exist harmoniously—and deliciously—in this easy baked pasta dish, which is a favorite in my family. (It's a delicious way to get your children to eat peas.) The word *lisce* means "smooth" (as opposed to "ridged"), referring to the type of penne. Because the pasta is cooked twice—boiled then baked—make sure it is al dente before baking.

Serving Suggestions
Serve this dish as a main course with a mixed green salad.

½ cup extra virgin olive oil

6 garlic cloves, pressed or finely chopped

1 onion, sliced in half

2 teaspoons salt

One 32-ounce jar homemade canned tomato puree (page 275), or one 35-ounce can whole plum tomatoes with juice, pureed in a blender or food processor for 3 to 5 seconds

Half a 32-ounce jar homemade canned tomato puree (page 275) or one 14½-ounce can whole plum tomatoes with juice, pureed in a blender for 3 to 5 seconds

¼ cup panna (see Mail-Order Sources, page 283) or heavy cream, or 2 tablespoons mascarpone

6 fresh basil leaves, coarsely chopped

3 garlic cloves, peeled and sliced lengthwise

½ pound prosciutto, smoked ham, or sopressata, diced

1½ pounds penne *lisce* (smooth) or penne *rigate* (ridged)

One 16-ounce package frozen peas, or 2 cups cooked fresh peas

1 teaspoon dried basil, preferably homemade (page 251)

4 cups (1 pound) grated whole-milk mozzarella cheese, preferably fresh dry (see page 10), or smoked mozzarella

½ cup grated Parmigiano-Reggiano cheese or Pecorino Romano cheese

1. Preheat the oven to 350°F.

2. Warm ¼ cup of the olive oil in a medium saucepan over medium heat. Add the pressed garlic, the onion, and ½ teaspoon of the salt. Cook, stirring, for 2 minutes, then add the tomato puree, panna, and basil. Simmer, partially covered, for 15 to 20 minutes, until the sauce has thickened. Discard the onion.

3. While the sauce cooks, roast the garlic: Place the sliced garlic in a ramekin or small baking dish. Add 3 tablespoons of the olive oil and sprinkle with ½ teaspoon of the salt. Roast uncovered for 15 to 20 minutes, until garlic turns slightly golden. Set aside, reserving the oil and the garlic. (Note: To roast garlic in the microwave, see page 67.)

(continued)

4. Warm the remaining 1 tablespoon olive oil in a small skillet over medium heat. Add the prosciutto and cook, stirring, for 2 to 3 minutes, until the prosciutto looks crispy and deep golden brown around the edges.

5. Combine 6 quarts of water and the remaining 1 teaspoon of salt in a large pot and bring to a boil. Add the pasta and cook for 1 to 2 minutes less than the time recommended on the package; the pasta must be al dente. While the pasta cooks, cook the peas in a separate saucepan according to the package directions; drain thoroughly.

6. Drain the pasta, then transfer it to a large bowl. Add the roasted garlic, peas, and prosciutto. Sprinkle with the dried basil. Use a ladle or a measuring cup and add $1^1/2$ cups of the tomato sauce and toss to blend.

7. Pour half of the pasta into a 10 X 12-inch baking dish; it should be about half full. Pour or ladle $^1/2$ cup of the tomato sauce evenly on top of the pasta mixture. Top the sauce with half the mozzarella, then sprinkle with $^1/4$ cup of the Parmigiano. Repeat the layers: Pour the remaining pasta mixture on top of the Parmigiano, pour or ladle on the remaining tomato sauce, then add the remaining mozzarella and the remaining Parmigiano.

8. Cover with foil and bake for 20 to 25 minutes. Remove from the oven and let the pasta settle for 5 minutes before serving. Scoop out portions with a large spoon and serve immediately.

Neapolitan Spaghetti Pie

Serves 10 to 12

Leave it to Neapolitans to transform leftover pasta into a delectable rustic pie made with eggs, soppressata, and mozzarella. My mother often made this easy dish for my father, especially when she was really busy with her household chores. Although I bake this pie in the oven, Mamma sometimes cooked it in a skillet on top of the stove. She'd make sure the pie was nice and crispy on both sides, turning it with a spatula right in the skillet. As a child, I always loved this hearty treat; I especially enjoyed eating the crispy spaghetti crust. Spaghetti pie can be made up to five days in advance and reheated or served at room temperature.

Serving Suggestions
Neapolitan Spaghetti Pie is delicious as a light lunch with a tossed green salad. I also find that it is a terrific addition to a buffet, and it travels well. I often serve it as a first course followed by a bowl of Turkey Wing Soup with Winter Vegetables (page 78), Tomato Soup with Fresh Basil (page 64), or another one of my comforting soups.

Light olive oil

6 large eggs, lightly beaten

1/4 cup heavy cream

1 pound dry-aged (see page 10) or processed whole-milk mozzarella cheese, grated

12 ounces hot soppressata sausage, cut into 1/4-inch dice

1 cup (1/4 pound) finely grated Pecorino Romano cheese

1 teaspoon dried parsley, preferably homemade (page 251), optional

Salt to taste

1/2 teaspoon freshly ground black pepper, plus more to taste

8 cups cooked spaghetti (1 1/4 pounds dried pasta)

1. Preheat the oven to 375°F, placing the oven rack in the middle position. Brush the bottom and sides of a 10-inch round cake pan that is 3 inches deep with olive oil. Line the bottom inside of the pan with parchment paper. Set aside.

2. Combine the eggs, cream, mozzarella, soppressata, Pecorino Romano, dried parsley (if using), salt, and pepper in a large bowl. Stir to combine. Add the spaghetti and stir again. Pour the mixture into the prepared pan.

3. Cover the pan with foil and bake for 40 minutes. Remove the foil, and bake for 20 minutes longer, or until lightly browned and crisp.

4. Remove from the oven and cool on a baking rack for about 10 minutes. Run a knife around the edge to loosen the pie. Place a large plate or platter on top of the pie, and invert to unmold, discarding the parchment paper. Place a plate or platter on top of the pie, and invert again. Cut into wedges and serve warm or at room temperature.

FISH AND SHELLFISH

*I*taly's long coastline—punctuated with lively ports and colorful fishing villages—is one of the main reasons that the country's cuisine is so rich in seafood. For Neapolitans in particular, love for the ocean, for the sun, and for seafood is in our blood. I have always enjoyed fish and shellfish for their versatility, flavor, and lightness—and of course they're very healthy as well.

I was born near the Bay of Naples, one of Campania's biggest and busiest ports, and my mother had access to a variety of fish and shellfish. When she did not travel to Naples, she would go to Montesarchio, a nearby town where fresh fish was sold at an open market every Wednesday. When we moved to America, we were fortunate to be near very good fish markets, some of which still stand today on Arthur Avenue. My mother—always a stickler for quality—taught me how to choose fish at the market. We had fish for dinner every Friday; Mamma would prepare whatever looked best in the market that day, whether it was flounder, calamari, cod, or eel. Traditionally, Christmas Eve is a holiday featuring an array of seafood, beginning with baked clams, and followed by Zuppa di Pesce (page 83), baccalà, and Insalata di Mare (page 148).

Neapolitans serve fish in numerous ways. It's enjoyed in pasta, in soups, and in salads, but most of all, we cook it simply and serve it without a lot of fuss. I often serve fish and shellfish throughout the menu, for an all-seafood feast. For example, an appetizer of Baked Littlenecks Oreganata (page 52) might be followed by Linguine with White Clam Sauce (page 102) as a first course, then Shrimp Marachiara (page 142) as the main dish.

The dishes in this chapter are all very flexible; all of them can be served as a first course, and most can be served as a main course. Some—such as Fried Calamari (page 144) and Baked Mussels Fra Diavolo (page 143)—can be offered as a hot appetizer. In some recipes, you'll see that I've combined the flavors of the old country with the riches of the new world, as is exemplified by Striped Bass alla Pizzaiola (page 139) or Oreganata (page 138). (Traditionally, pizzaiola sauce is an accompaniment to steak; and while shrimp and clams are often pre-pared *all'oreganata*, serving it with striped bass is my own creation.)

Whatever you choose to cook, be advised that the success of fish and shellfish begins at the marketplace. Patronize only those stores that are sparkling clean with fish that is odorless. Mollusks should be alive, and fish—whether it's whole or cut into steaks—should be on ice. If you're buying whole fish, check the eyes: They should be clear. Be loyal to your fishmonger, and he will keep you advised as to the best choices for the day.

Fried Flounder with Caper Sauce

Serves 6 to 8

This fast, easy dish is terrific for Friday night (fish night) supper. Fried flounder always gets a "two thumbs up" from my son, Steven. The caper sauce is something I learned to make from my godfather, Guerrino; it's a delicious, tangy complement to the crisp fried flounder.

Serving Suggestions

Serve as a main course with Eggplant alla Scarpetta (page 193) or Dandelion Greens with Potatoes and Sun-Dried Tomatoes (page 175).

FOR THE FLOUNDER

1 cup light olive oil

8 flounder fillets (about 1¹⁄₂ pounds total), or substitute tilapia, turbot, or perch

¹⁄₄ cup all-purpose flour

2 large eggs

1 teaspoon finely chopped fresh flat-leaf (Italian) parsley

1¹⁄₂ cups unseasoned dry bread crumbs, preferably homemade (page 6)

FOR THE CAPER SAUCE

2 teaspoons unsalted butter

2 tablespoons extra virgin olive oil

1 shallot, finely chopped

¹⁄₂ cup dry white wine

¹⁄₂ tablespoon Worcestershire sauce

2 tablespoons drained capers

¹⁄₂ teaspoon freshly ground black pepper

Juice of 1 lemon

¹⁄₂ teaspoon dried celery leaves, preferably homemade (page 251)

¹⁄₂ teaspoon dried basil, preferably homemade (page 251)

To make the flounder

1. Heat the olive oil in a large pot or deep-fat fryer until hot but not smoking, about 375°F. Place the flour and bread crumbs in separate shallow bowls. Beat the eggs with the parsley and ¹⁄₄ cup of water in a third bowl.

2. Place the flounder in the flour and turn to coat. Dip the flounder into the beaten egg mixture and transfer to the bread crumbs. Turn to coat on all sides. Cook in the hot oil until golden, 2 to 3 minutes on each side.

3. Transfer to a paper-lined sheet to absorb excess oil. Cover loosely with foil to keep warm while you make the sauce.

To make the sauce

4. Warm the butter and olive oil in a small saucepan over medium heat. Add the shallot and cook until softened. Stir in the wine, Worcestershire sauce, capers, pepper, lemon juice, celery, and basil. Heat for 1 to 2 minutes. Pour over the fried flounder and serve immediately.

Striped Bass Oreganata

Serves 4 to 6

Oreganata refers to any dish with oregano as the predominant herb. In southern Italian cooking, oregano is frequently used in rich tomato sauces, but the herb is also delicious used with a light hand to flavor fish and shellfish.

Serving Suggestions

For an all-seafood feast, serve over rice as a main course, or serve Linguine with White Clam Sauce (page 102) or Frittura di Mare (page 145) as a starter.

4 striped bass fillets (about
  1½ pounds), or substitute
  equivalent weight of cod, tilapia,
  perch, flounder, halibut, or
  turbot
¼ cup extra virgin olive oil
2 tablespoons unsalted butter
3 garlic cloves, pressed or finely
  chopped
¼ teaspoon salt

½ cup dry white wine
1 teaspoon dried oregano,
  preferably imported Italian
2 tablespoons finely chopped fresh
  flat-leaf (Italian) parsley
Juice of 2 lemons
½ teaspoon dried parsley,
  preferably homemade (page 251)
½ teaspoon dried basil, preferably
  homemade (page 251)

1. Preheat the oven to 350°F and place the fish in a baking dish large enough to hold the fillets flat in one layer.

2. Warm the olive oil and butter in a saucepan over medium heat. Add the garlic and salt. Cook, stirring, until fragrant, about 1 minute. Pour in the wine and add the oregano, fresh parsley, lemon juice, dried parsley, and basil. Cook, stirring often, for 3 to 4 minutes.

3. Pour the sauce over the fish, cover with foil, and bake for 12 to 15 minutes or until just cooked through. Turn on the broiler, remove the foil, and broil, watching carefully to avoid scorching, until lightly browned on top, 2 to 3 minutes.

VARIATION

Baked Striped Bass with Littlenecks Proceed with steps 1 and 2. Place 8 to 10 fresh littleneck clams around the fillets. Cover with foil and bake for 12 to 15 minutes. Uncover, then broil on high for 2 to 3 minutes, until the fish is slightly crisp.

Striped Bass alla Pizzaiola

Pizzaiola sauce is extremely versatile; it's a traditional accompaniment to grilled steak, but it's also delicious with striped bass. No matter how it's prepared—Oreganata, Pizzaiola, topped with Green Olive Pesto (page 92), or prepared very simply, with salt and lemon—I find striped bass irresistible. When shopping for striped bass, choose fish that has a sweet scent and is white in color.

Serving Suggestions
Serve as a main course over rice or angel hair pasta.

¼ cup extra virgin olive oil

3 garlic cloves, pressed or finely chopped

2 shallots or 1 small onion, finely chopped (about ⅓ cup)

1 teaspoon salt

1 teaspoon dried oregano, preferably imported Italian

¼ teaspoon dried parsley, preferably homemade (page 251)

¼ teaspoon dried basil, preferably homemade (page 251)

¼ teaspoon dried celery leaves, preferably homemade (page 251)

One 32-ounce jar homemade canned plum tomatoes (page 275), or 1¾ to 2 pounds very ripe, fresh plum tomatoes, crushed in a food processor or blender for 2 to 3 seconds

½ cup Gaeta or black oil-cured Sicilian olives, pitted

2 tablespoons drained oil-packed capers

6 fresh basil leaves, finely chopped

2 tablespoons finely chopped fresh flat-leaf (Italian) parsley

4 boneless striped bass fillets, 4 to 6 ounces each

1 cup dry white wine

1. Warm the olive oil in a deep skillet over medium heat. Add the garlic, shallots, ½ teaspoon of the salt, the dried oregano, dried parsley, dried basil, and dried celery. Cook, stirring, until the shallots are translucent, 2 to 3 minutes. Add the tomatoes, olives, capers, fresh basil, fresh parsley, and the remaining ½ teaspoon salt and cook for 3 to 5 minutes. (Note: Cook 10 minutes longer if using fresh tomatoes.)

2. Add the striped bass fillets and the wine. Ladle some of the tomato mixture over the fillets. Cover, reduce the heat to medium-low, and simmer for 10 to 15 minutes or until just cooked through. Serve over rice or pasta.

Note: Store-bought canned tomatoes are not recommended for this dish.

VARIATION

Oven-Baked Striped Bass Pizzaiola If you prefer, you can bake the fish in the oven. Preheat the oven to 375°F. Place the fillets in a baking dish that is large enough to hold them in one layer. Prepare the tomato mixture as the recipe directs in step 1. Pour the tomato mixture and the wine over the fish, cover with foil, and bake for 15 to 18 minutes. Turn the broiler on high, remove the foil, and broil for 2 to 3 minutes. Serve immediately.

Grilled Halibut with
Green Olive–Basil Pesto

Serves 4 to 6

Rich, robust, homemade olive-basil pesto is an unexpected accompaniment to grilled fish. This dish is easy and the pesto is extremely versatile. Add grated Pecorino Romano cheese to it and use it to sauce your favorite pasta or as a dressing with chops or steaks. Or spread it on homemade bruschette (page 39) to enjoy as a snack or as part of an antipasto platter.

3 garlic cloves, peeled and sliced

3 tablespoons extra virgin olive oil

1 teaspoon salt

6 to 8 fresh basil leaves

1 cup assorted imported green olives such as Sicilian, Castelvetrano, Calabrese, or Cerignola, pitted and halved (see Mail-Order Sources, page 283)

1/4 teaspoon freshly ground black pepper

3 pounds halibut steaks, or substitute tuna steaks or salmon fillets

1. Preheat the oven to 350°F.

2. Place the garlic in a ramekin or small baking dish. Add the olive oil and sprinkle with $^1/_2$ teaspoon of the salt. Roast uncovered for 15 to 20 minutes, until the garlic turns slightly golden. (Note: To roast garlic in the microwave, see page 67.)

3. Place the roasted garlic and its oil, the basil, olives, pepper, the remaining $^1/_2$ teaspoon salt, and $^1/_4$ cup of water in a blender or food processor and process for 2 to 3 seconds, until crushed.

4. Preheat a gas or charcoal grill or a grill pan to medium-high. Place the fish on the grill and cook for 4 to 5 minutes on each side, until just cooked through. Serve immediately, topped with 1 heaping tablespoon or more of the pesto.

Old-fashioned Tuna Loaf

My cousin in Italy introduced me to this summery dish. Although Tuna Loaf is an old-fashioned recipe—based on years of traditional cooking—it's perfect for modern menus since it's healthful, easy, and can be made in advance. Another plus: Tuna Loaf is made with on-hand ingredients—a few cans of tuna plus parsley and spices are transformed into something special.

Serving Suggestions
Serve as a first course on a bed of lettuce or as a light main dish with Hot and Spicy Eggplant Frittelle (page 48) or Preserved Artichoke Hearts (page 254).

3 large eggs

Three 6-ounce cans oil-packed tuna, drained, or 1½ pounds leftover cooked tuna or salmon, flaked

2 garlic cloves, finely chopped

1 teaspoon salt

½ teaspoon freshly ground black pepper

1½ cups crumbled Italian bread (from about 2 slices bread)

2 tablespoons finely chopped fresh flat-leaf (Italian) parsley

1 teaspoon extra virgin olive oil

2 tablespoons finely chopped fresh celery leaves, preferably the darkest leaves

¼ cup unseasoned dry bread crumbs, preferably homemade (page 6)

Extra virgin olive oil, vinegar, or mayonnaise, optional

1. Beat the eggs in a large bowl. Add the tuna and mash with a fork until well mixed. Add the garlic, salt, pepper, bread, parsley, olive oil, and celery leaves. Moisten the bread with water; squeeze out excess liquid with your hands and coarsely chop into the tuna mixture. Mix everything well with a wooden spoon. Use your hands to form an elongated loaf, about 9 inches long and 2 inches thick.

2. Place the loaf on a large cotton kitchen towel (see Mail-Order Sources, page 283). Fold the towel over the loaf and tie the ends with kitchen twine (or tie the ends into 2 separate knots).

3. Bring 3½ quarts water to a boil in a large pot. Add the tuna loaf and simmer for 18 to 20 minutes.

4. Drain, then let the loaf stand at room temperature for 10 to 15 minutes, until cool enough to handle. Remove the twine and the cheesecloth and place the loaf on a serving platter. Slice into 1-inch-thick slices and serve warm, at room temperature, or cool with olive oil, vinegar, or mayonnaise, if desired.

Shrimp Marachiara

Serves 4 to 6

The word *marachiara* means "light sea" (*mara* means "sea"; *chiara* means "light"). When referring to food, the term describes a thin tomato sauce for seafood that can be almost translucent. This dish is also light in calories and is quick and easy; perfect for hurried weeknight suppers, yet elegant enough for dinner parties.

¹/₄ cup extra virgin olive oil

2 shallots, finely chopped

3 garlic cloves, finely chopped

1 teaspoon salt

¹/₂ teaspoon dried parsley, preferably homemade (page 251)

¹/₂ teaspoon dried oregano, preferably imported Italian

¹/₂ teaspoon dried basil, preferably homemade (page 251)

¹/₂ teaspoon dried celery leaves, preferably homemade (page 251)

18 to 20 large shrimp, shelled and deveined, tails intact

1¹/₂ cups homemade tomato puree (page 275), or 1¹/₂ cups canned whole plum tomatoes with juice, pureed in a blender or food processor for 3 to 5 seconds

1 cup dry white wine

Serving Suggestions

Serve as a first course or with pasta for a main course. Make sure you serve plenty of crusty Italian bread to enjoy with the sauce.

Warm the olive oil in a large skillet over medium heat. Add the shallots, garlic, salt, parsley, oregano, basil, and celery. Cook, stirring often, until the shallots are softened, 2 to 3 minutes. Add the shrimp and cook for another 2 to 3 minutes. Add the tomato puree and the wine, cover, and cook for an additional 6 to 8 minutes. Serve immediately.

Note: If using canned tomatoes, cook 10 to 12 minutes before adding shrimp. Then add wine, cover, and cook for an additional 6 to 8 minutes.

Baked Mussels Fra Diavolo

Serves 6 to 8 as a first course

When I was about seven years old, living on Belmont Avenue in the Bronx, our landlady, Gina (who was Argentinean), used to prepare mussels frequently. She made them South American style: hot and spicy. They made a lasting impression on me; even at a young age I developed an affection for mussels with hot spices. Being Italian, I call this dish *fra diavolo* (*diavolo* means "devil"), a phrase used for just about any dish made with red peppers. This *piccante* dish is traditionally served with a wedge of bread and a glass of chilled white or rosé wine. Be sure to clean mussels well to eliminate sand and grit.

Serving Suggestions

Serve as a first course followed by Striped Bass Oreganata (page 138) or Linguine with Shrimp, Clams, and Arugula (page 100).

2¼ pounds live mussels, debearded and scrubbed, or littleneck clams, cleaned

¼ cup extra virgin olive oil

4 garlic cloves, finely chopped

2 to 3 dried whole hot red peppers, finely chopped or crushed, or 1 teaspoon red pepper flakes, or to taste

1 tablespoon dried oregano, preferably imported Italian

1 teaspoon salt

12 to 14 very ripe, fresh plum tomatoes (2 to 2½ pounds), cored and seeded

8 to 10 sprigs fresh flat-leaf (Italian) parsley, stems removed

6 fresh basil leaves

2 tablespoons unseasoned dry bread crumbs, preferably homemade (page 6)

1. Place the mussels in a large bowl of cold water and set aside for 10 minutes to remove excess sand or grit. Remove the soaked mussels from the water. (Note: If using farmed mussels, which are sold debearded and cleaned, you will only need to rinse them.)

2. Working with one mussel at a time, use a small, sharp knife to open the mussels and cut the meat from the shell, reserving the meat and one of the shells. Set aside.

3. Heat the olive oil in a medium saucepan over medium heat. Add the garlic, red pepper, oregano, and salt, and cook, stirring, for 1 to 2 minutes.

4. Place the tomatoes in a blender or food processor and process for 2 to 3 seconds. Add the parsley and basil and process for another 2 to 3 seconds.

5. Add the tomato mixture to the saucepan and simmer uncovered for 15 to 20 minutes, until the sauce has thickened.

6. Preheat the oven to 375°F.

7. Place the mussels in their shells in a medium baking dish. Spoon some of the sauce over each mussel. Sprinkle with bread crumbs, cover with foil, and bake for 18 to 22 minutes. Turn the broiler on high and broil for 1 to 2 minutes for a crispy topping. Serve immediately.

Fried Calamari

I love making fried calamari around the holidays but also in summertime. The batter is splashed with seltzer water, which lightens it, and the bread crumbs are applied gently.

1 1/2 pounds fresh calamari, cleaned (see page 7)

1/2 cup all-purpose flour

1 teaspoon salt

1/2 teaspoon freshly ground black pepper

3/4 cup seltzer water or club soda, plus a little more if necessary

3/4 cup unseasoned dry bread crumbs, preferably homemade (page 6)

1 teaspoon mixed dried herbs, such as parsley, basil, and imported Italian oregano

Light olive oil or vegetable oil

2 to 3 lemons, cut into wedges

Serving Suggestions
Serve Fried Calamari with a green leaf salad for lunch or as an appetizer followed by Striped Bass Oreganata (page 138).

1. Cut the cleaned torpedo-shaped bodies of the calamari into $1/2$-inch-thick rings. Pat the rings and the tentacles dry with paper towels. Lay the calamari pieces on paper towels to dry completely while you prepare the batter.

2. Pour the flour into a medium bowl, add the salt and pepper, and mix well. Whisk in $3/4$ cup of the seltzer, beating until smooth. It should be the consistency of heavy cream. Thin the batter with a little more seltzer if necessary. Set aside.

3. Combine bread crumbs and herbs in a wide shallow bowl or plate.

4. Pour enough olive oil into a large skillet to come $1/2$ inch up the sides of the skillet. Heat the oil until very hot but not smoking, about 375°F.

5. Add the calamari to the batter and toss to coat. One by one, transfer the battered calamari to the bread crumbs, letting the excess batter fall back into the bowl. Make sure the calamari are coated on all sides with the bread crumbs, then place them in a colander and shake gently to remove excess crumbs.

6. Cook the calamari in the hot oil in batches, making sure not to overcrowd the skillet. Cook for 1 to 2 minutes on each side, turning once, until the bread-crumb coating is golden all over. (Note: Do not overcook or the calamari will be tough and chewy.) Remove from the oil with a slotted spoon and drain on paper towels. Serve hot with lemon wedges on the side.

VARIATION

Frittura di Mare A fried seafood platter consisting of shrimp, scungilli, scallops, and fresh sardines. Remove the bones from $1/2$ pound fresh, cleaned sardines as follows: With a small sharp knife, split the sardines down the length of the belly. With your fingers, open up the sardines like a book. Grasp the skeleton at the tail end of the fish. Pull up on the skeleton to remove it; it will come away in one piece. Discard the bones; set the sardines aside.

Combine 1 cup flour, 1 teaspoon salt, and $1/2$ teaspoon freshly ground black pepper in a bowl with $1^1/2$ cups seltzer, beating until smooth and thin but not runny. Thin the batter with up to $1/4$ cup more seltzer if necessary. Set aside. Combine 1 cup unseasoned dry bread crumbs, preferably homemade (page 6), and 1 teaspoon mixed dried herbs in a shallow bowl. Heat the olive oil as directed in step 4. Place $1/2$ pound shrimp, $1/2$ pound scungilli, $1/2$ pound scallops, and $1/2$ pound fresh sardines (bones removed) in the batter, and toss to coat. Transfer each piece of seafood to the bread crumbs and coat on all sides. Place in a colander and shake gently to remove excess bread crumbs. Cook the seafood as directed in step 6; everything will require 3 to 5 minutes total cooking time. Serve hot.

Note: A light egg batter of 2 eggs beaten with $1/4$ cup water can also be used for fritta di mare. Dip the seafood in flour to coat lightly. Then dip the seafood into the batter, then into the bread crumbs to coat. Fry as the recipe directs in step 6.

Fried Baccalà

Serving baccalà, or salt cod, on Christmas Eve is an old Italian tradition. I prefer to cure my own baccalà, so I begin by searching for the best: The baccalà must be white with a slight yellow tint, at least one inch thick, and not appear too dry. Since curing takes time, I always make enough for several holiday dishes, such as Traditional Cold Baccalà Salad (see variation below) or Baccalà with Escarole and Capers (page 147).

Serving Suggestions

If serving this for Christmas Eve dinner the Italian way, offer it alongside Insalata di Mare (page 148). To serve Fried Baccalà for other occasions, try it with Mamma Rosina's Eggplant Pizzaiola (page 179) as a side dish.

Eight ¼-pound pieces of boneless baccalà (salt cod), each piece measuring about 3 x 4 inches

1½ cups light olive oil

¾ cup all-purpose flour

1 teaspoon freshly ground black pepper

Lemon wedges

1. Place the baccalà in a large bowl and pour in enough cold water to cover by 2 inches. Set aside in a cool spot, or in the refrigerator, and soak for 3 days, changing the water daily.

2. Remove the fish from the water, rinse, and pat dry with paper towels. Heat the olive oil in a large pot or deep-fat fryer until hot but not smoking, about 375°F. (Note: It's crucial that the oil be the correct temperature; if it is not hot enough, the baccalà will be heavy and oily.)

3. Mix the flour with the pepper in a large bowl. Add the baccalà and turn to coat on all sides. Fry in the hot oil until golden, 3 to 4 minutes on each side, turning to cook all sides. Transfer to a large platter lined with paper towels and set aside for 10 minutes to drain excess oil. Serve with lemon wedges.

VARIATION

Traditional Cold Baccalà Salad Soak the baccalà as the recipe directs in step 1. Place 4 pieces of baccalà in 3 quarts of water. Bring to a boil and cook for 4 to 5 minutes. Drain, then place the baccalà on a serving platter. Use a fork to break the baccalà into flakes. Let the baccalà cool to room temperature for 1 hour, then cover and refrigerate for 6 hours or until well chilled. Season the baccalà with 3 tablespoons extra virgin olive oil, 2 finely chopped garlic cloves, 1 tablespoon finely chopped fresh flat-leaf (Italian) parsley, the juice of 1 lemon, freshly ground black pepper, and Gaeta or Kalamata olives to taste.

Baccalà with Escarole and Capers

Serves 4 to 6

This old-fashioned dish is traditionally served around the holidays, but it's delicious anytime. My family prepares baccalà—dried, salt-cured cod—in many ways: fried, in salads, braised, with tomato sauce, or with greens. But no matter how it's served, Italians love it. In fall and winter—when baccalà is readily available—I crave it paired with escarole; it's such a comforting cold-weather dish.

Serving Suggestions

I usually serve this as a main course with Prosciutto Bread with Pancetta and Basil (page 200) or Taralli con Finochetti (page 206) and a glass of red wine. However, it can also be served on Christmas Eve as part of the traditional array of fish and shellfish.

1 1/4 pounds boneless baccalà (salt cod), cut into 3-inch squares

2 bunches of fresh escarole, dandelion greens, or Swiss chard, washed, rinsed, tough leaves and ends removed

1/4 cup extra virgin olive oil

4 garlic cloves, pressed or finely chopped

1/2 teaspoon salt

Half a 32-ounce jar homemade tomato puree (page 275), or one 14 1/2-ounce can whole plum tomatoes with juice, pureed in a blender or food processor for 3 to 5 seconds

1/4 cup drained capers

1/2 cup dry white wine

1. Place the baccalà in a large bowl and pour in enough cold water to cover by 2 inches. Set aside in a cool spot, or in the refrigerator, and soak for 3 days, changing the water daily.

2. Remove the fish from the water, rinse, and pat dry with paper towels. Bring a large pot of water to a boil over high heat. Add the escarole, return the water to a boil, and cook for 5 to 6 minutes. Drain the greens well.

3. Heat the olive oil, garlic, and salt in a large skillet over medium heat. Add the tomato puree and cook for 5 to 7 minutes. Add the escarole, stir once with a wooden spoon, then cook for 3 to 5 minutes. Place the baccalà on top. Spoon some of the tomato sauce on top of the baccalà. Add the capers and wine. Cover and cook for 15 to 20 minutes. Serve hot.

Insalata di Mare

Seafood Salad

Serves 8 to 10

Octopus (*pulpo* in Italian or *o'purpe* in Neapolitan dialect) is a must on Christmas Eve as part of the traditional seafood feast. I like to combine it with shrimp, calamari, and scungilli tossed with fresh parsley, garlic, and lemon. This light, refreshing dish is delicious all year round—particularly in summer—so don't wait until Christmas to serve it.

Serving Suggestions

If serving this as a first course, try Fried Baccalà (page 146) or Striped Bass Oreganata (page 138) as a main course.

1 medium octopus (about 1¾ pounds)

1 pound medium shrimp, deveined, shells and tails removed

¾ pound calamari, cleaned (see page 7)

¾ pound scungilli (conch), diced

2 tablespoons finely chopped, fresh flat-leaf (Italian) parsley

4 garlic cloves, finely chopped

¼ cup extra virgin olive oil

½ teaspoon dried basil, preferably homemade (page 251)

Juice of 2 lemons

1 teaspoon dried oregano, preferably imported Italian

⅛ cup white wine vinegar or white balsamic vinegar

1 teaspoon salt

½ teaspoon freshly ground black pepper

Lemon wedges, optional

1. Rinse the octopus under cold running water. Trim off the eyes and discard. In a large pot bring $3\frac{1}{2}$ quarts of water to a boil. Add the octopus and boil gently for 30 to 35 minutes, until tender. Drain, and let stand until cool enough to handle. Dice into 1-inch pieces and set aside.

2. In a large pot, bring $2\frac{1}{2}$ quarts of water to a boil. Add the shrimp, calamari, and scungilli, and boil for 3 minutes. Use a slotted spoon to remove the shrimp, set them aside, and boil the scungilli and calamari for 3 to 4 minutes longer, until tender. Drain, and let stand until cool enough to handle. Dice the scungilli into 3 or 4 small pieces each.

3. Mix the octopus, shrimp, calamari, and scungilli in a large bowl with the parsley, garlic, olive oil, basil, lemon juice, oregano, vinegar, salt, and pepper. Toss to blend and refrigerate to marinate for at least 3 to 4 hours or overnight. Serve chilled with lemon wedges, if desired.

MEAT AND POULTRY

*E*veryone knows that Italians are famous for pizza and spaghetti, but we're also well known for many meat dishes, including Veal Osso Buco (page 158), Veal Sorrentino (page 156), Grilled Steak Pizzaiola (page 164), and Chicken Cacciatore (page 167). Italian meat and poultry dishes are, by and large, straightforward and easy to make. Many are prepared in a skillet on top of the stove, some roast in the oven, and others sizzle on the grill. Most are quick enough for hurried weeknight suppers but sophisticated enough for a dinner party. Veal Marsala (page 151), Veal Francese (page 152), and my own creation, Veal Scarpetta (page 154), for example, take only minutes to cook, but they—and many other dishes in this chapter—are elegant, too.

Meat and poultry are an important part of my culinary heritage. Except for times when meat was scarce (during the Depression and World War II), my mother nearly always had some form of veal, lamb, beef, or pork on the table, since several members of my family were butchers. My mother also prepared rabbit, pheasant, and other game (my father loved to hunt in the mountains of Cervinara). Chicken was part of her repertoire, too; my older sisters Maria and Luigia used to pluck and clean freshly killed birds right near a small stream outside our home in Italy. We also enjoyed cured meats; I have vivid memories of my father coming home after a hard day's work with a whole prosciutto on his shoulder. That prosciutto was a blessing to have on hand—especially in winter—to flavor our soups and greens, to serve as an appetizer, and to add to pasta dishes.

Feast days and holidays often called for special meat dishes: We celebrated Easter with roast leg of lamb as well as *capozella* (head of lamb). Whenever we had large family gatherings or a *scampagnata*

149

(picnic), Mamma would cook a big batch of Italian-Style Sausage and Peppers (page 162). I can still smell them cooking in her kitchen! This chapter includes my recipes for many traditional meat and poultry dishes. To most, I've added my own personal touch, so they vary slightly from the classics. I hope you enjoy them as much as I do.

Veal Marsala

I like to serve Veal Marsala when I have unexpected company because it's quick and easy—everything cooks in one skillet—yet elegant. When I make this for my family, my son, Steven, is especially pleased, since he is quite fond of mushrooms. Turkey or chicken cutlets, by the way, can be substituted for the veal.

Serving Suggestions
Serve Veal Marsala as a main course following Fusilli with Zucchini, Eggplant, and Wild Mushrooms (page 98).

6 lean veal cutlets, about 1 pound total

1/4 cup plus one teaspoon all-purpose flour

1/2 teaspoon salt

1/2 teaspoon freshly ground black pepper

3 tablespoons extra virgin olive oil

2 garlic cloves, cracked

8 ounces white button mushrooms, wiped clean and sliced

2 tablespoons salted butter

1 cup sweet Marsala

Juice of 1 lemon, plus extra to taste

1. Have the butcher pound the veal cutlets for you or tenderize them yourself by placing the cutlets between sheets of plastic wrap and pounding them with a mallet. Mix 1/4 cup of the flour, the salt, and the pepper together in a shallow bowl or a plate. Lightly dredge the cutlets in the flour, gently shaking off any excess.

2. Heat the olive oil in a large skillet over medium heat. Add the garlic and cook for 1 minute. Add the mushrooms and cook until most of the oil has been absorbed and the mushrooms are slightly cooked, 2 to 3 minutes. Push the mushrooms to one side of the skillet.

3. Melt the butter in the middle of the skillet. Add the veal and cook on both sides until light golden brown, 1 to 2 minutes per side. Add the Marsala to the skillet and cook, partially covered, until the Marsala has evaporated slightly, 3 to 4 minutes. Add the lemon juice and the remaining 1 teaspoon flour and whisk until smooth and slightly thickened. Cover the pan and cook for an additional 2 to 3 minutes. Remove from the heat and discard the garlic. Serve hot with sauce from the skillet and additional lemon juice, if desired.

Veal Francese

Culinary lore has it that Italians created this dish to honor Napoleon Bonaparte. Whether or not the French general was indeed the inspiration, this dish is terrific to have in your repertoire: It's fast, easy, and elegant, too. Classic Veal Francese is flavored with white wine, lemon, and butter; I've added garlic for additional flavor. You can substitute chicken cutlets, turkey cutlets, or butterflied jumbo shrimp for the veal.

Serving Suggestions
This dish is delicious with sautéed spinach and garlic. I like to serve Fettuccine with Green Olive Pesto (page 92) or Pasta Mare e Monte (page 104) as the first course.

FOR THE VEAL

6 lean veal cutlets, about 1 pound total

1 cup vegetable or light olive oil, or more if necessary

1/4 cup all-purpose flour

2 cups unseasoned dry bread crumbs, preferably homemade (page 6)

3 large eggs

2 tablespoons grated Pecorino Romano cheese (omit if using shrimp)

1/2 teaspoon freshly ground black pepper

2 tablespoons finely chopped fresh flat-leaf (Italian) parsley

FOR THE WHITE WINE AND LEMON SAUCE

2 tablespoons salted or unsalted butter

1/4 cup extra virgin olive oil

3 garlic cloves, cracked

1 teaspoon salt

1 cup dry white wine

1 teaspoon all-purpose flour, or more if necessary

Juice of 1 large lemon

1 tablespoon finely chopped fresh flat-leaf (Italian) parsley

To make the veal

1. Have the butcher pound the veal cutlets for you or tenderize them yourself by placing the cutlets between sheets of plastic wrap and pounding them with a mallet. Heat the vegetable oil in a large skillet over medium heat until hot but not smoking. Meanwhile, place the flour and bread crumbs in separate shallow bowls. Beat the eggs with the Pecorino Romano, pepper, and parsley in a third bowl.

2. Dredge the veal cutlets, one at a time, in the flour, then in the egg batter, then in the bread crumbs. Place them in the skillet, one by one, without crowding the pan. Depending on the size of the skillet and the size of the veal cutlets, you may need to fry the veal in batches. Cook until golden brown, 3 to 4 minutes per side. Remove from the skillet and place on a baking sheet lined with paper towels to absorb excess oil.

To make the sauce

3. Melt the butter and the olive oil in a large skillet over medium heat. Add the garlic and $1/2$ teaspoon of the salt and cook for 1 to 2 minutes, being careful not to burn the garlic. Add the wine and flour and whisk until the sauce is smooth and slightly thickened. Immediately add the veal and season with the lemon juice, parsley, and remaining $1/2$ teaspoon salt. Cover the skillet and cook over medium-low heat for 8 to 10 minutes. Discard the garlic and serve immediately with the sauce from the skillet.

Veal Scarpetta

Veal Cutlets with Artichokes, Mushrooms, and Sun-Dried Tomatoes   *Serves 4 to 6*

I created this dish for my husband, Michael, who simply loves veal, no matter how it is prepared. The dish combines several of his and my favorite things: veal, mushrooms, and artichoke hearts. If you favor chicken over veal, try this dish using thin chicken cutlets. Whether you use veal or chicken, this dish is very easy, but special enough for a dinner party.

Serving Suggestions

Serve Veal Scarpetta as a main course following Spaghetti Puttanesca (page 87), Fettuccine with Green Olive Pesto (page 92), or Gemelli with Pesto Napoletano (page 96).

4 to 6 baby artichokes (about ¼ pound total), outer leaves removed, with stems

2¼ cups dry white wine

6 lean veal cutlets, about 1 pound total

Salt and freshly ground black pepper to taste

¼ cup heavy cream

¼ cup extra virgin olive oil

3 garlic cloves, pressed or finely chopped

2 shallots, finely chopped

1 large portobello mushroom, wiped clean and diced

6 to 8 sun-dried tomatoes, cut into thirds

Half a 32-ounce jar homemade canned plum tomatoes (page 275) or one 14½-ounce can whole plum tomatoes with juice, crushed in a blender or food processor for 2 to 3 seconds

1 tablespoon coarsely chopped fresh flat-leaf (Italian) parsley

1 tablespoon coarsely chopped fresh basil

1. Prepare the artichokes: Trim off ¼ inch from the bottom of the stems and remove coarse outer leaves. Trim ½ inch from the tips of the artichokes. Quarter the artichokes through the stem. Bring 2 cups of the wine and 2 cups of water to a boil in a saucepan. Add the artichokes and cook uncovered for 20 minutes or until the artichokes are tender. Let the artichokes cool in the wine for 30 minutes. Drain, and set aside.

2. Have the butcher pound the veal cutlets for you or tenderize them yourself by placing the cutlets between sheets of plastic wrap and pounding them with a mallet. Season the cutlets on both sides with salt and pepper. Pour the cream into a shallow bowl, dip the cutlets into the cream to coat on both sides, then set aside.

3. Heat the olive oil in a large skillet over medium heat. Add the garlic and shallots and cook, stirring frequently, until the garlic turns slightly golden.

4. Add the artichokes, mushroom, and sun-dried tomatoes to the skillet and cook until the mushroom begins to brown and starts to look slightly crisp, about 2 minutes.

5. Add the veal and cook, turning once, for 2 or 3 minutes on each side, until no pink remains. Add the remaining wine and cook for 1 minute longer. Add the tomatoes, parsley, and basil, cover, and simmer until the veal is tender, about 6 minutes. Taste the sauce, and season with salt and pepper, if desired. Serve immediately.

Veal Sorrentino

Veal Cutlets with Prosciutto, Eggplant, and Mozzarella

Serves 6 to 8

This dish originated in Sorrento, but is enjoyed throughout Italy. It has been a staple in my home for years, and it's one of my favorite company dishes. Veal topped with prosciutto, grilled eggplant, and melted mozzarella—all simmered in a rich tomato-wine sauce—is a mouthwatering *secondo*. Chicken or turkey cutlets can be used in place of the veal, if you prefer.

Serving Suggestions

Serve Veal Sorrentino as a main course with crusty Italian bread and a salad. I usually like to serve an antipasto platter or Baked Littlenecks Oreganata (page 52) as a starter.

FOR THE VEAL

6 lean veal cutlets (about 1 pound)

1/4 cup all-purpose flour

3 large eggs

1/2 teaspoon freshly ground black pepper

3 tablespoons grated Pecorino Romano cheese

1 cup unseasoned dry bread crumbs, preferably homemade (page 6)

1 cup light olive oil

FOR THE EGGPLANT

1 Italian baby eggplant (about 1/4 pound) with skin, cut lengthwise into 1/8-inch-thick slices

2 tablespoons extra virgin olive oil

FOR THE MARINARA SAUCE

1/4 cup extra virgin olive oil

1 sprig of fresh rosemary

4 to 6 garlic cloves, pressed or finely chopped

1 teaspoon salt

One 32-ounce jar homemade canned plum tomatoes (page 275) or one 35-ounce can whole plum tomatoes with juice, crushed in a blender or food processor for 2 to 3 seconds

Half a 32-ounce jar homemade tomato puree (page 275), or one 14 1/2-ounce can whole plum tomatoes with juice, pureed in a blender or food processor for 3 to 5 seconds

1/4 cup dry red wine

6 fresh basil leaves, coarsely chopped

ASSEMBLING THE DISH

1/4 pound prosciutto, thinly sliced

1/2 pound fresh dry or processed whole-milk mozzarella cheese, sliced (page 10)

To make the veal

1. Have the butcher pound the veal cutlets for you or tenderize them yourself by placing the cutlets between sheets of plastic wrap and pounding them with a mallet. Place the flour in a shallow bowl. Beat the eggs, pepper, and Pecorino Romano in another bowl. Place the bread crumbs in a third bowl. Dip the cutlets in the flour, then shake off any excess. Dip the cutlets into the egg mixture, then into the bread crumbs.

2. Heat the olive oil in a large, nonstick skillet over medium-high heat until hot but not smoking, 1 to 2 minutes. Add the prepared cutlets and cook until golden brown, 2 to 3 minutes on each side. Drain on paper towels.

To make the eggplant

3. Preheat a gas or charcoal grill or a grill pan. Brush the eggplant with the olive oil and grill for 2 to 3 minutes on each side, until slightly golden. Set aside.

To make the sauce

4. Heat the olive oil in a skillet over medium heat. Sweep the rosemary sprig around the skillet to lightly flavor the oil. Add the garlic and salt, and cook, stirring, for about 2 minutes. Stir in the tomatoes and tomato puree and cook for 10 to 15 minutes. (Note: If using canned tomatoes, cook for 20 to 25 minutes.) Add the wine and basil and continue to cook for 5 more minutes.

To assemble the dish

5. Place the veal on top of the tomato sauce. Top each cutlet with slices of prosciutto, eggplant, and mozzarella. Cover, reduce the heat to medium-low, and cook until the veal is tender and the cheese has melted, about 10 minutes. Serve hot.

Veal Osso Buco

My mother sometimes prepared osso buco in a Traditional Sunday Sauce alla Russo (page 109) or added it to her Chicken and Veal Soup with Tiny Meatballs (page 80). I enjoy it both ways, but I also like to braise it in wine and add zucchini to make a light stew.

Serving Suggestions
Serve as a main course with orzo or rice that has been seasoned with roasted garlic (page 67).

½ cup extra virgin olive oil

4 garlic cloves, pressed or finely chopped

1 large onion, diced

2 veal osso buco (about 1¼ pounds each)

1 teaspoon salt

1 teaspoon freshly ground black pepper

1½ cups dry red wine

Half a 32-ounce jar homemade tomato puree (page 275), or one 14½-ounce can plum tomatoes with juice, pureed in a blender or food processor for 3 to 5 seconds

1 teaspoon dried parsley, preferably homemade (page 251)

2 tablespoons finely chopped fresh flat-leaf (Italian) parsley

2 tablespoons finely chopped fresh basil

¼ cup finely chopped celery with leaves

½ teaspoon dried rosemary

1 zucchini (about ¼ pound), trimmed and diced, optional

1. Place the olive oil, garlic, and onion in a large saucepan and cook over medium heat for 2 to 3 minutes, until the onion is translucent. Season the veal with salt and pepper, then add to the saucepan and cook for 2 to 3 minutes on each side, until light golden brown.

2. Add the wine and cook for 5 minutes, or until some of the wine has evaporated. Add the tomato puree, dried parsley, fresh parsley, basil, celery, rosemary, and 2 cups of water, cover, and cook for 30 to 35 minutes, until the veal is tender.

3. Add the zucchini, if using, and cook for 8 to 10 minutes more, until the zucchini is tender but not mushy. Serve immediately.

Pork Loin Roast

I often make this for Sunday dinner when I don't have enough time to make the braised meats that go into Traditional Sunday Sauce alla Russo (page 109). I prefer Smithfield brand pork, because the meat is more tender and has less fat than other brands.

Serving Suggestions
This easy main course is delicious with Dandelion Greens with Potatoes and Sun-Dried Tomatoes (page 175) or Stuffed Escarole with Sun-Dried Tomatoes and Capers (page 192) on the side. For a first course, try pasta with Rich Marinara Sauce (page 127).

One 4- to 5-pound pork loin roast, preferably Smithfield (See Mail-Order Sources, page 283)

1 teaspoon salt

½ teaspoon freshly ground black pepper

½ cup honey

3 garlic cloves, sliced

1 medium Vidalia onion, chopped

1 cup red wine vinegar

¼ cup Worcestershire sauce

1 cup dry red wine

½ teaspoon dried basil, preferably homemade (page 251)

½ teaspoon dried parsley, preferably homemade (page 251)

1. Season the pork with salt and pepper. Combine the honey, garlic, onion, vinegar, Worcestershire sauce, wine, dried basil, and dried parsley in a large, deep bowl. Mix well and add the pork. Cover and marinate in the refrigerator, turning occasionally, for 3 to 4 hours or overnight.

2. Preheat the oven to 425°F. Transfer the pork to a large roasting pan, pour on the marinade, and roast uncovered for 20 minutes. Add 1 cup of water to the roasting pan. Lower the oven temperature to 350°F, cover, and cook for 1 hour and 20 minutes longer, or until a meat thermometer plunged into the center registers 160°F. The meat should be cooked through with no signs of pink. Place the pork roast on a large platter, carve, and serve with any juices that have collected on the platter.

Pork Chops al Forno

Baked Pork Chops with Seasoned Bread Crumbs

Serves 4 to 6

The secret ingredient for these pork chops is the heavy cream, which makes them tender. You can substitute veal or lamb chops with equally good results. For lamb chops, you need not bake them if you prefer your lamb medium-rare. Veal chops will take less time in the oven than pork (15 to 20 minutes).

Serving Suggestions

Serve this dish as a main course with Preserved Sweet Italian Peppers Vinaigrette (page 263), Swiss Chard with Prosciutto and Cipolline (page 176), Stuffed Escarole with Sun-Dried Tomatoes and Capers (page 192), or Fava Beans alla Pomodoro (page 177).

1 1/2 cups heavy cream

2 cups unseasoned dry bread crumbs, preferably homemade (page 6)

1/2 teaspoon dried basil, preferably homemade (page 251)

1/2 teaspoon dried parsley, preferably homemade (page 251)

1 teaspoon salt

1 teaspoon freshly ground black pepper

1 teaspoon dried oregano, preferably imported Italian

6 lean pork chops, about 1 inch thick (about 3 pounds)

1 cup light olive oil

1. Pour the heavy cream into a shallow bowl. In a separate bowl, combine the bread crumbs, basil, parsley, salt, pepper, and oregano, and mix to combine. Dip the chops one at a time into the cream, making sure to coat both sides completely. Then dredge each chop in the bread crumbs, coating each side generously. Set aside.

2. Preheat the oven to 375°F.

3. Heat the olive oil in a large skillet over medium heat until hot but not smoking. Add the chops and fry until golden brown, 4 to 6 minutes per side. Transfer to a baking sheet lined with paper towels to absorb excess oil.

4. Place the pork chops in one layer in a nonstick baking dish and cover with foil. Bake for 30 to 35 minutes. Serve immediately.

Braised Pork Chops with Marinated Artichoke Hearts and Vinegar Peppers

Serves 2 to 4

I often serve this on cold winter nights when I want something hearty and flavorful but easy to make. Using already-prepared marinated artichoke hearts and vinegar peppers makes this dish a snap. Boneless chicken breasts or veal chops can be used instead of the pork chops. The cooking time for pork chops, veal, or chicken will be the same. If using purchased artichoke hearts—which tend to fall apart more easily than homemade artichoke hearts—add them during the final two to three minutes of cooking time to avoid overcooking.

8 to 10 oil-packed artichoke hearts, preferably homemade (page 254), along with 3 tablespoons of the marinating oil

Four 1-inch-thick lean pork chops (about 2½ pounds total)

6 sweet vinegar peppers, preferably homemade (page 263)

1 teaspoon salt

½ teaspoon freshly ground black pepper

1. Drain the marinating oil from the artichoke hearts into a large skillet. Warm the oil over medium heat, add the pork chops, and cook for 8 to 10 minutes on one side.

2. Add the artichoke hearts (if using purchased artichoke hearts, do not add at this time; see Note) and vinegar peppers to one side of the skillet. Turn the chops over and cook for 8 to 10 minutes more, until golden brown. Season with salt and pepper and serve immediately.

Note: If using purchased artichoke hearts, add them to the skillet after the chops have cooked for 6 to 7 minutes.

Serving Suggestions
Serve this as a main course with Creamy Potato Gratin with Smoked Mozzarella (page 186), Potato Croquettes (page 184), or Mamma Rosina's Eggplant Pizzaiola (page 179).

Italian-Style Sausage and Peppers

Serves 4 to 6

This traditional dish—offered at Italian festivals and street fairs—is easy and tasty for quick suppers, lunch, or snacks. I often make a large platter of sausage and peppers when I have outdoor parties. I offer two cooking methods here: baking in the oven and frying on the stovetop. Frying is more traditional; it requires the cook to be more attentive, but it fills the kitchen with a mouthwatering aroma. No matter how you cook them, leftover sausages and peppers are wonderful in hot or cold hero sandwiches.

4 long red Italian cubanelle peppers

4 long green Italian cubanelle peppers

1 large Vidalia or yellow onion, sliced

$1/2$ cup extra virgin olive oil

$1/2$ teaspoon salt

10 sweet or hot Italian pork sausages (about $2^{1}/2$ pounds total)

3 garlic cloves, cracked

$1/4$ cup white balsamic vinegar or red wine vinegar, optional

1. Preheat the oven to 350°F.

2. Remove the stems, cores, and seeds from the peppers. Slice the peppers crosswise into $1/2$-inch-thick round slices. Toss the peppers and onion slices in a bowl with $1/4$ cup of the olive oil and the salt. Set aside.

3. Place the sausages in a 3-inch-deep baking pan. Add the garlic and drizzle with the remaining $1/4$ cup olive oil. Bake in the oven for 45 minutes. Place the peppers and onions on top of the sausages, cover with foil, and cook for 30 minutes, until the sausages look very crisp and browned. If using the vinegar, add it 10 minutes before the peppers are done. Serve immediately.

Serving Suggestions

Serve with crusty Italian hero bread as a main course. Or serve as a second course following Tomato Soup with Fresh Basil (page 64) or Pasta with Peas (page 76).

VARIATION

Instead of baking, you can fry the sausage and peppers: Prepare the peppers as the recipe directs in step 2. Place the sausages in a large, nonstick skillet with $1/4$ cup olive oil and 3 cracked garlic cloves and cook, stirring occasionally, for 40 to 45 minutes, until the sausages look very crisp and browned. Add the peppers and onion slices, cover, and cook over medium heat for 35 minutes, or until the peppers and onions have softened. If using the vinegar, add it 10 minutes before the peppers are done.

Marinated Grilled Baby Lamb Chops with Fresh Mint

Serves 4 to 6

My mother never used bottled barbecue sauce, so we enjoyed our meats marinated and seasoned with basic ingredients such as oil, vinegar, wine, spices, and herbs. Lamb with mint is a classic combination, but this mint-flavored marinade is also delicious with steaks, ribs, veal chops, and pork chops.

Serving Suggestions
Serve as a main course with a mixed green salad and Grilled Eggplant and Portobello Pizzaiola (page 180), Traditional Stuffed Artichokes (page 190), or Roasted Red Bell Peppers with Olive Oil and Garlic (page 41).

¼ cup extra virgin olive oil
½ cup white wine vinegar or white balsamic vinegar
¼ cup dry white wine
3 garlic cloves, finely chopped
½ teaspoon salt
½ teaspoon freshly ground black pepper
½ cup coarsely chopped fresh mint

1 teaspoon dried oregano, preferably imported Italian
2 dried hot red peppers, finely chopped or crushed, or
½ teaspoon red pepper flakes, or more to taste
2½ to 3 pounds baby lamb chops
Lemon wedges

1. Mix the olive oil, vinegar, wine, garlic, salt, black pepper, mint, oregano, and red pepper in a bowl until well combined. Pour the mixture into a flat baking dish or into a Ziploc plastic bag and add the lamb chops. Coat the chops with the marinade, seal tightly, and then marinate overnight in the refrigerator.

2. Preheat a gas or charcoal grill or a grill pan to medium. Place the chops on the grill and pour a little bit of the marinade on the chops. Grill the chops for 3 to 4 minutes on each side. When the chops are almost done, drizzle the remaining marinade on top. Serve immediately with lemon wedges.

Grilled Steak Pizzaiola

Serves 2 to 4

When I was growing up, Saturdays were busy days filled with chores and errands so we usually had steaks for dinner, since they're quick and easy. Because we lived in an apartment, we didn't have an outdoor grill, and since my father liked his steak charred, my mother would hold the steak right over the gas flame in the kitchen! Of course, it spattered everywhere and made quite a mess, but it tasted marvelous. My mother made Steak Pizzaiola often. My version is different from hers (I add mushrooms and dried herbs), but the Saturday night tradition is the same. Whether you char the steak on the grill or pan-fry it, it will be delicious.

Serving Suggestions
Serve with Italian bread, Potato Croquettes (page 184), or rice and cooked dandelion greens. Follow with a mixed green salad and dessert.

2 porterhouse or T-bone steaks, 1/2 to 3/4 inch thick

3 tablespoons extra virgin olive oil, plus additional for brushing

1/2 teaspoon freshly ground black pepper

3 garlic cloves, pressed or finely chopped

3 shallots or 1 medium onion, finely chopped

1 teaspoon dried oregano, preferably imported Italian

1 teaspoon salt

1/2 teaspoon dried parsley, preferably homemade (page 251)

1/2 teaspoon dried basil, preferably homemade (page 251)

1/2 teaspoon dried celery leaves, preferably homemade (page 251)

1 large portobello mushroom with stem, wiped clean and sliced

1 cup dry red wine

Half a 32-ounce jar homemade canned plum tomatoes (page 275), crushed in a blender or food processor for 2 to 3 seconds, or 1 1/2 to 1 3/4 pounds very ripe, fresh plum tomatoes, cored, seeded, and diced

1/2 cup Gaeta olives, pitted

2 tablespoons drained brine-packed capers

4 fresh basil leaves, finely chopped

2 tablespoons finely chopped fresh flat-leaf (Italian) parsley

1. Preheat the oven to 200°F.

2. Prepare a charcoal grill and allow the coals to burn down to a gray ash, or heat a large grill pan over medium-high heat. Brush both sides of the steaks with olive oil, sprinkle with black pepper, and grill for 3 to 4 minutes per side. Cover loosely.

3. Warm the 3 tablespoons of olive oil in a large skillet over medium heat. Add the garlic, shallots, oregano, 1/2 teaspoon salt, the dried parsley, dried basil, and celery. Cook, stirring often, until the shallots are translucent. Add the mushroom and cook for 2 to 3 minutes longer. Place the steaks in the pan, add the wine, and continue cooking for 2 more minutes. Add the tomatoes, olives, capers, fresh basil, fresh parsley, and the remaining 1/2 teaspoon salt. Cover and cook for 20 to 25 minutes. Place the steaks on a platter with the sauce from the skillet, and serve each person a half or whole steak with some of the sauce.

PIZZAIOLA

Pizzaiola is derived from "pizza." If a dish is *alla Pizzaiola,* it is served with a quickly prepared sauce made with chopped or crushed tomatoes and their skins. A Pizzaiola sauce also usually has garlic, onions, and herbs. It is a versatile Neapolitan sauce that's delicious on many things, including chicken, veal, vegetables, and fish (Striped Bass Pizzaiola, page 139).

Beef Amburg

Italian Hamburgers

Makes 10 to 12 patties

Instead of American-style hamburgers, my mother made these, flavored with Pecorino Romano and lots of fresh parsley. My kids love these as much as regular hamburgers, and we enjoy them often for quick suppers and weekend lunches. "Amburg," by the way, is what my cousins in Italy call hamburger.

3 large eggs

$1/2$ teaspoon salt

1 teaspoon freshly ground black pepper

$1/2$ cup freshly grated Pecorino Romano cheese

1 tablespoon extra virgin olive oil

2 garlic cloves, pressed or finely chopped

1 tablespoon finely chopped fresh flat-leaf (Italian) parsley

5 fresh basil leaves, finely chopped, optional

2 pounds lean ground beef

$3/4$ cup unseasoned dry bread crumbs, preferably homemade (page 6)

$3/4$ cup light olive oil or vegetable oil

1. Beat the eggs in a large bowl. Add the salt, pepper, Pecorino Romano, extra virgin olive oil, garlic, parsley, and basil, and mix well.

2. Add the ground beef. Use your hands or a wooden spoon to mix thoroughly, adding the bread crumbs slowly as you mix.

3. Wet your hands with cold water, then shape 10 to 12 plump, rounded patties, using about $3/4$ cup of the beef mixture for each.

4. Heat the light olive oil in a nonstick skillet over medium-high heat. Carefully place the patties in the oil and cook until well-browned on each side, turning once, 3 to 4 minutes per side. Drain on paper towels. Let cool for 5 minutes before serving. (Note: Leftovers can be reheated in a preheated 350°F oven for 10 to 15 minutes.)

VARIATION

Pork and Smoked Mozzarella Patties Substitute ground pork for the ground beef and add $1/2$ cup crumbled smoked whole-milk mozzarella cheese. (Note: You can crumble the mozzarella yourself in a food processor or blender or you can ask the butcher to grind the meat with the smoked mozzarella.) Omit the eggs from the mixture. After cooking the pork-mozzarella patties, leave the oil in the skillet. Crack eggs into the skillet (one egg for each patty) and cook them sunny-side-up. Serve the eggs on top of the pork-mozzarella patties. (Note: You can reheat leftover patties in a 350°F oven and top them with eggs when ready to serve.)

Chicken Cacciatore

Chicken with Tomatoes, Mushrooms, and Olives

Serves 6 to 8

Cacciatore means "hunter's style" and refers to chicken, rabbit, and other dishes prepared with mushrooms, wine, herbs, and tomatoes. Chicken Cacciatore is one of my weeknight staples, since it's fast, easy, and the family loves it. My father, Francesco, enjoyed hunting for rabbit, pheasant, quail, and other game, and my mother often prepared them *alla cacciatore*. When wild game was not available, she prepared it with chicken. This hearty dish is delicious in cold weather; try it with a glass of rustic red wine.

Serving Suggestions

Serve Chicken Cacciatore over pasta or rice as a main course with a tossed salad to follow. And don't forget to enjoy this dish *alla scarpetta;* Scarpetta is not only my last name, but in Italian the term refers to the roughly shoe-shaped piece of bread used to mop up all the delicious sauce. Plenty of *panella,* or Italian bread, is a must with this dish.

1/4 cup olive oil

3 garlic cloves, pressed or finely chopped

1 large onion, diced

1 teaspoon dried oregano, preferably imported Italian

1 teaspoon salt

1/2 teaspoon dried parsley, preferably homemade (page 251)

1/4 teaspoon dried rosemary

1 small dried hot red pepper, finely chopped or crushed, or 1/2 teaspoon red pepper flakes

4 chicken thighs and drumsticks, about 3 pounds

2 whole split chicken breasts, about 1 3/4 pounds

2 chicken wings, about 1/2 pound

1/2 cup red wine vinegar

One 32-ounce jar homemade canned plum tomatoes (page 275) or one 35-ounce can whole plum tomatoes with juice, crushed in a blender or food processor for 2 to 3 seconds

1/4 cup roughly chopped fresh basil leaves

1/4 cup dry white wine

1/2 cup pitted Gaeta olives

6 small sweet Italian red peppers, cored, seeded, and halved, or 2 red bell peppers, cored, seeded, and cut into 1-inch strips

4 ounces oyster mushrooms, cleaned, trimmed, and torn with your hands, if large

1. Warm the olive oil in a large skillet over medium heat. Add the garlic, onion, 1/2 teaspoon of the oregano, 1/2 teaspoon of the salt, the dried parsley, dried rosemary, and red pepper. Cook, stirring often, until the onion is translucent but not browned.

2. Add the chicken thighs, drumsticks, breasts, and wings, and cook, turning occasionally, until browned on both sides, about 30 minutes. Add the vinegar and cook until reduced by half, 10 to 12 minutes.

3. Add the tomatoes, the remaining 1/2 teaspoon oregano, and the remaining 1/2 teaspoon salt. Cook, stirring often, until the tomatoes have reduced and slightly thickened, about 20 minutes.

4. Add the basil, wine, olives, sweet peppers, and mushrooms. Cook until the peppers have softened and the chicken is very tender, about 15 minutes.

Stuffed Chicken Breast with Mozzarella

Serves 6 to 8

When they're stuffed with mozzarella and simmered in a marinara sauce, chicken breasts become a deliciously comforting dish. For a slightly different flavor and texture, you can add a diced eggplant (with skin) or one cup of diced portobello or cremini mushrooms to the sauce after adding the red wine.

Serving Suggestions
Serve as a main course with Sun-Dried Tomato Bread (page 201) or Homemade Italian Bread (page 198) with a mixed green salad to follow.

FOR THE CHICKEN

Six 4-ounce boneless chicken breasts, trimmed

3 tablespoons extra virgin olive oil

½ teaspoon freshly ground black pepper

½ pound fresh dry or processed whole-milk mozzarella cheese (see page 10), cut into 6 slices

¼ cup all-purpose flour

3 large eggs

½ cup grated Pecorino Romano or Parmigiano-Reggiano cheese

2 tablespoons finely chopped fresh flat-leaf (Italian) parsley

2 cups unseasoned dry bread crumbs, preferably homemade (page 6)

1 cup light olive oil or vegetable oil

FOR THE MARINARA SAUCE

¼ cup extra virgin olive oil

3 to 4 garlic cloves, pressed or finely chopped

1 teaspoon salt

One 32-ounce jar homemade canned plum tomatoes (page 275) or one 35-ounce can whole plum tomatoes with juice, pureed in a blender or food processor for 3 to 5 seconds

Half a 32-ounce jar homemade canned tomato puree (page 275), or one 14½-ounce can whole plum tomatoes with juice pureed in a blender for 3 to 5 seconds

4 to 5 fresh basil leaves, coarsely chopped

¼ cup dry red wine

To make the chicken

1. Working with one breast at a time, trim off all excess skin and fat. Place one hand on top of the chicken breast and place a sharp knife at the thickest side to butterfly the breast. Cut the breast nearly in half horizontally, being careful not to cut all the way through the breast.

2. Open the breast so that the cut side is facing up. Brush the cut side of the breast with a little extra virgin olive oil, then sprinkle with some of the black pepper. Place one slice of mozzarella on one side of the breast, then fold the other side of the breast on top of the mozzarella. Repeat with the remaining chicken breasts.

3. Place the flour in a shallow bowl. In a separate bowl, beat the eggs with the Pecorino Romano and the parsley. Place the bread crumbs in a third bowl.

4. Place the breasts in the flour and turn them to coat all sides. Shake off any excess flour. Dip the breasts into the egg mixture, then transfer them to the bread crumbs and turn to coat on all sides. Set aside for 1 to 2 minutes.

5. Heat the olive oil in a large nonstick skillet over medium-high heat until hot but not smoking, about 5 minutes. Add the prepared breasts and cook until golden, 4 to 5 minutes on each side. Drain on paper towels and set aside for at least 20 to 25 minutes.

To make the marinara sauce

6. Heat the olive oil with the garlic and the salt in a saucepan over medium heat and cook, stirring, for 2 to 3 minutes, being careful not to let the garlic burn. Add the tomatoes, tomato puree, and basil and simmer for 5 to 10 minutes. Add the wine and simmer for 5 minutes longer.

7. Add the chicken breasts and spoon some of the sauce over each cutlet. Cover and simmer for 15 to 20 minutes longer. (Note: If using canned tomatoes, the cooking time should be increased to 45 minutes after adding the tomatoes.) If the sauce condenses too much, add a little water. Serve immediately.

VEGETABLE AND SIDE DISHES

Of all the food groups, I think I am most passionate about vegetables. It may be because of my heritage: In Campania, the rich, dark volcanic soil and long growing season result in an abundance of incredibly delicious vegetables. Or it may be conditioning from my childhood, when vegetables were always an important part of the meal; even as small children, we always enjoyed the taste of escarole, chicory, and dandelion greens.

Thanks to today's farmers' markets, the growth of organic gardening, and the emphasis on health and nutrition, things that were once considered exotic—wild mushrooms, arugula, and baby artichokes, for example—can now be found in nearly every supermarket across America. In fact, the market is often my inspiration for what to cook for dinner. A bushel basket of shiny, deep purple–black eggplants sets my mind spinning in a hundred different directions: Should I make Eggplant Rollatini (page 44) or Eggplant alla Scarpetta (page 193)? If the zucchini looks fresh, I'll probably make Vegetable Carbonara (page 107) or Zucchini with Fresh Mint (page 173) for dinner. And I can never pass up tender, just-picked dandelion greens, which I may add to soup or simply sauté with oil and garlic.

Most of the recipes in this chapter are for side dishes, but some—such as Mamma's Stuffed Italian Peppers (page 189)—can be served as a hot antipasto or as a light meal. Others—like Grilled Eggplant and Portobello Pizzaiola (page 180)—can be served as a side or alone as lunch. Some of the recipes here (Broccoli Rabe Vinaigrette, page 174) can be served cold or at room temperature, and others can be made a day in advance. Although Italians cook daily and eat freshly prepared foods, some vegetables are delicious as leftovers: Eggplant Parmigiana hero sandwich, anyone?

I encourage you to shop with the seasons: Swiss chard in winter, baby artichokes in fall, fava beans in spring, and zucchini blossoms—stuffed and fried—for a delicious treat at the end of summer.

Zucchini with Fresh Mint

Serves 6 to 8

My mother made this refreshing cold zucchini dish from the first warm days of spring through Indian summer. She always used fresh mint leaves that she would pinch off a plant in our apartment. Whenever she made this dish, there were plenty of leftovers for sandwiches. When selecting zucchini, choose those that are firm to the touch. The color of zucchini can range from dark green to light green, and the skin should be smooth and tight without ripples. When frying zucchini, it's important to keep the heat consistent to keep the oil from burning. Medium heat is best. Remember to turn the zucchini pieces gently— and only once or twice—so they don't break.

½ cup plus 2 tablespoons extra virgin olive oil
6 small zucchini (about 1¾ pounds total), trimmed and cut into ⅛-inch-thick rounds

2 garlic cloves, finely chopped
1 teaspoon salt
¼ cup red wine vinegar
¼ cup coarsely chopped fresh mint leaves

1. Warm ½ cup of the olive oil in a large skillet over medium heat. Add the zucchini rounds and cook until they begin to turn slightly golden, 6 to 8 minutes. Remove from the heat and set aside to cool to room temperature.

2. Transfer the zucchini to a serving dish and add the garlic, salt, vinegar, and mint. Drizzle with the remaining 2 tablespoons olive oil, if desired. There is no need to toss the ingredients; doing so may cause the zucchini to tear. Refrigerate for 4 to 6 hours or overnight. Serve cold.

Serving Suggestions
During the hot days of summer, this is a delicious, refreshing side dish with Grilled Halibut with Green Olive–Basil Pesto (page 140), or a simple grilled steak. It also makes a delicious sandwich filling with sliced turkey, mortadella, prosciutto, or Genoa salami.

Broccoli Rabe Vinaigrette

Serves 2 to 4

Broccoli rabe is naturally bitter, but if it's blanched, much of the bitterness is diminished. It's important, however, not to overcook broccoli rabe, so I recommend using a kitchen timer. When making this dish, do not season before refrigerating; the seasoning will cause the vegetable to discolor and lose some of its flavor. This is a cold dish. For a hot broccoli rabe dish, see the variations below.

Serving Suggestions
Serve with grilled steaks or Pork Loin Roast (page 159).

1 bunch of broccoli rabe (about 1 pound), washed

1/4 cup extra virgin olive oil

1/4 cup red wine vinegar or balsamic vinegar

2 garlic cloves, finely chopped

1/2 teaspoon salt

1. Bring a large pot of water to a boil. Add the broccoli rabe and boil for 3 to 4 minutes, until crisp-tender. Drain, and place in a bowl. Set aside to cool to room temperature, then refrigerate for 2 to 4 hours.

2. Add the olive oil, vinegar, garlic, and salt to the broccoli rabe, and toss lightly to mix. Serve cold.

VARIATIONS

Broccoli Rabe with Garlic Bring a large pot of water to a boil. Add the broccoli rabe and boil for 2 to 3 minutes; drain. In a medium skillet, heat 1/4 cup extra virgin olive oil over medium heat. Add 2 pressed garlic cloves, and cook, stirring, for 1 to 2 minutes, until the garlic is slightly golden. Add the drained broccoli rabe and cook, stirring occasionally, for 5 minutes. Season with salt to taste and serve hot.

Broccoli Rabe with Sausage (a hearty main course) Bring a large pot of water to a boil. Add the broccoli rabe and boil for 2 to 3 minutes. Drain, reserving 2 cups of the cooking water. Set the broccoli rabe aside to cool to room temperature, then chop it coarsely. Heat 1/4 cup extra virgin olive oil in a large skillet over medium-high heat. Add 3 pressed garlic cloves, 1/2 teaspoon salt, and 1 pound sweet Italian pork sausage cut into 1/4-inch-thick pieces. Cook, stirring frequently, for 15 to 20 minutes. Add the broccoli rabe and the reserved cooking liquid and cook for 5 to 7 minutes longer. Toss with 1 pound of cooked pasta and serve immediately.

Dandelion Greens with Potatoes and Sun-Dried Tomatoes

Serves 4 to 6

This is one of my favorite ways to enjoy dandelion greens in spring, when they first come to the market. The concentrated flavor of the sun-dried tomatoes slightly diminishes the natural bitterness of the greens. There are two types of dandelion greens: Some have leaves with jagged edges; the others have smooth edges. The smooth-edged dandelion greens are less bitter and deliver a sweeter flavor.

Serving Suggestions
Try this side dish with Pork Chops al Forno (page 160) or Grilled Steak Pizzaiola (page 164).

4 boiling potatoes (about 1½ pounds), scrubbed and peeled

1 large bunch of tender dandelion greens (about 1¼ pounds), washed, trimmed, and drained

¼ cup extra virgin olive oil

½ teaspoon salt

4 garlic cloves, pressed or finely chopped

¼ teaspoon freshly ground black pepper

8 to 10 oil-packed sun-dried tomatoes, drained (see page 13)

1. Bring 6 quarts of water to a boil in a large pot. Add the potatoes and cook at a low boil for 40 to 45 minutes, until the potatoes are tender when pierced with a fork. Add the dandelion greens and cook for 5 to 7 minutes longer. Drain the potatoes and the greens and set aside until the potatoes are cool enough to handle.

2. Heat the olive oil, salt, and garlic in a large skillet over medium heat. Cook for 1 to 2 minutes, until the garlic is slightly golden. Add the potatoes and use a potato masher or a fork to mash them with the garlic. Add the black pepper and the sun-dried tomatoes and cook for 1 to 2 minutes. Add the drained dandelion greens, toss to mix, and cook for 2 to 3 minutes, until heated through. Serve hot.

VARIATION

Dandelion Greens with Shallots and Fresh Tomatoes Bring a large pot of water to a boil. Add 1 pound washed dandelion greens and cook for 5 to 7 minutes. Drain thoroughly. Heat ¼ cup extra virgin olive oil and ½ teaspoon salt in a large skillet over medium heat and add ½ cup diced shallots (or onions) and 8 to 10 very ripe plum tomatoes, chopped, with seeds and core, and cook, covered, for 1 to 2 minutes. Mix in the drained dandelion greens, cover, and cook for 2 to 3 minutes, until heated through.

Swiss Chard with Prosciutto and Cipolline

Serves 4 to 6

Cooked Swiss chard is delicious on its own, added to soups, or sautéed with garlic and oil. It's also wonderful combined with pancetta and cipolline—flat, shallot-like bulbs. I make this side dish regularly when cipolline are in season (September through February).

Serving Suggestions
Serve this as a side dish or toss it with a pound of your favorite pasta for a main course.

¼-pound piece of pancetta (preferably spicy, see page 11) or Canadian bacon

½ teaspoon red pepper flakes (omit if using spicy pancetta)

1 pound Swiss chard, washed, trimmed, and chopped

¼ cup extra virgin olive oil

½ pound cipolline, peeled, trimmed, and finely sliced

3 garlic cloves, pressed or finely chopped

1 teaspoon salt

¼ pound prosciutto, diced

Gorgonzola cheese, crumbled, optional

1. Place the pancetta in a large pot of water and bring to a boil. (If you are using Canadian bacon, add the red pepper flakes.) Add the Swiss chard and cook for 4 to 5 minutes. Drain, reserving the pancetta and 1 cup of the cooking liquid. (Note: If serving with pasta, reserve all of the cooking liquid.)

2. Heat the olive oil in a large skillet over medium heat. Add the pancetta, cipolline, garlic, and ½ teaspoon of the salt, and cook, stirring, until the cipolline have turned light golden, 2 to 3 minutes. Add the prosciutto and cook, stirring, for 2 to 3 minutes more.

3. Add the Swiss chard, 1 cup of the reserved cooking liquid, and the remaining salt, and cook, stirring occasionally, for 4 to 5 minutes. Discard the pancetta. Serve hot, topped with Gorgonzola, if desired. If serving with pasta, cook the pasta in the reserved Swiss chard cooking liquid according to the package instructions, until al dente. Drain, and toss the pasta with the chopped Swiss chard.

Fava Beans alla Pomodoro

Serves 4 to 6

Neapolitans love fava beans. My mother grew them in her garden in Italy, as did my grandmother, aunts, and uncles. Today, my cousins continue the tradition. Although I can't grow them in my Connecticut garden, I enjoy fava beans from the market when they are in season.

Serving Suggestions
This dish pairs up nicely with just about any beef, lamb, or fish dish.

1 1/4 pounds fresh unshelled fava beans

1 teaspoon salt

1/4-pound piece of pancetta (preferably spicy, see page 11) or Canadian bacon

1 celery stalk with leaves

1 to 1 1/4 very ripe plum tomatoes, cored, seeded, and chopped

3 shallots, sliced, or 1 medium onion, sliced

3 garlic cloves, pressed or finely chopped

6 fresh basil leaves, coarsely chopped

1/2 teaspoon dried parsley, preferably homemade (page 251)

8 oil-packed sun-dried tomatoes, drained and chopped (see page 13)

1/4 cup extra virgin olive oil

1. Shell the fava beans and set aside. Bring 4 cups of water and 1/2 teaspoon of the salt to a boil in a large pot. Add the beans, pancetta, and celery and cook for 20 to 25 minutes. Drain the beans and discard the celery and pancetta.

2. Mix the tomatoes, shallots, garlic, basil, parsley, sun-dried tomatoes, olive oil, and the remaining 1/2 teaspoon salt in a medium bowl.

3. Warm a large dry skillet for 1 minute over medium heat. Add the tomato mixture and cook for 2 to 3 minutes, stirring often. Add the fava beans and cook for 5 to 7 minutes more, stirring often. Serve warm or at room temperature.

VARIATIONS

Fava Beans with Tuna This is a great, easy main dish for summer. Proceed as the recipe directs and allow the mixture to cool at room temperature. Transfer the mixture to a bowl and refrigerate for 2 to 4 hours. Drain one 6-ounce can of oil-packed tuna and add it to the mixture; toss gently before serving.

Fava Beans with Onions Prepare the beans as directed in step 1. Heat 1/4 cup extra virgin olive oil, 1 teaspoon red pepper flakes (optional), and 1/2 teaspoon salt in a small skillet and cook for 1 to 2 minutes. Add

$1^1/_2$ cups sliced onions and cook until soft, 5 to 6 minutes. Add the beans and cook for 5 to 7 minutes, stirring often. Serve immediately or at room temperature.

Pasta with Fava Beans   Proceed as the recipe directs, then toss with 1 pound cooked small pasta, such as baby shells or orecchiette. Serve as a first course or a light meal.

Mamma Rosina's Eggplant Pizzaiola

Serves 4 to 6

This old-fashioned recipe is quick, easy, and can be cooked on the stove or in the oven. I remember my mother making this dish when she had a few small eggplants on hand and little time to cook. She would top the eggplant with fresh tomatoes, oregano, garlic, and basil. I like to add capers.

Serving Suggestions
Serve as a side dish to Braised Pork Chops with Marinated Artichoke Hearts and Vinegar Peppers (page 161), grilled steaks, Stuffed Chicken Breast with Mozzarella (page 168), or Striped Bass Oreganata (page 138).

4 small Italian eggplants (about 1 pound total), with skin, stems removed, sliced in half lengthwise

One 32-ounce jar homemade canned plum tomatoes (page 275), chopped, or 1¾ to 2 pounds very ripe, fresh plum tomatoes, cored and chopped

4 tablespoons extra virgin olive oil

2 garlic cloves, finely chopped

1 tablespoon dried oregano, preferably imported Italian

4 to 6 fresh basil leaves, finely chopped

1 teaspoon salt

¼ cup drained capers, optional

1. Use the tip of a sharp knife to score the cut side of the eggplant, creating a tic-tac-toe pattern. The slits should almost reach the skin of the eggplant. Set aside.

2. Mix the tomatoes, 2 tablespoons of the olive oil, the garlic, oregano, basil, salt, and optional capers in a bowl and toss to mix.

To cook on the stove

3. Heat 2 tablespoons of the olive oil in a large skillet. Add the eggplant cut side up. Place some of the tomato mixture on top of each eggplant, pressing it into the slits so that the flavors can blend. Pour the remaining tomato mixture into the skillet. Cover and cook on medium to low heat for 25 to 30 minutes. (Note: If the tomatoes condense too much, add ½ cup water.)

To cook in the oven

4. Preheat the oven to 350°F. Grease a baking dish or an ovenproof skillet with 2 tablespoons of the olive oil. Add the eggplant cut side up. Place some of the tomato mixture on top of each eggplant, pressing it into the slits so that the flavors can blend. Pour the remaining tomato mixture into the baking dish or skillet. Cover with foil and bake for 25 minutes. Heat the broiler, remove the foil, and broil for about 2 minutes, until the top is slightly crispy.

Grilled Eggplant and Portobello Pizzaiola

Serves 4 to 6

My friends and family know that I am in love with eggplants. They're so beautiful and so versatile! This dish is a particular favorite, because it's such a nice accompaniment to just about any simply prepared roasted, baked, or grilled meat, fish, or poultry. Salting the eggplant ahead of time tenderizes it, and releases some of the natural juices. I adore the natural bitterness of eggplant, and that is what attracts me to this dish. Look for baby eggplants, which have fewer seeds and are firmer in texture than larger eggplants. Although this is delicious all year round, I particularly like to make it in summer when the grill is at the ready. (However, you can also use an indoor grill or a grill pan.)

Serving Suggestions
This dish is very versatile; it goes with just about any meat, fish, poultry, game, or lamb dish. Try it with Marinated Grilled Baby Lamb Chops with Fresh Mint (page 163). It's also delicious in sandwiches!

5 baby eggplants with skin (about 1 1/2 pounds total), preferably Italian

2 tablespoons salt plus 1/2 teaspoon

3 large portobello mushrooms with stems, wiped clean

3/4 cup extra virgin olive oil

3 to 4 garlic cloves, pressed or finely chopped

3 teaspoons dried oregano, preferably imported Italian

One 32-ounce jar homemade canned plum tomatoes (page 275), crushed in a blender or food processor for 2 to 3 seconds, or 2 1/4 to 2 1/2 pounds fresh, very ripe plum tomatoes, cored and coarsely chopped (about 2 1/2 cups chopped tomatoes)

6 fresh basil leaves, coarsely chopped

1/3 cup fresh dry or processed whole-milk mozzarella cheese (page 10), optional

1. Trim off the stems of the eggplants and discard. Slice the eggplants vertically into $1/8$-inch-thick slices. Use 2 tablespoons of the salt to sprinkle both sides of all the eggplant slices, or toss the eggplant slices and the 2 tablespoons of salt in a bowl.

2. Place the eggplant in a deep baking dish. You will have 4 to 5 layers of eggplant. Place another baking dish on top of the eggplant, then place a weight (such as a large can of tomatoes) in the second baking dish. Set aside for 20 to 25 minutes. (This process will rid the eggplant of excess moisture.)

3. Prepare a fire in a gas or charcoal grill or heat an indoor grill or a grill pan to medium.

4. Drain the excess juices from the eggplant. Slice the mushrooms vertically into $1/8$-inch-thick slices through the stem. Brush each slice of eggplant and each mushroom slice with some of the olive oil. (You will use about $1/2$ cup for brushing the vegetables.)

5. Place the eggplant and mushrooms on the grill and cook for 2 to 3 minutes on each side. Transfer to a baking dish or platter and set aside.

6. Warm the remaining $1/4$ cup olive oil in a 2-quart saucepan over medium heat. Add the garlic and the remaining $1/2$ teaspoon salt, and cook for 1 minute. Add 1 teaspoon of the oregano, the tomatoes, and the basil, and cook for 8 to 10 minutes. (If using fresh tomatoes, cook for 15 minutes.)

7. Preheat the oven to 350°F.

8. Pour $1/2$ cup of the tomato sauce on the bottom of an 8 X 8-inch baking dish that is about $2^{1}/2$ inches deep. Place one layer of eggplant and mushrooms in the bottom of the dish, then top with $1/2$ cup of the tomato sauce, and sprinkle with $1/2$ teaspoon oregano. Repeat the layers, adding the tomato sauce and the oregano between each layer; you will have 4 to 5 layers.

9. Cover with foil and bake for 20 minutes. Remove the foil, and sprinkle the top with mozzarella, if using. Return the uncovered dish to the oven and bake for 10 minutes more, or until the mozzarella has melted. Serve immediately. (Note: The mozzarella topping is optional, but the final 10 minutes of baking time are necessary with or without the mozzarella.)

VARIATION

Grilled Eggplant and Portobello Pizzaiola with Extra Mozzarella
You will need 1 cup total shredded whole-milk mozzarella cheese.

Proceed as the recipe directs through step 7. In step 8, add $1/3$ cup mozzarella on top of the oregano between each of the layers. Bake and serve according to step 9.

Fried Asparagus with Cheese

Serves 4 to 6

I created this recipe simply because I love asparagus. This side dish is fancier than just plain steamed asparagus spears, so I enjoy serving it when I have company. It's easy to make and reheats well, too.

Serving Suggestions
Serve this extremely versatile side dish with just about any fish, meat, or poultry dish. It can also be served as an appetizer.

1 pound fresh thick or medium-thick asparagus spears, tough ends trimmed

3 large eggs

Three ³⁄₄-ounce packages Bel Paese cheese

2 tablespoons grated Pecorino Romano cheese

1 teaspoon freshly ground black pepper

1 cup unseasoned dry bread crumbs, preferably homemade (page 6)

¹⁄₂ teaspoon dried basil, preferably homemade (page 251)

¹⁄₂ teaspoon dried parsley, preferably homemade (page 251)

¹⁄₄ cup all-purpose flour

1 cup light olive oil or vegetable oil

1. Bring 4 quarts of water to a boil in a 6-quart asparagus steamer or medium pot. If using a steamer, place the asparagus spears upright in the water, leaving the tips exposed. If using a pot, put the spears in the water. (Note: if you are using a pot, you can arrange the asparagus spears with a pair of tongs so that the stems are not submerged. This will keep the tips from overcooking.) Do not cover the pot. Cook for 2 minutes, or until al dente. Remove from the water and drain. Set aside to cool.

2. Combine the eggs, Bel Paese, Pecorino Romano, and pepper in a blender; blend until thick and smooth, about 30 seconds. Pour into a shallow dish.

3. Place the bread crumbs in a separate shallow dish and mix in the basil and parsley.

4. Place the flour in a third shallow dish. Toss the asparagus in the flour mixture; shake off any extra flour. Then dip the asparagus into the cheese mixture, then directly into the bread crumbs. Cover the asparagus spears completely, then gently shake off any extra bread crumbs.

5. Heat the olive oil in a medium skillet until hot but not smoking. Add the asparagus and fry until crisp, 3 to 5 minutes. Remove from the pan and drain on paper towels to absorb excess oil. Transfer to a platter and serve immediately.

VARIATION

Instead of asparagus, try using 6 medium zucchini: Cut each zucchini in half lengthwise, then cut each piece into thirds. Do not blanch the zucchini; proceed as the recipe directs, starting with step 2. Increase the total frying time to 5 to 6 minutes, until the zucchini is crisp.

Eleanora's Tips

When frying asparagus, it is very important to keep the cooking temperature at medium-high. If the temperature is too hot, the oil will smoke and may burn. When blanching asparagus, since the tips cook more quickly than the stems, it's important not to place the tips in the water when you begin the cooking process. If asparagus tips are overcooked, they will get mushy and break off.

Potato Croquettes

Makes about 26 croquettes; serves 10 to 12

These fancy potato "sticks" are great for parties, appetizers, or snacks, or to serve as a side dish to just about any meat, chicken, or fish dish. My sister Natalina loves my potato croquettes and whenever she joins us for dinner, I always make an extra batch for her to take home.

Serving Suggestions
Potato Croquettes are delicious with Veal Sorrentino (page 156) or Grilled Steak Pizzaiola (page 164).

3½ pounds boiling potatoes, such as Yukon Gold or Red Bliss

3 large eggs

1 cup shredded fresh dry or processed whole-milk mozzarella cheese (page 10)

½ pound sweet soppressata or prosciutto, finely diced

Two ¾-ounce packages Bel Paese cheese, diced

3 heaping tablespoons grated Pecorino Romano cheese

2 tablespoons extra virgin olive oil

2 tablespoons finely chopped fresh flat-leaf (Italian) parsley

1 teaspoon salt

Freshly ground black pepper to taste

1½ cups unseasoned dry bread crumbs, preferably homemade (page 6)

1 cup light olive oil

1. Place the potatoes in a large pot filled with water. Bring to a boil and cook for 45 to 50 minutes or more, until the potatoes are tender when pierced with a fork. Drain and set aside until cool enough to handle. Remove the skins under lukewarm running water.

2. Place the potatoes in a bowl and coarsely mash them with a potato masher. Let the potatoes cool for 20 to 25 minutes.

3. Whisk the eggs in a separate bowl with a fork or a whisk and add to the potatoes. Mix in the mozzarella, soppressata, Bel Paese, and Pecorino Romano, extra virgin olive oil, parsley, and salt. Season to taste with pepper. Stir in ¼ cup of the bread crumbs (which will bind the mixture and make it easier to form the croquettes).

4. Moisten your hands with water, and form the potato mixture into cylinders approximately 2½ inches long, using about ¼ cup of the mixture for each croquette.

5. Pour the remaining bread crumbs into a flat dish. Place the croquettes in the bread crumbs, pressing the crumbs gently onto all sides of the croquettes, rolling each croquette several times until it cannot incorporate any additional bread crumbs.

6. Heat the light olive oil in a large, heavy skillet until very hot but not smoking. Add the croquettes and cook for 8 to 10 minutes, turning them every 3 to 4 minutes, until golden brown. Drain on paper towels and serve hot. (To reheat leftovers, place on a baking sheet in a preheated 350°F oven and cook for 15 minutes or until heated through.)

Eleanora's Tips

Be sure to let the potatoes cool completely before making the croquettes so that they'll be easier to form. It's also important to coat the croquettes generously in bread crumbs so that they won't absorb too much oil. In addition, make sure the oil is very hot—but not smoking—before adding the croquettes.

Creamy Potato Gratin with Smoked Mozzarella

Serves 6 to 8

Everyone loves potatoes, but when they're combined with smoked mozzarella, prosciutto, and panna, and baked in the oven, the humble tuber is even more delicious. The panna adds richness; if you like sour cream and butter with your potatoes, you'll love panna. I like to serve this side dish with meat or poultry when I want something a little more special than baked potatoes.

Serving Suggestions
Serve as a side dish with Veal Marsala (page 151), Pork Loin Roast (page 159), or Pork Chops al Forno (page 160).

3½ pounds boiling potatoes, such as Yukon Gold or Red Bliss

½ teaspoon salt

½ cup grated Pecorino Romano or Parmigiano-Reggiano cheese

½ pound smoked whole-milk mozzarella cheese, diced

½ pound prosciutto or ham, diced

2 tablespoons unsalted butter

1 cup panna (see Mail-Order Sources, page 283) or heavy cream

1. Place the potatoes in a large pot filled with water. Bring to a boil and cook for 45 to 50 minutes or more, until the potatoes are tender when pierced with a fork. Drain and set aside until cool enough to handle. Remove the skins under lukewarm running water.

2. Preheat the oven to 350°F.

3. Place the potatoes in a large bowl and mash them with a potato masher until smooth.

4. Add the salt, Pecorino Romano, mozzarella, prosciutto, butter, and panna. Mix well with your hands until all the panna is absorbed.

5. Transfer the mixture into an ungreased 8½ X 10-inch baking dish. Wet a spatula and flatten the top of the mixture. For a decorative top, use the tines of a fork to create shallow diagonal lines in the mixture. Bake for 45 minutes to 1 hour, until the top looks golden.

Eggplant Parmigiana

When I was a schoolgirl, my mother would often pack my lunch with a big hero sandwich filled with leftover Eggplant Parmigiana. My lunches were so big, it looked like I was going to work at a construction site! In the school cafeteria, everyone else had peanut butter and jelly sandwiches and little bags of celery stalks and carrot sticks. It was embarrassing to pull out that huge hero, so I would try to hide it inside the lunch bag. I couldn't really fool my schoolmates, however, because they would look at me with raised eyebrows, wondering if I was really going to eat the whole sandwich. I always did, and I can do so to this day, when I still make Eggplant Parmigiana sandwiches for my family.

Serving Suggestions
Serve as a side with Pork Loin Roast (page 159), or as a small meal with bread and a salad. Leftovers, served hot or cold, are delicious reheated or in sandwiches.

FOR THE EGGPLANT

3 to 4 medium eggplants (about 2 1/2 pounds total), with skin

2 cups all-purpose flour

1 teaspoon dried basil, preferably homemade (page 251)

1 teaspoon dried parsley, preferably homemade (page 251)

7 extra-large eggs

1 1/4 cups grated Pecorino Romano cheese

3 cups unseasoned dry bread crumbs, preferably homemade (page 6)

3 cups light olive oil

FOR THE MARINARA SAUCE

3 tablespoons extra virgin olive oil

1 large onion, finely chopped

2 garlic cloves, pressed or finely chopped

Two 32-ounce jars homemade canned plum tomatoes (page 275) or two 35-ounce cans whole plum tomatoes with juice, pureed in a blender or food processor for 3 to 5 seconds

One 32-ounce jar homemade tomato puree (page 275), or one 35-ounce can whole plum tomatoes with juice, pureed in a blender or food processor for 3 to 5 seconds

1 teaspoon salt

6 fresh basil leaves, coarsely chopped

ASSEMBLING THE DISH

2 tablespoons dried oregano, preferably imported Italian

1/4 cup Pecorino Romano cheese

1/2 pound fresh dry or processed whole-milk mozzarella cheese, grated (page 10)

To make the eggplant

1. Cut the eggplants lengthwise into $1/4$-inch-thick slices. Combine the flour, dried basil, and dried parsley in a large bowl. In another bowl, beat the eggs with the Pecorino Romano. Place the eggplant slices in the flour and turn to coat. Shake off any excess flour. Dip the slices in the egg mixture, transfer to the bread crumbs, and turn to coat on all sides. Set aside for 10 minutes so that the bread crumbs absorb some of the egg batter.

2. Heat the olive oil in a large nonstick skillet until hot but not smoking. Add the prepared eggplant slices and cook until golden, about 3 minutes on each side. Drain on paper towels. *(continued)*

To make the marinara sauce

3. Warm the olive oil in a large skillet over medium heat. Add the onion and garlic. Cook, stirring often, until the onion is translucent, 3 to 5 minutes. Stir in the tomatoes, tomato puree, salt, and basil. Cook for 20 minutes, stirring often.

To assemble the dish

4. Preheat the oven to 350°F. Pour about 1 cup of the sauce into a large baking dish, sprinkle with a little dried oregano, and top with a layer of eggplant. Sprinkle on some of the Pecorino Romano and about $1/2$ cup of the mozzarella. Continue layering until the dish is filled. Reserve about $1/3$ cup of the mozzarella.

5. Cover the dish with foil and bake for 30 minutes. Remove the foil, sprinkle on the remaining $1/3$ cup mozzarella, and bake uncovered for 8 to 10 minutes longer. Remove from the oven and set aside for 15 to 20 minutes before serving.

Mamma's Stuffed Italian Peppers

Serves 6 to 8

Many years ago, on Arthur Avenue, there was a vendor who sold his wares out of his horse-drawn wagon. He'd ride up and down the avenues selling fresh produce, yelling at the top of his lungs, *"Frutti! Verdure!"* All the housewives would come out—in their housedresses, aprons, and sometimes with rollers in their hair—clutching their purses and wallets. Whenever my mother found Italian peppers (called *frevarelli* in Neapolitan dialect) that were fresh enough to suit her taste, she'd proudly show them to her neighbors. They would wonder what she was going to do with them. When the aroma of her sweet stuffed peppers wafted through the building, their question was answered.

Serving Suggestions
I like to serve this as a side dish to Beef Amburg (page 166), Pork Loin Roast (page 159), simply prepared grilled steak, or grilled or pan-fried pork or veal chops. Or serve for lunch with a generous chunk of hearty Italian bread.

6 long red or green Italian peppers *(frevarelli)* or cubanelle peppers

Two ½-inch-thick slices Italian bread

3 large eggs

¼ cup plus 1 tablespoon extra virgin olive oil

1 teaspoon dried oregano, preferably imported Italian

5 garlic cloves pressed or finely chopped (2 for the stuffing, 3 for the sauce)

½ teaspoon freshly ground black pepper

2 very ripe, fresh plum tomatoes, diced

½ cup grated Pecorino Romano cheese

½ cup finely chopped celery with leaves

2 tablespoons finely chopped fresh flat-leaf (Italian) parsley

8 salt-packed anchovy fillets, rinsed and chopped, or 8 oil-packed anchovies, drained and chopped

1 cup unseasoned dry bread crumbs, preferably homemade (page 6)

One 32-ounce jar homemade tomato puree (page 275), or one 35-ounce can whole plum tomatoes with juice, pureed in a blender or food processor for 3 to 5 seconds

6 fresh basil leaves, finely chopped

1 teaspoon salt

1. Use a small sharp knife to cut off the stem end of each pepper. Remove the seeds, leaving the peppers intact.

2. Hold the bread quickly under cold running water. Squeeze out the excess water, then tear or crumble into small pieces and set aside.

3. Beat the eggs, 1 tablespoon of the olive oil, the oregano, 2 of the pressed garlic cloves, and the black pepper in a large bowl. Mix in the diced tomatoes, cheese, ¼ cup of the celery, the parsley, anchovies, and moistened bread pieces. Mix in the bread crumbs.

4. Stuff the peppers with the mixture, dividing it evenly among the peppers.

5. Heat the remaining ¼ cup olive oil and the remaining 3 pressed garlic cloves in a very large skillet over medium heat until the garlic just begins to turn golden, about 2 minutes. Add the tomato puree, the remaining ¼ cup celery, the basil, and the salt and simmer until thickened, about 10 minutes for homemade puree and about 20 minutes for canned tomatoes.

6. Add the peppers to the tomato sauce, so that they are lying flat. Cover and simmer for 40 to 45 minutes. Serve hot.

Traditional Stuffed Artichokes

Serves 4 to 6

My father, Francesco, loved this simple, down-to-earth dish, and I love it, too. I have vivid memories of my mother making this dish; she'd stuff the artichokes with ingredients she kept on hand, fry them quickly, then simmer them gently with tomatoes and fresh celery.

When buying artichokes, choose those that are round in shape, free of blemishes, and heavy for their size. (Lighter artichokes are tasteless and full of choke.) The outer leaves should be tender, not coarse or dry.

4 large artichokes

2½ cups dry white wine

2 large eggs, beaten

3 heaping tablespoons grated Pecorino Romano cheese

One ½-inch-thick slice Italian bread, moistened, torn, and crumbled

½ pound fresh, ripe plum tomatoes, cored and diced

1 celery stalk with leaves, finely chopped

1 tablespoon finely chopped fresh flat-leaf (Italian) parsley

4 fresh basil leaves, finely chopped

½ teaspoon freshly ground black pepper

1 tablespoon dried oregano, preferably imported Italian

1 cup unseasoned dry bread crumbs, preferably homemade (page 6)

1½ tablespoons finely chopped fresh mint

¼ cup plus 2 tablespoons extra virgin olive oil

6 garlic cloves

1½ cups homemade tomato puree (page 275), or 1½ cups canned whole plum tomatoes with juice, pureed in a blender or food processor for 3 to 5 seconds

1 teaspoon salt

Serving Suggestions

This versatile side dish is delicious with roast chicken or pork chops. It can also be served as a first course. For a light lunch, serve it with a piece of crusty Italian bread.

1. Remove the tough outer leaves of the artichokes and discard. Trim off the spiky, pointed tops with kitchen shears. Cut the stems off to make a flat base for the artichokes and coarsely chop the stems.

2. Combine 4 cups of water with 2 cups of the wine in a large pot and bring to a boil. Add the artichokes and stems and boil for 20 to 25 minutes uncovered. Drain, reserving ½ cup of the artichoke cooking broth.

3. Mix the eggs, Pecorino Romano, bread, diced tomatoes, half the celery, the parsley, basil, pepper, oregano, bread crumbs, chopped artichoke stems, and mint in a large bowl. Warm 2 tablespoons of the olive oil in a small skillet over medium heat. Put 2 of the garlic cloves through a garlic press, add them to the skillet, and cook for 1 minute. Add to the egg mixture.

4. Separate the leaves of the artichoke to reveal the fuzzy choke in the center. Use the point of a sharp knife to cut around the choke; remove the choke, chop coarsely, and add to the filling. Fill the cavity with enough stuffing so that it comes to the very top of the artichoke.

5. Warm 2 tablespoons of the olive oil in a large, deep skillet over medium heat. Crack 2 garlic cloves with the flat side of a large knife. Add them to the skillet and cook until fragrant, 1 to 2 minutes. Add the artichokes, stuffing side down. (Note: The stuffing will not fall out.) Cook for 5 to 7 minutes, until the stuffing is golden brown. Discard the cracked garlic and add the remaining 2 tablespoons olive oil to the skillet. Put the remaining 2 garlic cloves through a garlic press and add to the skillet. Add the tomato puree, the remaining celery, and the salt. Cook, partially covered, for 10 minutes or until the sauce has condensed. Add the $1/2$ cup of reserved artichoke cooking broth and the remaining $1/2$ cup wine. Cover, lower the heat to medium-low, and simmer for 15 to 20 minutes. Serve immediately.

Stuffed Escarole with Sun-Dried Tomatoes and Capers

Serves 4 to 6

Offering a head of fresh escarole stuffed with sunny, Mediterranean ingredients makes everyone at my table happy. Braised in a mixture of tomatoes, wine, and capers, it's a flavorful, simple side dish that can even be served as a light lunch.

Serving Suggestions
Serve as a side dish to Veal Osso Buco (page 158) or simply prepared chicken, veal, or steak.

2 small heads escarole

1/4 cup plus 2 tablespoons extra virgin olive oil

Freshly ground black pepper

6 oil-packed sun-dried tomatoes, drained and diced (see page 13)

1 3/4 to 2 pounds very ripe, fresh plum tomatoes, chopped (about 2 1/2 cups)

2 tablespoons drained capers (see page 7)

1/4 cup toasted pine nuts, optional (toast in a 350°F oven for 5 to 6 minutes, then broil on high for 1 to 2 minutes, or until slightly golden)

2 garlic cloves, finely chopped

1/4 cup finely diced shallots or onions

1/2 teaspoon salt, or to taste

4 fresh basil leaves, coarsely chopped

1/2 cup dry white wine

1. Rinse the escarole and remove the tough outer leaves and discard.

2. Working with one head of escarole at a time, place the head—stem side down—on a flat work surface and flatten it slightly to expose the inner leaves as much as possible.

3. Drizzle each escarole head with 1 tablespoon of the olive oil. Sprinkle each head with pepper to taste and half of the diced sun-dried tomatoes. Scatter about 2 of the chopped tomatoes and $1^{1}/2$ teaspoons of the capers into each head. Add half the pine nuts, if using. Fold in the leaves of the escarole to close it up. Hold the ends of the leaves together with one hand while you secure the escarole bundle with kitchen twine.

4. Warm the remaining $^{1}/4$ cup olive oil in a large saucepan over medium heat. Add the garlic, shallots, salt, the remaining chopped tomatoes, the basil, the remaining tablespoon of capers, the wine, and 1 cup of water. Simmer for 5 minutes. Add the escarole bundles and ladle some of the sauce over them. Cover tightly and simmer for 15 to 20 minutes, until the leaves are tender. Serve hot with Prosciutto Bread with Pancetta and Basil (page 200).

Eggplant alla Scarpetta

Stuffed Eggplant

I've taken the traditional stuffed eggplant my mother used to make and added wild mushrooms, capers, and basil to make it even more appealing. By the way, the menus at some Italian restaurants will describe stuffed eggplant as *alla scarpetta,* which means "little shoe."

Serving Suggestions
Serve as a side dish to roast meats, chops, or chicken.

FOR THE SAUCE

1/4 cup extra virgin olive oil

1 shallot, finely diced, or
    2 tablespoons finely chopped
    onion

2 garlic cloves, pressed or finely
    chopped

1/2 teaspoon salt

One 32-ounce jar homemade canned
    plum tomatoes (page 275), or
    one 35-ounce can whole plum
    tomatoes with juice, crushed in a
    blender or food processor for
    2 to 3 seconds

1/2 cup dry red wine

1 celery stalk with leaves, finely
    diced

2 tablespoons drained capers

1 teaspoon dried oregano,
    preferably imported Italian

4 fresh basil leaves, coarsely
    chopped

**FOR THE EGGPLANT AND
STUFFING**

4 Italian baby eggplants (about 1 1/4
    pounds), with skin, trimmed and
    cut in half lengthwise

2 tablespoons extra virgin olive oil

2 garlic cloves, finely chopped

1/2 teaspoon salt

1/4 pound fresh shiitake, oyster,
    porcini, or white button
    mushrooms, diced

2 large eggs, beaten

1/2 teaspoon freshly ground black
    pepper

2 tablespoons grated Pecorino
    Romano cheese

1/2 cup unseasoned dry bread
    crumbs, preferably homemade
    (page 6)

1/2 teaspoon dried parsley,
    preferably homemade (page 251)

1/2 teaspoon dried basil, preferably
    homemade (page 251)

1/2 teaspoon dried oregano,
    preferably imported Italian

2 slices Italian bread, moistened
    with water and torn into small
    pieces

2 tablespoons chopped fresh flat-
    leaf (Italian) parsley

To make the sauce

1. Combine the olive oil, shallot, garlic, and salt in a skillet, and cook, stirring, for 2 to 3 minutes over medium heat. Add the tomatoes and wine and bring to a boil. Add the celery, capers, oregano, and basil. Simmer for about 10 minutes. If the sauce condenses too much, add a little cold water. Set aside. *(continued)*

To make the eggplant and the stuffing

2. Use the tip of a sharp knife to remove the center portion of each egg-plant, leaving about $1/4$ inch of the skin. You will need to stuff each egg-plant with about $1/4$ cup of the stuffing, so make sure to cut out enough of the eggplant to make room for the stuffing. Dice the eggplant flesh and set aside the carved-out eggplant shells.

3. Heat 2 tablespoons of the olive oil in a skillet. Add the garlic, salt, mushrooms, and the diced eggplant, and cook, stirring, for 5 minutes or until golden. Set aside.

4. Combine the eggs and black pepper in a bowl and whisk to blend. Add the Pecorino Romano, bread crumbs, dried parsley, basil, oregano, and the moistened bread. Add the sautéed mushrooms and eggplant and the fresh parsley. Stir to mix.

5. Place about $1/4$ cup of the stuffing into each eggplant half. The stuffing should mound slightly above the top of the eggplant. Pat the mixture down with moistened hands (or use a spoon and press gently).

To cook on the stove

6. Place the eggplant, stuffed side up, in a skillet with the tomato sauce. Add $1 1/2$ cups of water, cover, and cook on medium to low heat for 25 to 30 minutes, until the eggplant looks tender. If the sauce condenses too much, add water as needed.

To cook in the oven

7. Preheat the oven to 350° F. Spoon the tomato sauce into a baking dish. Place the stuffed eggplants stuffing side up in the dish. Cover with foil and bake for 25 to 30 minutes. For a crisp topping, bake only 25 minutes, un-cover, and broil for 2 minutes. Serve hot.

VARIATION

Stuffed Artichoke Halves

1. Trim $1/2$ inch from the tips of 6 to 8 medium artichokes and $1/4$ inch from the stem end. Cut off the stems and peel them. Discard the coarse, outer leaves.

2. Bring 6 cups of water to a boil in a large, non-aluminum pot, add the artichokes and artichoke stems, and boil for 15 to 20 minutes, until slightly tender. Drain and set aside to cool to room temperature. Slice the artichokes in half; scoop out the choke and discard. Finely chop the artichoke stems.

3. Preheat the oven to 350°F. Heat $1/4$ cup olive oil in a large skillet over medium heat. Add 2 finely chopped garlic cloves, $1/2$ teaspoon salt, $1/4$ pound sliced mushrooms, and the finely chopped artichoke stems, and cook, stirring, for 5 minutes or until golden.

4. Proceed as the stuffing recipe directs, adding 2 tablespoons chopped fresh mint in step 4. Stuff the artichokes as the recipe directs in step 5.

5. Place the stuffed artichokes stuffing side up in one layer in a lightly oiled baking dish. Cover with foil and bake for 20 to 25 minutes. Remove the foil and broil on high for 2 to 3 minutes, until the stuffing is slightly golden.

BREAD, PIZZA, AND SAVORY PIES

When I was growing up, it seemed as though a loaf of *panella* was always on the table, as if it were part of every meal's table setting. My mother made her own bread, but when time was limited she purchased freshly baked loaves from the bakery down the street. I take after my mother: Even though there are very good Italian bakeries nearby, I nearly always bake my own bread. I particularly like to bake on a sunny day, when I can let the dough rise on the kitchen table in the warm rays of the sun. Making bread takes a little time, but I find the process relaxing and therapeutic. Plus, nothing can compare to the taste, texture, and aroma of your own home-baked loaves.

My basic bread recipe—a version of *panella,* the country-style loaf from my homeland—makes four generous loaves so that some can be frozen for later use. The basic dough can then be used to make other breads, such as Prosciutto Bread with Pancetta and Basil (page 200), Tomato Focaccia (page 202), or Olive Bread (page 201). This same versatile dough can also be used to make Pizza Napoletana with Anchovies (page 203) and Calzones (page 211).

In this chapter I also include the recipe for my Sweet Easter Bread (page 207), a braided loaf perfumed with liqueur and studded with golden raisins. You'll also find recipes for Taralli con Finochette (page 206), which is made from dough flavored with white wine, fennel seeds, and black pepper, and Panzarotti (page 209)—little pillows of fried dough stuffed with mozzarella. Both make tasty snacks or appetizers to serve with aperitivi. Finally, I've included recipes for the renowned Italian savory pies, Pizza Rustica (page 215) and Toma Pie (page 213). Both are as versatile as they are delicious, since they can be served as appetizers, snacks, or for lunch or supper.

Homemade Italian Bread

Makes 4 large loaves

Almost one hundred years ago, when my Nonna Cristina was growing up in Italy, she had a job helping the local bakeries deliver bread. Carrying thirty or forty loaves in a wicker basket on top of her head, she walked three or four miles a day going to various shops and bakeries around town. Her pay at the end of the day? A loaf of bread to take home to her family. When I see the sun's rays beaming through my kitchen window, I immediately want to take advantage of the warm sun and make my homemade bread. My recipe for basic table bread or "house bread" (referred to as *panella*) originated in the Campania region. Homemade bread is an all-day process, since the dough needs to rise twice. Therefore, I recommend making it on a day when you have leisure time. My recipe makes four large loaves, so I serve one for the evening meal and freeze two or three loaves to enjoy later.

2 ounces fresh compressed yeast or
  2 packages active dry yeast
2 tablespoons salt
1 large egg, beaten

1 teaspoon olive oil
20 cups (one 5-pound bag)
  unbleached bread flour, plus
  additional flour for kneading

1. Combine the yeast and the salt in a large measuring cup or a bowl with 2 cups of warm (105 to 115°F) water. Stir to mix, then set aside in a warm place for 10 minutes, until the yeast and salt have dissolved.

2. Combine the dissolved yeast mixture, the egg, olive oil, and 4 cups of warm water in a very large bowl and stir to mix. Add the flour gradually, stirring constantly, until you have a soft, but not sticky, dough.

3. Knead the dough on a lightly floured work surface for 7 to 10 minutes, until smooth and elastic. Place the dough in a lightly floured bowl, cover with plastic wrap, and top with a tea towel. Place the bowl in a warm area and let rise for 3 to 4 hours, until doubled in bulk.

4. Turn the dough out onto a lightly floured work surface and knead for 5 to 7 minutes, adding a little more flour if the dough seems sticky. Form it into a loose loaf; you should have an oblong piece of dough about 8 inches wide and 14 inches long. Divide the dough into 4 equal pieces. (Note: To make Prosciutto Bread with Pancetta and Basil [page 200], Tomato Focaccia [page 202], Pizza [page 203], or the other flavored breads in this book, divide the dough into 5 equal pieces. One piece is sufficient for a medium loaf of bread or for pizza or foccacia.)

5. Working with one piece of dough at a time (keep the other pieces of dough covered with a kitchen towel as you work), knead the dough for 1 to 2 minutes before shaping it. To make *panella* (round loaves with a domed top), take one of the pieces of dough and pat it into a round, slightly domed shape about 10 inches in diameter. Use a very sharp knife to cut several $1/2$-inch-deep slashes on top of the bread. To make oblong loaves, pat the dough into an oblong shape, about 14 inches long and about 5 inches wide. Use a very sharp knife to cut several $1/2$-inch-deep slashes on top of the bread.

6. Place the shaped loaves on 4 separate lightly floured baking sheets, cover each with a kitchen towel, and place in a warm area to rise for 1 to 2 hours, until doubled in bulk.

7. Preheat the oven to 375°F.

8. Bake each loaf for 1 hour or until golden brown (see Note). Place the loaves on a rack and let them cool at room temperature at least 20 to 25 minutes before slicing. Note: If your oven will not accommodate 4 loaves at once, bake 2 loaves at a time, keeping the other 2 loaves covered with a kitchen towel until ready to bake.

Prosciutto Bread with Pancetta and Basil

Makes five 6-inch wreath-shaped loaves or five 14-inch oblong loaves

When I was growing up, my brother-in-law, Angelo, would always bring store-bought prosciutto bread to the family Sunday dinner. Now, I prefer to make my own homemade prosciutto bread, which I find much more delicious than store-bought bread. I like to add pancetta, basil, pepper, and garlic-flavored oil to my prosciutto bread for even more richness and flavor. This robust bread does not need any company; it's delicious for snacking all by itself. Or try it, as we do in our home, as part of an antipasto platter with provolone or Fiore di Sardegna. This hearty bread is also delicious with just about any soup—particularly Nonna's Homemade Minestrone (page 62) or anything that includes greens, such as Peasant-Style Escarole and White Bean Soup (page 70). The bread can be made in advance and kept at room temperature for several days or frozen for several months.

Dough for Homemade Italian Bread (page 198), prepared through step 4

6 garlic cloves, peeled and sliced lengthwise

¾ cup extra virgin olive oil

1 teaspoon salt

2½ teaspoons freshly ground black pepper

5 teaspoons dried basil, preferably homemade (page 251)

5 teaspoons dried parsley, preferably homemade (page 251)

2½ cups (about 1¼ pounds) diced prosciutto (diced into ½-inch pieces)

1¼ pounds sliced pancetta (preferably spicy, see page 11), diced into ½-inch pieces, or thinly sliced Canadian bacon, diced

1. Prepare the dough as the recipe directs through step 4, dividing the dough into 5 pieces, and set aside.

2. Preheat the oven to 350°F.

3. Place the sliced garlic in a small baking dish. Add the olive oil and salt and roast uncovered in the oven for 15 to 20 minutes, until the garlic turns slightly golden. Set aside, reserving the oil and the garlic. (Note: To roast garlic in the microwave, see page 67.)

4. To make oblong loaves: Working with one piece of dough at a time, knead the dough briefly on a lightly floured work surface. Roll out the dough into an oblong shape that is about 14 inches long and 8 inches wide. Brush with some of the roasted garlic oil, then sprinkle with ½ teaspoon black pepper, 1 teaspoon dried basil, 1 teaspoon dried parsley, ½ cup of the prosciutto, and ¼ cup of the pancetta for each loaf. Roll up the dough to form a long, narrow rectangle. (You can twist it several times, if desired.) Use a knife to make small incisions on the top of the loaf.

5. Make wreath-shaped loaves *(taralli)* as follows: Working with one piece of dough at a time, knead the dough briefly on a lightly floured surface. Roll out each piece into a long, narrow rectangle, about 14 inches long and 8 inches wide. Brush with additional roasted garlic oil, then sprinkle with black pepper, basil, parsley, ½ cup of the prosciutto, and ¼ cup of the pancetta. Roll up the dough to form a rectangle about 20 inches long and 4 inches wide. Continue to shape the dough into a long, thick rope by stretching it vertically. Twist the dough and join the two ends so they adhere. Transfer the loaf to a lightly floured baking sheet. Use a sharp knife to make small incisions on top of the loaf. Repeat with the remaining dough.

6. Place each loaf on a lightly floured baking sheet, cover with kitchen towels and place in a warm place to rise for 2 hours or until doubled in bulk.

7. Preheat the oven to 375°F.

8. Brush the dough with the remaining garlic oil.

9. Bake each loaf in the oven for 50 minutes to 1 hour, until golden brown. (Note: Oblong loaves and wreath-shaped loaves will bake in the same amount of time.) Remove from the oven, place the loaves on a baking rack, and let cool for 20 to 25 minutes at room temperature before slicing. Serve warm.

VARIATIONS

Sun-Dried Tomato Bread Substitute $^1/_2$ pound diced sun-dried tomatoes for the prosciutto and pancetta.

Olive Bread Substitute $3^3/_4$ cups of homemade Cured Green Olives (page 272), Cerignola olives, or green Sicilian olives for the prosciutto and pancetta. (Note: If you want only 1 or 2 loaves flavored with olives, use $^3/_4$ cup olives per loaf.)

Tomato Focaccia

Focaccia al Pomodoro

Serves 4 to 6

One look at my pantry shelf and anyone can see how much I love tomatoes! But I not only love home-canned tomatoes, I'm crazy about fresh tomatoes, too, and find that they're delicious as a topping for focaccia. Although my mother didn't make focaccia, she often scattered chopped, fresh tomatoes on top of home-made pizza bread, which is similar to my focaccia. Try Tomato Focaccia as a snack, with soups, salads, or as sandwich bread. One of my favorite ways to enjoy Tomato Focaccia is with prosciutto, sliced black figs, fresh arugula, a drizzle of extra virgin olive oil, and a sprinkle of black pepper.

Dough for Homemade Italian Bread (page 198), prepared through step 4
Light olive oil
1 garlic clove, finely chopped
2 tablespoons extra virgin olive oil
1/4 teaspoon dried parsley, preferably homemade (page 251)
1/4 teaspoon dried basil, preferably homemade (page 251)
1/4 teaspoon dried oregano, preferably imported Italian
1 cup roughly chopped, very ripe, fresh plum tomatoes, with skin

1. Prepare the dough as the recipe directs through step 4, dividing the dough into 5 pieces. (The remaining dough can be used to make Prosciutto Bread with Pancetta and Basil [page 200] or any of its variations.)

2. Grease a 9 1/2-inch round pizza pan or a 10-inch cake pan with light olive oil. Place one piece of the dough in the pan. If using a cake pan, press the dough to fit inside the pan. Cover the dough with a kitchen towel and set it in a warm place to rise for 2 hours or until doubled in bulk.

3. Preheat the oven to 350°F.

4. Press the garlic into the dough at evenly spaced intervals. Brush with extra virgin olive oil, then sprinkle with the parsley, basil, and oregano. Scatter the tomatoes on top.

5. Place on the center rack in the oven and bake for 45 to 50 minutes, until golden and the bottom is crusty. Slice into wedges and serve warm.

VARIATIONS

Garlic Focaccia Substitute 1/2 teaspoon dried rosemary for the parsley, if desired, and omit the tomatoes.

Onion Focaccia Proceed as the recipe directs through step 2. (Note: The dough does not need to rise.) Preheat the oven to 375°F. Warm 1/4 cup extra virgin olive oil in a skillet over medium heat. Add 2 cups thinly sliced onions, 1 teaspoon red pepper flakes, and 1/2 teaspoon salt. Cook, stirring, for 5 to 6 minutes, until the onions have softened. Scatter the onions on top of the dough and bake for 45 to 50 minutes, until golden brown.

Pizza Napoletana with Anchovies

Pizza with Tomatoes, Oregano, and Anchovies

Makes 1 pizza; serves 4 to 6

Neapolitans invented it, but everyone everywhere loves it. My recipe is classic Neapolitan-style, topped with quick-cooked tomatoes seasoned with garlic, oregano, olives, and anchovies—but no cheese.

If you don't care for anchovies—or want a more standard pizza—omit the anchovies and sprinkle with mozzarella and fresh basil (see the variations below). I make pizza using the dough for Homemade Italian Bread (page 198), which will make four to five large pizzas. The recipe and variations here are for one pie, using a portion of the dough recipe. If you want to make more pies, simply use the remaining portions of dough for this or other pizzas and double, triple, or quadruple the topping amounts. Or, place the dough in plastic bags and seal tightly. Refrigerate for up to one week or until ready to use.

Dough for Homemade Italian Bread (page 198), prepared through step 4 (Note: Use ¼ of the dough for a large pizza or ⅕ of the dough for a smaller pizza)

Light olive oil

3 tablespoons extra virgin olive oil

3 garlic cloves, pressed or finely chopped

½ teaspoon coarse salt

Half a 32-ounce jar homemade canned plum tomatoes or 1½ to 1¾ pounds very ripe, fresh plum tomatoes, cored, seeded, and coarsely chopped

6 anchovy fillets, chopped into ½ inch pieces

1 cup pitted Gaeta olives, halved

½ teaspoon dried oregano, preferably imported Italian

4 fresh basil leaves, coarsely chopped

1. Prepare the dough as the recipe directs through step 4.

2. Preheat the oven to 350°F with the oven rack in the second lowest position. Grease a 12- or 14-inch pizza pan or heavy-duty non-aluminum cookie sheet with light olive oil, and set aside.

3. Warm the extra virgin olive oil in a saucepan over medium heat. Add the garlic and salt and cook, stirring, for 1 minute. Add the tomatoes and cook for 3 to 5 minutes more.

4. Stretch or roll the dough to fit into the prepared pizza pan.

5. Spread the tomato sauce on top of the dough. Add the anchovies, olives, and oregano.

6. Bake for 45 to 50 minutes, until the crust looks golden brown and the bottom of the pie is crispy.

7. Top with basil and return to the oven for 2 to 3 minutes more. Slice into wedges and serve hot.

VARIATIONS

Cheese Pizza Prepare Pizza Napoletana as the recipe directs in steps 1, 2, and 4. Spread 2 cups Pizza Sauce (page 205) on top of the dough. Bake for 35 to 40 minutes, then top each pie with 8 ounces fresh dry or processed whole-milk mozzarella cheese (2 cups shredded) (page 10). Return pizza to the oven and bake for another 10 minutes until the crust looks golden brown and the bottom of the pie is crisp.

Spinach Pizza   Prepare Pizza Napoletana as the recipe directs through step 4. Spread the tomato sauce on top of the dough. Prepare 2 bunches of fresh spinach (about $1^1/2$ pounds) as directed on page 212. (Note: It is very important to squeeze out as much liquid as possible from the cooked spinach.) For each pie, warm 2 tablespoons extra virgin olive oil in a small skillet with the spinach, $^1/2$ teaspoon salt, and 2 cracked garlic cloves. Cook, stirring, for 2 to 3 minutes, until the spinach looks dry and free of moisture. Discard the garlic. Bake the pizza as directed in step 6, but 10 minutes before it is done, distribute the spinach evenly on top of the tomato sauce. Serve hot. (Note: You can top with 1 cup shredded whole-milk mozzarella cheese, if desired.)

Broccoli Rabe Pizza   Prepare Pizza Napoletana as the recipe directs through step 4. Spread the tomato sauce on top of the dough. For each pie, rinse and trim 1 pound fresh broccoli rabe. Trim off $^1/2$ inch of the stem and discard any coarse or discolored leaves. Bring a large pot of water to a boil, add the broccoli rabe, and cook for 2 minutes. Drain, and cut into 1-inch pieces. Warm 2 tablespoons extra virgin olive oil in a small skillet and add the broccoli rabe, $^1/2$ teaspoon salt, and 2 cracked garlic cloves. Cook, stirring, for 2 to 3 minutes, until the broccoli rabe is slightly crisp. Bake the pizza as directed in step 6, but 10 minutes before it is done, distribute the broccoli rabe evenly on top of the tomato sauce. Serve hot. (Note: You can top with 1 cup shredded whole-milk mozzarella cheese, if desired.)

Wild Mushroom Pizza   Prepare Pizza Napoletana as the recipe directs through step 4. Spread the tomato sauce on top of the dough. Clean and dice $^1/4$ pound mushrooms (about 1 cup diced) for each pie. (Note: Choose from porcini, shiitake, oyster, or white button mushrooms). Warm 2 tablespoons extra virgin olive oil in a skillet with $^1/2$ teaspoon salt and 2 cracked garlic cloves. Add the mushrooms and cook, stirring, for 2 to 3 minutes, until slightly crisp. Bake the pizza as directed in step 6, but 10 minutes before it is done, top with the mushrooms. Serve hot.

PIZZA SAUCE

Makes 2 cups; enough for 1 large pizza or five 5- to 6-inch small pizzas (pizzelle)

Heat ¼ cup extra virgin olive oil, ½ teaspoon salt, and 2 cracked garlic cloves in a saucepan for 1 to 2 minutes. Place 2 cups homemade canned plum tomatoes (page 275) in a blender or food processor and process for 2 to 3 seconds to puree. (Or use 2 cups canned whole plum tomatoes with juice, processed in a blender or food processor; 2 cups homemade canned tomato puree (page 275); or 10 to 12 very ripe, fresh plum tomatoes, processed in a blender or food processor for 2 to 3 seconds.) Add the tomatoes and 1 or 2 fresh basil leaves to the saucepan and cook for 15 to 20 minutes. (Note: If using fresh plum tomatoes, increase the cooking time to 30 to 35 minutes.) Discard the garlic. Use the sauce to top homemade pizza using Homemade Italian Bread dough (page 198).

Eggplant Pizza Prepare Pizza Napoletana as the recipe directs through step 4 and set aside. Slice 1 eggplant with skin into small, thin slices about ¼ inch thick. Season with 1 tablespoon salt and place in a small bowl. Place another dish on top and compress it for 1 hour. Discard the juices, and squeeze the eggplant dry with your hands. Warm 2 tablespoons extra virgin olive oil in a skillet with ½ teaspoon salt and 2 cracked garlic cloves. Add the eggplant and cook, stirring, for 2 to 3 minutes, until slightly crisp. Spread the tomato sauce on top of the dough. Bake the pizza as directed in step 6, but 10 minutes before it is done, distribute the eggplant evenly on top of the tomato sauce. Add 1 cup shredded whole-milk mozzarella cheese, if desired. Serve hot.

Ricotta Pizza Prepare Pizza Napoletana as the recipe directs in steps 1, 2, and 4. (Note: This pizza has no tomatoes.) Mix 1 pound drained fresh dry (page 45) or processed whole-milk ricotta cheese with ½ pound shredded whole-milk mozzarella cheese and 1 teaspoon freshly ground black pepper. Bake the dough without the topping for 25 minutes. Remove from the oven and spread the cheese mixture on the pie. Return it to the oven and bake for 15 to 20 minutes longer, until the bottom is crisp.

Pizza with Peppers Prepare Pizza Napoletana as the recipe directs through step 4. Warm 2 tablespoons extra virgin olive oil and 2 cracked garlic cloves in a large skillet. Slice red or green sweet Italian peppers (cubanelle peppers) into long strips about ½ inch wide. Add them to the skillet and cook, stirring, until slightly wilted; set aside. Bake the pizza for 25 minutes. Add the peppers (and 1 cup shredded whole-milk mozzarella cheese, if desired) and bake for 15 to 20 minutes longer, until the bottom is crisp.

Taralli con Finocchetti

Fennel Knots

Makes about 60 taralli

This is a recipe I learned from my cousin Maria Domenica Barbato, who lives in my hometown, Cervinara. She's a teacher in the nearby town of Sante Agate, where these taralli are always served at local festivals and celebrations. She and other townspeople refer to these fragrant snacks as "vrennoli de Sante Agata"—*vrennoli* is Neapolitan dialect for taralli. I love to have homemade taralli on hand so if unexpected company drops by, I can offer them with a glass of wine for instant hors d'oeuvres. Taralli make an excellent savory snack, and they're terrific with just about any kind of cheese. Wrap them with a slice of prosciutto and add them to your antipasto platter or enjoy them instead of bread with cooked greens or soups. Taralli also make a great addition to holiday gift baskets.

2 1/2 ounces fresh compressed yeast or 2 packages active dry yeast

1 1/2 cups dry white wine

1 1/4 cups extra virgin olive oil

4 teaspoons salt

1/3 cup fennel seeds

1 teaspoon freshly ground black pepper

6 1/4 cups all-purpose flour

1. Place the yeast in a small bowl and add 1/2 cup of warm (105 to 115°F) water. (Note: Make sure the water is not too hot or it will kill the yeast.) Set aside in a warm place until the yeast has dissolved, about 5 minutes.

2. Pour the mixture into a large bowl. Add the wine, olive oil, salt, fennel seeds, and pepper, and stir to mix. Add the flour gradually while mixing constantly, until all the flour has been incorporated.

3. Transfer the dough to a lightly floured work surface and knead for 10 minutes or until smooth and elastic and not sticky. Cover with a kitchen towel and set aside in a warm place for 45 minutes to 1 hour.

4. Preheat the oven to 375°F.

5. Remove the dough from the bowl and knead on a clean work surface for 1 to 2 minutes. Shape the dough into an oval approximately 9 inches long and 6 inches wide. Cut the dough into pieces that equal a heaping tablespoon of dough.

6. Roll out each piece one at a time into ropes that are about 8 inches long and 1/2 inch thick. (Note: Do not use flour when rolling out the taralli dough. Excess flour will make the dough too dry.) Form a pretzel shape by overlapping one end on top of the other end and pressing together with your fingertips to bind. Place the shaped taralli about 1 inch apart on an ungreased baking pan.

7. Bake for 20 to 25 minutes, until golden brown. (Note: If the taralli do not look golden brown, broil them for 2 minutes or until golden brown.) Remove from the oven and let the taralli cool on the baking sheet for at least 10 minutes. Serve warm or at room temperature. To keep the taralli crisp, store them in a cookie jar or canister or in a brown paper bag in a bread drawer. (Note: If the taralli are stored in a tightly sealed plastic bag, they will lose their crunchy texture and become soft and chewy.)

Sweet Easter Bread

Makes three 8-inch loaves; serves 8 to 10

"Beautiful" is the word for this sweet, traditional Easter bread. The eggs, cooked in their shells (which my children often color before I entwine them in the dough), are an age-old symbol of renewal. Baking several loaves on Easter morning, I fill the house with their yeasty aroma and serve a freshly made loaf to my family for breakfast. A second loaf goes on the table as a centerpiece, where it is a festive addition to the big family meal that follows later in the day. The third loaf I offer to my neighbor as a gift to welcome spring and to celebrate all the beauty and freshness of the season.

1 ounce fresh compressed yeast or
   1 package active dry yeast

2 teaspoons salt

3 large eggs

2 egg yolks

1 cup milk

Two $1/2$-gram packages imported
   vanilla powder (see page 14) or
   2 teaspoons pure vanilla extract

1 cup sugar

Grated zest and juice of 1 lemon

2 tablespoons olive oil

$1/3$ cup homemade Arancello (page
   248), Triple Sec, Grand Marnier,
   or Strega

9 cups unbleached bread flour, plus
   additional flour for kneading
   surface and bowl

$1 1/2$ cups golden raisins

4 large eggs

Easter Bread Icing (recipe follows)

Multicolored candy sprinkles,
   optional

1. Place the yeast and the salt in a small bowl and add 2 cups of warm (105 to 115°F) water. (Note: Make sure the water is not too hot or it will kill the yeast.) Set aside in a warm place for 10 to 12 minutes, until dissolved.

2. Pour the yeast mixture into a large bowl. Add the eggs and egg yolks and mix well. Then add the milk, vanilla, sugar, lemon zest and juice, olive oil, and liqueur. Stir until well combined.

3. Slowly add the flour while mixing constantly, until a dough forms.

4. Place the dough on a lightly floured work surface and knead for 12 to 15 minutes or until smooth and elastic. Transfer to a lightly floured bowl and cover with plastic wrap, then cover with a clean white kitchen towel. Place the bowl in a warm place and let it rise until doubled in bulk, 3 to 4 hours.

5. Remove the dough from the bowl to a lightly floured work surface. Knead for 2 to 3 minutes, gradually adding a little more flour if necessary to keep the dough from becoming sticky.

6. Divide the dough into 3 equal pieces. Roll out each piece into a rectangle that is approximately 8 inches wide and 24 inches long; sprinkle each with $1/2$ cup of the raisins. Fold over each piece of dough and roll into a rope shape 32 to 36 inches long and 3 to $3 1/2$ inches thick.

7. Arrange the rope on the work surface so that it forms a horseshoe shape. Take one end in each hand and twist them until you reach the end. Connect the two ends to form a wreath shape.

8. Place one egg in the center of each bread, as if it were in the center of a nest. (Note: The eggs are for decorative purposes only.) Place the breads on lightly floured baking sheets and let them rise until doubled in bulk, about 2 hours.

9. Preheat the oven to 350°F.

10. Bake the breads for 35 to 45 minutes, until golden brown. Remove from the oven and let cool to room temperature on the baking sheets.

11. Brush the icing on top of the cooled loaves. Sprinkle with candy sprinkles, if desired, and let the icing set before slicing.

Easter Bread Icing

¹/₂ cup confectioners' sugar

1 teaspoon lemon extract

Combine the confectioners' sugar and lemon extract in a bowl with 2 tablespoons of water, and mix until it's the consistency of heavy cream. (Note: If the mixture is too thick, add a little more water; if it is too thin, add a little more confectioners' sugar.)

Panzarotti

Panzarotti are sweet dough puffs filled with mozzarella. They're one of the most popular snacks in my hometown, Cervinara. The word *panzarotti* means "little bellies." Panzarotti can be round or half-moon in shape and either savory or sweet. Serve them as snacks or appetizers, or enjoy them as a side dish instead of bread. They reheat well, so you can make them in advance and serve them piping hot to your guests.

1 ounce fresh compressed yeast or 1 package active dry yeast

3 cups warm (105 to 115°F) whole milk

1 tablespoon salt

1 tablespoon sugar

4 tablespoons unsalted butter, melted

9 to 10 cups unbleached bread flour, sifted

2 cups light olive oil or vegetable oil

1 pound fresh dry whole-milk mozzarella cheese (see page 10), cut into 1 1/2 x 1/8-inch pieces

1. Place the yeast and 2 cups of the milk in a small bowl and set aside for 10 minutes, until dissolved. Pour the yeast mixture into a large bowl, then add the remaining 1 cup milk, the salt, sugar, and butter.

2. Add 9 cups of the flour gradually while whisking constantly, until a dough forms. Use a spatula to transfer the dough to a clean work surface and knead until smooth and elastic, 5 to 7 minutes, adding additional flour as needed to keep the dough from becoming too sticky. Knead the dough for 5 to 7 minutes longer, then place in a large, floured bowl. Cover with plastic wrap, top with a kitchen towel, and set aside in a warm spot to rise for 2 hours, until doubled in bulk.

3. Take one piece—about 1 1/4 cups—of the dough and roll it out into a rope that is 8 to 10 inches long. Cut the rope into five 2 X 4-inch pieces and roll each piece into a round ball; each ball will be slightly larger than an egg. Continue with the rest of the dough.

4. Place the dough balls on a lightly floured baking pan. Place a kitchen towel over the dough balls and let them rise for 1 hour, until doubled in bulk.

5. Cook the panzarotti in 2 batches. For the first batch, pour 1 cup of the olive oil into a deep skillet and heat until the oil is hot but not smoking, about 375°F. Add the dough balls one by one and cook for 2 to 3 minutes total or until golden brown.

6. Remove from the skillet and drain on paper towels. While still warm, split the panzarotti open with a knife—like a sandwich—and stuff each with 1 piece of mozzarella. Keep them warm while you make the second batch.

7. Discard the oil; add the remaining oil to the same skillet and heat until hot but not smoking. Cook the remaining dough pieces, drain, split them open, and stuff with mozzarella just as you did for the first batch. Serve immediately. To store panzarotti, place them in one layer in a baking dish, cover with foil, and refrigerate. When ready to serve, place in a pre-heated 350°F oven and bake for 15 minutes or until hot.

VARIATIONS

Half-Moon Panzarotti

2 pounds fresh or processed whole-milk ricotta cheese,
**   drained overnight (see page 45)**
3 tablespoons Pecorino Romano cheese
2 large eggs
1 teaspoon freshly ground black pepper
1 teaspoon dried basil, preferably homemade (page 251)
Dough for Panzarotti (above) prepared through step 4
2 cups light olive oil or vegetable oil

1. Mix the ricotta, Pecorino Romano, eggs, pepper, and basil in a bowl with a wooden spoon until well combined. Set the filling aside.

2. Working with one piece of panzarotti dough (about $1/4$ cup dough) at a time, roll out each piece with a rolling pin in a 5-inch circle. Place 1 tablespoon of the filling in the center. Overlap the dough to cover the filling and to form a half-moon shape. Seal the edges with a fork.

3. Pour 1 cup of the olive oil into a deep skillet and heat until hot but not smoking, about 375°F. Add the panzarotti and cook each for 2 to 3 minutes, turning once, until both sides are golden brown. Drain on paper towels. As you continue to fry, refresh the oil in the skillet between batches when it becomes low, but be sure to bring the oil back up to about 375°F before adding the next batch of panzarotti. Serve warm.

Chocolate Half-Moon Panzarotti   Drain 2 pounds fresh or processed whole-milk ricotta cheese as directed on page 45. Mix the drained ricotta with $1/2$ cup finely grated semisweet chocolate and set the filling aside. Proceed as the Half-Moon Panzarotti recipe directs, from step 2 on, substituting the chocolate filling for the filling in step 2. Sprinkle with confectioners' sugar and serve warm.

Calzone with Spinach and Anchovies

Makes 1 large calzone; serves 4 to 6

Because I am a true Neapolitan at heart, I am not only crazy about *acciughe* (anchovies) on my pizza, I also love them in my spinach calzone. I must admit that my husband and children are not too fond of anchovies, but much to my surprise, they too enjoy this Italian classic. This old-world dish makes a wonderful, savory appetizer; it's also perfect for lunch.

Dough for Homemade Italian Bread (page 198), prepared through step 4

1/4 cup extra virgin olive oil, plus extra for brushing the calzone

2 large yellow onions or Vidalia onions, sliced, or 1 1/2 cups finely chopped scallions (white and light green parts)

1 teaspoon red pepper flakes, optional

1/2 teaspoon salt

2 bunches of fresh spinach (about 1 1/2 pounds), stems discarded and leaves cleaned (see page 212)

6 anchovy fillets (preferably salt-cured; see Mail-Order Sources, page 283), diced

1/4 teaspoon dried oregano, preferably imported Italian

1/4 teaspoon dried parsley, preferably homemade (page 251)

1/4 teaspoon dried basil, preferably homemade (page 251)

1. Prepare the dough as the recipe directs through step 4. You will need 1 piece of the dough for this recipe; reserve the remaining 3 pieces of dough for another use, such as the Ricotta-Mozzarella Calzone (below), pizza (page 203), seasoned breads like Prosciutto Bread with Pancetta and Basil (page 200), and Sun-Dried Tomato Bread (page 201), or Homemade Italian Bread (page 198). Or, place the dough in plastic bags and seal tightly. Refrigerate until ready to use or for up to 1 week.

2. Roll out the dough on a lightly floured work surface into a circle about 5 1/2 inches in diameter. With the rolling pin, flatten the dough to a thickness of 1/4 inch. Hold the dough at its outer ends and rotate the dough by passing it through your hands. Place your knuckles in the center of the dough and rotate them. This enlarges the dough circle. When 10 inches in diameter, place it on a lightly floured 12-inch pizza pan. Stretch the dough with your hands so that it reaches the outer rim of the pan.

3. Preheat the oven to 375°F and arrange a rack in the middle position.

4. Warm the olive oil in a large skillet over medium heat. Add the onions, red pepper flakes (if using), and salt. Cook, stirring, until the onions have softened, 2 to 3 minutes. Add the prepared spinach and cook, stirring, for 1 to 2 minutes, until wilted. Remove from the heat and let cool.

(continued)

5. Spoon the filling onto half of the dough circle. Create a half-moon shape by spreading the filling out evenly, keeping it 1 inch away from the outer edge of the circle.

6. Top with the anchovies. Bring the other half of the dough over the filling, press the edges, and crimp to seal. Your calzone should look like a half-moon. Brush lightly with oil and sprinkle with oregano, parsley, and basil.

7. Bake for 35 to 40 minutes, until golden. Slice into wedges and serve warm.

VARIATION

Ricotta-Mozzarella Calzone Mix $3/4$ pound drained fresh or processed whole-milk ricotta cheese (page 45) with 1 cup fresh dry or processed shredded whole-milk mozzarella cheese (page 10), 1 teaspoon freshly ground black pepper, and $1/2$ teaspoon (or more) salt in a bowl until combined. Stir in $1/2$ cup finely diced prosciutto or soppressata, if desired. Proceed as the recipe directs through step 3. Spread the ricotta-mozzarella mixture onto half of the dough circle, leaving 1 inch of the outer edge of the dough free. Fold the other half of the dough over the filling and press the edges to crimp and seal. Bake as the recipe directs in step 7.

Eleanora's Tips **Preparing Spinach**

To prepare the spinach for calzones, proceed as follows: Submerge 2 pounds of spinach in a pot of cold water and let it stand for 10 minutes so the grit can settle. Lift the spinach out of the water, discard the water, and repeat the process until no grit is visible. Discard any wilted or discolored leaves. (Note: Flat-leaf spinach is usually less gritty than standard spinach since there are no crevices to hold the sand and grit.) Place the cleaned spinach in a colander while you bring a large pot of water to a boil. Add the spinach and cook for 3 to 5 minutes. Drain thoroughly. When the spinach is cool enough to handle, squeeze out any excess liquid with your hands, making sure that the spinach is completely dry. Chop the spinach and set aside. Proceed as the recipe directs.

Toma Pie

Savory Rice and Ricotta Pie

Makes 1 pie; serves 8 to 10

Customarily made on Good Friday, this savory pie is made with such simple ingredients—rice, ricotta, and lots of parsley—but is oh-so-delicious! Every year, I make this traditional pie and place it on the table for family and friends to enjoy throughout the day. (Since meat is forbidden on Fridays, Toma Pie is served and no one feels deprived.) We enjoy leftover Toma Pie throughout the holiday weekend as a snack and as a light lunch. It also makes a terrific accompaniment to soups. By the way, this pie is named after the famous cheese from the Lombardy and Piedmont regions of Italy; the shape of the pie resembles the shape of the cheese.

FOR THE FILLING

3 large eggs

1 1/2 pounds fresh or processed whole-milk ricotta cheese

6 heaping tablespoons grated Pecorino Romano cheese

1 teaspoon freshly ground black pepper

1 teaspoon salt

3/4 cup finely chopped fresh flat-leaf (Italian) parsley

1/2 cup uncooked white rice

FOR THE DOUGH

2 large eggs

1 tablespoon extra virgin olive oil, plus extra for greasing the pan and brushing the crust

1/4 teaspoon freshly ground black pepper

1/4 teaspoon salt

2 cups bread flour or all-purpose flour

To make the filling

1. Beat the eggs in a bowl with a fork until blended. Add the ricotta and mix well. Add the Pecorino Romano, pepper, salt, and parsley and mix well. Add the rice and mix together gently. Set aside.

To make the dough

2. Beat the eggs, 1 tablespoon olive oil, the pepper, salt, and 1/4 cup of cold water in a bowl by hand or with an electric mixer.

3. Gradually add 1 1/2 cups of the flour while mixing constantly until all the flour is incorporated.

4. Transfer the dough to a clean work surface. Knead the dough for 3 to 4 minutes by hand, incorporating the remaining 1/2 cup flour. Knead for 3 to 4 minutes longer, until smooth and elastic and tiny holes appear in the dough when you split it open with a knife.

5. Cut the dough into 2 pieces, one slightly larger than the other. (The large piece will be for the bottom crust; the smaller piece for the top crust.) Wrap each piece with wax paper and rest at room temperature for 10 minutes.

6. Preheat the oven to 400°F, arranging a rack in the bottom position.

7. Lightly grease a deep, round baking pan (9 1/2 inches in diameter and 3 inches deep) with olive oil and set aside.

8. On a lightly floured work surface, roll out the larger piece of dough into a circle that is about 14 inches in diameter and about $1/8$ inch thick. Fit the circle into the prepared baking pan, letting the excess dough hang over the sides. Add the filling and spread it evenly with a spatula.

9. On a lightly floured work surface, roll out the top crust to a circle about 12 inches in diameter and about $1/8$ inch thick. Place the top crust over the filling. Use a paring knife to trim the excess dough to hang over the edge of the pan by $1/2$ inch. Fold the edges over and seal with a fork. Prick the surface of the dough several times with a fork to allow steam to escape. Brush the surface lightly with olive oil. Place on the bottom rack in the oven and bake for 35 to 40 minutes, until golden.

10. Remove from the oven and set the pie aside at room temperature for 2 to 3 hours. Run a paring knife around the edge of the pan to loosen the pie. Place a large, round plate or platter on top of the pie, then invert to unmold. Place a plate or platter on the pie and turn it over again. Slice and serve at room temperature. Leftover pie can be stored in the refrigerator for 3 to 5 days, and is delicious served cold or at room temperature.

Pizza Rustica

Savory Cheese and Prosciutto Pie

Every Easter without fail my mother would make this classic Italian pie. It is one of the most traditional, old-world recipes in the Neapolitan repertoire. Nevertheless, I created my own version, adding basket cheese. Despite its name, Pizza Rustica is not really a pizza at all. It is a savory, deep-dish pie filled with assorted cheeses and cured Italian meats, such as prosciutto and soppressata. If you can't find soppressata, substitute an equivalent amount of diced salami or capicollo. I always make Pizza Rustica the day before Easter so we can enjoy it Easter Sunday and throughout the week. (Because it contains meat—which is forbidden from Good Friday until Easter—we have to wait until Easter to enjoy it.) Pizza Rustica is exceptionally filling; one wedge with a glass of wine is very satisfying.

Serving Suggestions

This pie is traditionally placed on the table for family and guests to enjoy on Easter Sunday as a snack or later in the evening after dinner. It could be served for lunch, along with a mixed green salad and a glass of red wine.

- 2½ cups bread flour, plus additional flour for rolling out the dough
- 16 large eggs
- 1 tablespoon olive oil, plus extra oil for greasing the pan and brushing the crust
- ½ teaspoon freshly ground black pepper
- ¼ cup grated Pecorino Romano cheese
- 2 pounds fresh or processed whole-milk ricotta cheese
- 1 pound sweet soppressata, casing removed, cut into ½-inch cubes
- 4 ounces hot soppressata, casing removed, cut into ½-inch cubes
- ½ pound prosciutto, cut into ½-inch cubes
- 1 pound dry-aged whole-milk mozzarella cheese, cut into ½-inch cubes (see page 10)
- 1½ pounds fresh, finely crumbled fresh cheese (see page 9)
- ½ pound dry basket cheese (see page 6), cut into ½-inch cubes

1. Preheat the oven to 350°F. Grease a 10 X 3-inch round baking pan and line the bottom with parchment paper. Set aside.

2. Mound the flour on a clean work surface and make a well in the middle. Break 3 of the eggs into the well. Beat the eggs with a fork until smooth; add the tablespoon of olive oil and beat until incorporated. Gradually work some of the flour and ½ cup of water—a few drops at a time—into the egg mixture and mix with a fork until the dough comes together.

3. Knead the dough, slowly drawing in the remaining flour, until the dough is soft but not sticky, 5 to 7 minutes.

4. Divide the dough into 2 pieces; one piece should be slightly larger than the other. Knead each piece for 2 to 3 minutes longer. Wrap each piece with wax paper and let rest for 10 to 15 minutes.

5. On a lightly floured work surface, roll out the larger piece of dough into an 18-inch circle. Drape the dough loosely over the prepared pan. Gently fit the dough into the pan, letting the excess hang over the sides. Trim the dough, leaving a 1½-inch border around the edge.

6. On a lightly floured work surface, roll out the remaining piece of dough into a 14-inch circle and set aside.

7. Whisk together the remaining 13 eggs, the pepper, and the Pecorino

Romano. Gradually stir in the ricotta until well combined. Add the sweet and hot soppressata, prosciutto, mozzarella, fresh cheese, and basket cheese. Pour the mixture into the dough-lined pan and smooth the surface. Cover with the 14-inch dough circle and press the edges together to seal in the mixture.

8. Use a paring knife to trim the dough to hang over the edge of the pan by $^1/_2$ inch. Fold the edges over, and seal with a fork. Prick the surface of the dough in several places to allow steam to escape.

9. Brush the surface lightly with olive oil. Place in the oven and bake for 1 hour and 45 minutes, until golden brown and a wooden skewer inserted in the center comes out clean.

10. Cool on a rack for 2 hours. Run a paring knife around the edge of the pan to loosen it. Place a large, round plate or platter on top of the pie, then invert to unmold. Place a plate or platter on the pie, and turn it over again. Chill completely before slicing. Serve chilled or at room temperature.

DESSERTS

*I*talians are proud of their exquisite desserts, as can be seen in the dazzling displays in *pasticcerie* and *gelaterie* throughout the country. In Campania, panettone studded with candied fruit, rows of cannoli on doily-lined platters, and gelati in every color imaginable are only a few of the offerings from which to choose. In addition to purchased desserts (sofigliatelle and cannoli, for example, which are not usually made in the home), there are legions of mouthwatering cakes, biscotti, pies, and tortes regularly prepared by the home cook for holidays and for special occasions.

Neapolitan desserts are often flavored with regional ingredients—lemons, hazelnuts, walnuts, and chestnuts—as well as locally made liqueurs such as Strega and Limoncello. Some Neapolitan desserts are served up only at holiday time and are therefore anticipated all year long. Struffoli (page 244)—shimmering with honey syrup and as pretty as an ornament on the tree—is perhaps the ultimate Neapolitan Christmas tradition. Migliaccio di Cervinara (semolina and ricotta pie, page 230) is prepared for Carnevale feasting, and Pizza Gran (ricotta and wheat grain pie, page 234) is a must for Easter.

In this chapter, I also include a recipe for homemade Limoncello (page 248), which can be served as an aperitivo or as a refreshing after-dinner drink followed by a quick espresso and sometimes dessert. What a lively finish!

Pignoli Cookies

Pine Nut Cookies with Orange Liqueur

Makes about 34 cookies

My brother Giuseppe used to work at the local *pasticceria* (bakery) on Arthur Avenue and would often bring a box of pignoli cookies home at the end of the day. Now that I'm living in Connecticut and not able to get those pignoli cookies from my old neighborhood, I created my own recipe. When you pull them out of the oven, there's an intoxicating scent of orange, vanilla, and toasted pine nuts. They are delicious with coffee, tea, or a glass of milk. Make them for a party, a picnic, or any time at all.

1^3/$_4$ cups all-purpose flour, plus additional flour for kneading the dough

3 large eggs, separated

One ^{1}/$_2$-gram package imported vanilla powder (see page 14) or 1 teaspoon pure vanilla extract

1 teaspoon baking powder

1 teaspoon orange extract

2 tablespoons orange-flavored liqueur, such as Grand Marnier, Cointreau, or Triple Sec

2 heaping tablespoons orange marmalade

^{1}/$_2$ cup plus 2 tablespoons granulated sugar

^{1}/$_2$ cup (1 stick) unsalted butter, diced, plus extra for greasing the pans

1 cup (8 ounces) almond paste

^{1}/$_2$ pound pine nuts (pignoli)

To make the dough by hand

1. Sift the flour into a mound on a large work surface and make a well in the center. Put the egg yolks, vanilla, baking powder, orange extract, orange liqueur, orange marmalade, and ^{1}/2 cup of the sugar in the well and beat with a fork until blended. Add the butter and almond paste to the well and mix into the egg mixture with a fork until well blended. Gradually draw the flour into the egg mixture, little by little, and mix and combine until a dough forms. Knead the dough for 3 to 5 minutes, until it is no longer sticky, adding additional flour if necessary. Place the dough in a bowl and cover with wax paper or aluminum foil and refrigerate for 20 minutes.

To make the dough with an electric mixer

2. Beat the egg yolks, vanilla, baking powder, orange extract, orange liqueur, and ^{1}/2 cup of the sugar in a bowl with an electric mixer with the paddle attachment. Add the orange marmalade and the butter and beat until smooth. Add the almond paste and beat until well combined. Add the flour gradually while beating constantly, until all the flour has been incorporated. Transfer the dough to a large work surface and knead for 1 minute. Form into a round that is about 5^1/2 inches in diameter. Cover with wax paper or aluminum foil and refrigerate for 20 minutes.

3. Preheat the oven to 350°F and adjust the rack to the middle position. Grease 2 baking sheets with butter and set aside.

4. Remove the dough from the refrigerator and place it on a cutting board. Cut the dough into 1-inch-thick slices. Cut each slice into smaller pieces, each equal to about 1 tablespoon of dough. Working with one piece of dough at a time, flour your hands and roll each into a ball, then gently press to flatten the top of the cookie.

5. Beat the egg whites in a small bowl. In another bowl, mix the pine nuts with the remaining 2 tablespoons sugar. Dip the tops (the flattened side) of each cookie into the egg whites then into the pignoli-sugar mixture, and gently press the mixture into the top of each cookie slightly. The cookies will be about $1^{3}/4$ inches in diameter.

6. Place the cookies about $1^{1}/2$ inches apart on the prepared baking sheets. Bake for 18 to 20 minutes, until the cookie bottoms are golden brown. Turn the broiler on high, and broil the cookies for 1 to 2 minutes, until toasted. Let the cookies cool on the baking sheets for 10 to 15 minutes before removing them. Transfer to a doily-lined platter or plate and serve warm, or store in an airtight container to serve later.

Biscotti with Almonds and Hazelnuts

Makes about 60 cookies

Although both my grandmother and my mother made biscotti, their recipes aren't like mine. Their biscotti were delicious, but fairly straightforward and simple. I like to add roasted almonds and hazelnuts, orange zest, and orange liqueur—plus a bit of cocoa and cinnamon—for an enhanced version. Unlike traditional biscotti, which are baked twice (the word *biscotti* means just that), mine are baked only once, so the resulting cookie is not as hard as classic biscotti. (Baking them once is also easier and saves time.) These crunchy, not-too-sweet cookies are delicious with coffee, tea, or a glass of Italian dessert wine, such as a Moscato.

½ pound almonds, sliced in half crosswise

½ pound hazelnuts, sliced in half (Note: To save time, the nuts can be left whole. However, the biscotti will have a nuttier flavor if the nuts are sliced)

4 cups all-purpose flour

4 large eggs

1 large egg yolk

2 teaspoons baking powder

1 teaspoon unsweetened cocoa powder

1 teaspoon cinnamon

¼ cup whole milk

One ½-gram package imported vanilla powder (see page 14) or 1 teaspoon pure vanilla extract

Grated zest of 2 oranges

1 teaspoon orange extract

1 teaspoon olive oil, optional

2 tablespoons Pergoné liqueur or a nut-flavored liqueur such as Nocelle (see Mail-Order Sources, page 283)

2 cups granulated sugar

1. Preheat the oven to 350°F, and adjust the rack to the middle position.

2. Spread the almonds and hazelnuts out in one layer on a large baking sheet and roast for 20 to 22 minutes or until golden. Check the nuts from time to time, making sure they're not overcooking. Cool slightly, then rub off the dark brown papery skins. Set the nuts aside.

3. Increase the oven temperature to 400°F.

To make the dough by hand

4. Mound the flour on a large work surface and make a well in the center. Place the eggs and the egg yolk in the well and beat them gently with a fork. Add the baking powder, cocoa, cinnamon, milk, vanilla, orange zest, orange extract, olive oil (if using), and liqueur, and beat with a fork until well blended. Add the sugar to the egg mixture in the well and mix to blend. Draw the flour slowly into the well and mix until a medium-soft dough forms.

To make the dough with an electric mixer

5. Combine the eggs, egg yolk, baking powder, cocoa, cinnamon, milk, vanilla, orange zest, orange extract, liqueur, and olive oil (if using) in the bowl of an electric mixer and beat to blend. Add the sugar and continue to beat until well combined. Add the flour little by little while beating constantly, until you have a medium-soft, slightly moist dough.

MAKING CHOCOLATE SHAVINGS

I like to have a large slab of semisweet chocolate on hand for chocolate shavings, which make an attractive and tasty garnish for Tiramisù (page 236) and other desserts. To make chocolate shavings, break off about 2 ounces from a large slab of chocolate (or use a smaller bar of good-quality semisweet chocolate) and use a citrus zester to grate the chocolate into fine shavings.

6. On a lightly floured work surface, flatten and shape the dough into a rectangle about 20 X 12 inches. Scatter the cooled nuts on top, then knead the nuts into the dough until they are evenly distributed. (Note: Do not add too much flour as you knead or the biscotti will be dry.)

7. Moisten your hands with cold water and divide the dough into 4 equal pieces. Working with one piece at a time, pat the dough into a long rectangular shape about 14 inches long, $1\frac{1}{2}$ to 2 inches wide, and $\frac{3}{4}$ inch thick. Repeat with the remaining dough pieces. Place the loaves 3 inches apart on a lightly buttered baking sheet.

8. Bake in the center of the oven for 15 to 18 minutes, until the bottom is golden brown. Remove from the oven and let cool for 45 minutes.

9. Transfer the loaves to a large work surface. Use a large serrated knife to cut the loaves into $\frac{1}{4}$-inch-thick diagonal slices to make the biscotti. (Note: The approximate size of each biscotti is $3\frac{1}{2}$ inches long, 1 inch wide, and $\frac{1}{4}$ inch thick.) Arrange the biscotti on a doily-lined platter and serve or store in an airtight container.

VARIATION

Chocolate Biscotti with Figs Omit the cinnamon and use half the amount of nuts, but add 8 to 10 chopped dried figs and $\frac{1}{3}$ cup shaved semisweet chocolate with the egg.

Biscotti con Marmellata

Makes about 24 cookies

In the Italian countryside, the word *marmellata* is used to refer to jams, jellies, and preserves as well as marmalade. My *zia* (aunt) Matilda—who lived next door to us in Italy—used to make wonderful blackberry jam, *marmellata di more*. What delicious memories; I can still taste it. I make these cookies with whatever jam, preserves, or marmalade I have on hand, but I'll always prefer them with blackberry jam. These buttery treats are easy to make and are wonderful with afternoon tea or coffee. They're also a nice addition to holiday cookie platters or to give as gifts.

1³⁄₄ cups sifted all-purpose flour

2 large eggs, separated

1 teaspoon baking powder

One ¹⁄₂-gram package imported
    vanilla powder (see page 14) or
    1 teaspoon pure vanilla extract

2 tablespoons orange-flavored
    liqueur, such as Grand Marnier,
    Cointreau, or Triple Sec

¹⁄₂ cup (1 stick) butter, softened

¹⁄₂ cup granulated sugar

1¹⁄₂ cups (6 ounces) coarsely
    crushed walnuts, pecans,
    almonds, or hazelnuts

¹⁄₄ cup of your favorite jam,
    preserves, or marmalade

Confectioners' sugar, optional

To make the dough by hand

1. Mound the flour on a large work surface and make a well in the center. Place the egg yolks, baking powder, vanilla, orange liqueur, butter, and sugar in the well, and mix with a fork until well blended. Gradually draw the flour into the liquid mixture until you have a smooth, tender dough. Place the dough in a bowl, cover with wax paper, and refrigerate for 15 minutes. (Note: The dough should be slightly sticky; do not add too much flour or the dough will be dry and difficult to work with.)

To make the dough with an electric mixer

2. Combine the egg yolks, baking powder, vanilla, liqueur, butter, and sugar in the bowl of an electric mixer and beat to blend. Add all but ¹⁄₄ cup of the flour gradually while beating until the mixture forms a dough ball. Flour a spatula and use it to transfer the dough to a lightly floured work surface. Knead in the remaining ¹⁄₄ cup flour for 1 to 2 minutes. Return to the bowl, cover with wax paper, and refrigerate for 15 minutes. (Note: It is important to let the dough rest before forming the cookies. During the resting period, the gluten relaxes and the dough will be easier to work with.)

3. Preheat the oven to 350°F. Lightly grease 2 cookie sheets with butter and set aside.

4. Place the reserved egg whites in a bowl and whisk with a fork until slightly foamy. Place the crushed walnuts in a separate bowl.

5. Remove the dough from the bowl. Pinch off about 1 tablespoon of dough and roll it into a ball with your hands. Gently press the ball to flatten the top of the cookie, so that it is about 1¹⁄₂ inches in diameter. Dip the cookie into the egg whites, then into the walnuts, coating both sides. Place it on one of the baking sheets. Continue forming cookies this way with the rest of the dough.

6. Make an indention in the middle of each cookie with the end of a wooden spoon, taking care not to press all the way through the cookie. The holes should be only about $1/8$ inch deep. Spoon about $1/2$ teaspoon of the jam into each indentation.

7. Bake for 18 to 20 minutes, until the bottoms of the cookies are golden brown. Remove from the oven and let them cool for 15 minutes before removing them from the baking sheet. Transfer the cookies to a platter and dust with confectioners' sugar before serving, if desired. The cookies may be made up to 1 week in advance. Store them in an airtight container or in a deep platter or dish covered with plastic wrap at room temperature.

Lemon Drop Cookies

Makes about 3 dozen cookies

I created this recipe because I love lemon-flavored cookies, especially with tea. I always make Lemon Drop Cookies at holiday time, adding them to the other biscotti and cookies on the platter. Appealing to all ages, Lemon Drops are a favorite in our house, and I hope they will be a favorite in yours, too. For a simpler cookie, omit the Lemon Icing and dust the cooled cookies with confectioners' sugar.

2 1/2 cups all-purpose flour, sifted

2 large eggs

1/2 cup (1 stick) unsalted butter, softened and diced

1 1/2 teaspoon baking powder

1 teaspoon olive oil

Grated zest and juice of 1 lemon (about 1/4 cup lemon juice)

1 teaspoon lemon extract

One 1/2-gram package imported vanilla powder (see page 14) or 1 teaspoon pure vanilla extract

1 tablespoon homemade Limoncello (page 248) or lemon-flavored liqueur

3/4 cup granulated sugar

Sweet Lemon Icing (recipe follows)

To make the dough by hand

1. Mound the flour on a large work surface and make a well in the center. Place the eggs in the well and beat them gently with a fork. Add the butter, baking powder, olive oil, lemon zest and juice, lemon extract, vanilla, lemon liqueur, and sugar to the well. Mash the butter with a fork, and mix with the other ingredients in the well until well combined. Gradually draw in the flour little by little and mix until all the flour has been incorporated. Knead the dough for 5 minutes or until smooth and elastic.

To make the dough with an electric mixer

2. Beat the eggs, butter, baking powder, olive oil, lemon zest and juice, lemon extract, vanilla, lemon liqueur, and sugar in the bowl of an electric mixer until well combined. Add the flour slowly while beating constantly with the flat beater (if your mixer has one; if not, use the regular beaters) until the flour is incorporated and the mixture forms a dough ball. Remove the dough with a spatula to a lightly floured work surface and knead for 1 to 2 minutes, until smooth and elastic. (Note: If using an electric mixer, the kneading time is shorter than if mixing the dough by hand.)

3. Pat the dough into a round that is about 5 1/2 inches in diameter. Transfer to a lightly floured bowl, cover, and refrigerate for 20 minutes.

4. Preheat the oven to 350°F and adjust the rack to the middle position. Lightly grease 2 cookie sheets with butter and set aside.

5. Remove the dough from the bowl and place it on a lightly floured work surface. Cut the dough into 1-inch-thick slices, then cut each slice into pieces of about 1 tablespoon of dough each.

6. Roll each piece into a dome shape by tucking in the bottom of the cookies. You will have dome-shaped cookies that are 1 to $1^1/4$ inches in diameter.

7. Place the cookies about 1 inch apart on the prepared cookie sheets. Bake for 15 to 18 minutes, until the bottoms are slightly golden. Let the cookies cool for 20 to 25 minutes before icing.

8. Dip each cookie into the icing (dip the domed side into the icing; the flat side is the bottom of the cookie). Place the iced cookies back on the cookie sheet. Let the icing set for 2 to 3 minutes before serving.

Sweet Lemon Icing

Makes about 1 cup icing

$1^1/2$ **cups confectioners' sugar**

2 tablespoons freshly squeezed lemon juice

2 tablespoons granulated sugar

2 tablespoons homemade Limoncello (page 248)

 or lemon-flavored liqueur

1 teaspoon lemon extract

1 teaspoon orange extract

Blend all the ingredients together with an electric mixer until thick and creamy.

Orange and Lemon Sunrise Cake

Serves 8 to 10

This rich, golden cake is easy to make and keeps well, too. Because the cake has to stand for two hours before unmolding, I like to make it early in the morning as the sun is rising, hence the name. I find that this cake, topped with cream and berries, is particularly delicious in summer.

1 cup golden raisins

1/4 cup Strega liqueur (see page 13)

4 large eggs

1 cup (2 sticks) salted butter, melted and cooled

1 teaspoon orange extract

One 1/2-gram package imported vanilla powder (see page 14), or 1 teaspoon pure vanilla extract

2 teaspoons baking powder

1 tablespoon orange-flavored liqueur, such as homemade Arancello (page 248), Grand Marnier, Cointreau, or Triple Sec

Grated zest of 1 orange

1/4 cup fresh orange juice

Grated zest of 1 lemon

1/4 cup fresh lemon juice

2 1/2 cups granulated sugar

1 pound (2 cups) fresh or processed whole-milk ricotta or mascarpone cheese

2 tablespoons orange marmalade

3 cups all-purpose flour

1/2 cup sliced almonds

Confectioners' sugar, optional

Panna (Italian heavy cream, see Mail-Order Sources, page 283), whipped cream, or mascarpone, lightly sweetened (see page 227), optional

Fresh strawberries, blueberries, or raspberries, optional

1. Preheat the oven to 375°F. Grease and flour a 10 1/2-inch Bundt pan and set aside.

2. Combine the raisins and the Strega in a small bowl and set aside for 10 to 15 minutes.

3. Combine the eggs, butter, orange extract, vanilla, baking powder, orange liqueur, orange zest, orange juice, lemon zest, lemon juice, and sugar in a large bowl and beat with an electric mixer until well combined. Add the ricotta and continue to beat until smooth and creamy with no visible lumps.

4. Add the orange marmalade and the raisins with the Strega and stir with a wooden spoon. Add the flour gradually while stirring, until the flour has been incorporated; do not overmix. The batter should be thick and creamy.

5. Pour the batter into the prepared pan and smooth the top with a spatula. The batter will be about 2 inches deep. Sprinkle the almonds on top. Bake for 1 hour and 10 minutes, or until a toothpick inserted in the cake comes out clean and the almonds are slightly toasted. Turn the broiler on high and place the cake under the broiler for 1 minute.

6. Remove the cake from the oven and let it cool in the pan for 2 hours. Loosen the edges of the cake with a butter knife. Place a large, flat plate on the Bundt pan and invert to unmold.

7. Cut the cake into thin wedges, and garnish each serving with confectioners' sugar, a heaping tablespoon of the panna, and about $1/4$ cup of berries, if desired.

Eleanora's Tips Garnishing with Cream: Three Ways

Panna

I prefer serving this cake with panna—Italian heavy cream—that I whip and sweeten slightly with a little bit of sugar. Panna is available at many specialty food stores in the dairy case. To sweeten it, beat 1 cup panna with a whisk or an electric mixer to thicken it slightly. Then gradually add 2 tablespoons sugar, little by little, and whisk or beat for 2 to 3 minutes until fluffy. Place the beaten cream in the freezer for 8 to 10 minutes to chill before using.

Whipped Cream

Beat 1 cup whipping cream or heavy cream with a whisk or an electric mixer until slightly thickened. Gradually add 2 tablespoons sugar, little by little, and continue to beat until stiff.

Mascarpone

For a very rich topping, try a heaping tablespoon of mascarpone cheese (Italian cream cheese).

Fig and Hazelnut Torta

Serves 8 to 10

My paternal grandmother had a variety of fig trees in her garden. When there was an overabundance of ripe figs, she dried them. She would pick them, then spread them out in a flat wicker basket, and let them dry in the sun for at least three to five days. To ensure that the figs were completely dry, she would place them in a warm oven to dry further. The dried figs were then stored in small wicker baskets to enjoy year round, particularly in winter, when fresh fruit might not be available.

I've always loved figs—both fresh and dried—so I added them to this cake, which is similar to one that my mother used to make. Her version had walnuts; I use hazelnuts, but pecans or almonds work well, too.

1½ cups shelled hazelnuts, walnuts, pecans, or almonds

2½ cups plus 1 tablespoon granulated sugar

2 teaspoons unsweetened cocoa powder

4 large eggs

1 cup (2 sticks) salted butter, melted and cooled

2 teaspoons baking powder

1 teaspoon cinnamon

One ½-gram package imported vanilla powder (see page 14) or 1 teaspoon pure vanilla extract

1 pound (2 cups) fresh or processed whole-milk ricotta or mascarpone cheese

3 cups all-purpose flour or bread flour

12 dried figs, chopped

Confectioners' sugar, optional

1. Preheat the oven to 350°F.

2. Place the nuts in a blender and chop for 2 seconds. Spread the nuts out on a baking sheet.

3. Mix 1 tablespoon of the sugar with the cocoa in a small bowl. Sprinkle the mixture over the nuts and toss to combine. Roast in the oven for 5 minutes, then set aside to cool.

4. Increase the oven temperature to 375°F. Grease a 10½-inch Bundt pan or an 8 X 10-inch baking pan and set aside.

5. Combine the eggs, the remaining 2½ cups sugar, the butter, baking powder, cinnamon, and vanilla in a large bowl and beat with an electric mixer until smooth and creamy.

6. Add the ricotta gradually while beating constantly with the electric mixer. Then slowly add the flour, mixing constantly with a rubber spatula or a wooden spoon until well combined. Fold in the figs and nuts with a clean rubber spatula until incorporated.

7. Pour the batter into the prepared pan. Moisten a rubber spatula with water and smooth the top of the batter.

8. Bake for 1 hour and 10 minutes, or until a toothpick inserted in the center comes out clean. Turn the broiler on high and broil for 2 minutes, or until the top is crisp.

9. Cool the cake in the pan for 2 to 3 hours. Loosen the edges of the cake with a butter knife, place a large, flat plate on the pan, and invert to unmold.

10. Cut the cake into 1-inch wedges (or if using an 8 X 10-inch pan, cut into 3 X 3-inch slices), and dust with confectioners' sugar, if desired. Serve at room temperature.

Migliaccio di Cervinara

Sweet Semolina and Ricotta Pie

Serves 8 to 10

Traditionally made at carnival time, this dessert is something that my family looks forward to all year long. It is usually decorated with colored candy and party favors. Although migliaccio (the word *migliaccio* refers to semolina puddings and desserts) is made throughout southern Italy, my hometown, Cervinara, is particularly known for this pie. It's made with simple, earthy ingredients—except for the addition of that luscious liqueur known as Strega. (You can also make a chocolate-flavored migliaccio by substituting one cup of grated, semisweet chocolate for the citron.) The pie can be topped with liqueur and fruit or with a dusting of confectioners' sugar. Whether you celebrate *Carnevale* or not, I think you'll enjoy this dessert as much as I do; it's delicious any time of year.

1 lemon

1 orange

3½ cups whole milk

½ cup (1 stick) salted butter

2 cups granulated sugar

1 cup semolina

¼ cup plus 2 tablespoons Strega liqueur (see page 13), Grand Marnier, or homemade Arancello (page 248)

1¼ pounds fresh or processed whole-milk ricotta cheese (Note: If using processed ricotta, place in a colander set over a bowl and let drain in the refrigerator for 2 hours)

3 large eggs

One ½-gram package imported vanilla powder (see page 14) or 1 teaspoon pure vanilla extract

¼ cup diced citron (see page 8) or candied fruit

Fresh fruit, optional

Confectioners' sugar, optional

1. Preheat the oven to 350°F. Butter the bottom and sides of a 10- or 11-inch springform pan or pie plate.

2. With a sharp paring knife remove the peel—including the white pith—from the lemon and the orange in one continuous spiral. (Reserve the fruit for making juice or for another use.) Combine the milk, lemon peel, orange peel, butter, and sugar in a large saucepan. Bring to a boil over medium-high heat. Stirring constantly, gradually add the semolina and cook until thick and creamy, about 2 minutes. (Note: It is important to stir constantly, otherwise the semolina may stick to the pan or bind up.) Remove from the heat and set aside for 20 minutes at room temperature.

3. Remove the lemon and orange peels and discard. Add ¼ cup of the Strega. Beat the ricotta with the eggs in a bowl until smooth and creamy. (Note: If the mixture is lumpy, you can sieve or strain it at this point for a smoother texture.) Add the ricotta-egg mixture to the semolina mixture and stir to blend. Add the vanilla and citron and stir to mix.

4. Pour the mixture into the prepared pan and bake for 50 minutes to 1 hour, or until the top is slightly golden and the center of the pie is set. Remove from the oven and cool to room temperature.

5. If using a springform pan, open the pan and transfer to a flat serving plate. Brush the cake with the remaining 2 tablespoons Strega and top with fresh fruit or dust with confectioners' sugar, if desired. Serve warm or chilled.

Sweet Lemon-Ricotta Pie with Brandied Cherries

Serves 8 to 10

The "ricotta lady" would walk door to door through our town of Cervinara with fresh ricotta in a basket nestled in a turban perched on her head. *"Ricottella! Ricottella!"* she would sing out as she hawked her wares. My mother used it in a variety of dishes, including this light, custardlike pie that we enjoyed at Christmas and Easter. She included orange and lemon zest in her recipe; I like to add lemon liqueur and sambuca for extra flavor. The brandied cherry topping is sublime! I use dried cherries when fresh ones are not in season. And this dessert is also delicious without any topping at all. Don't wait for a holiday to make this pie; it is delicious any time of year.

FOR THE PIE

4 large eggs

2 large egg yolks

2 cups granulated sugar

1/4 cup sambuca or other anise-flavored liqueur, Grand Marnier or other orange-flavored liqueur, or homemade Limoncello (see page 248) or other lemon-flavored liqueur

Grated zest and juice of 1 lemon

Grated zest and juice of 1 orange

One 1/2-gram package imported vanilla powder (see page 14), or 1 teaspoon pure vanilla extract

1 tablespoon Limoncello, preferably homemade (page 248)

3 pounds fresh or processed whole-milk ricotta cheese

FOR THE BRANDIED CHERRY TOPPING

1 cup brandy

3 tablespoons granulated sugar

1/2 pound fresh, ripe cherries, stemmed and pitted, or 6 ounces dried cherries

To make the pie

1. Preheat the oven to 375°F and adjust the rack to the middle position. Lightly butter the bottom and sides of a 10-inch springform pan and set aside.

2. Beat the eggs, egg yolks, sugar, sambuca, lemon zest and juice, orange zest and juice, vanilla, and lemon liqueur in a bowl with an electric mixer or in a blender or food processor until very smooth. Add the ricotta and blend again until very smooth and creamy. (Note: It is important to beat the mixture until there are no lumps to ensure that the pie is silky-smooth.)

3. Transfer the mixture into the prepared pan and bake for 45 to 60 minutes, until the tip of a knife comes out clean when inserted in the center.

4. Remove from the oven and let cool to room temperature on a baking rack. Cover loosely with foil and refrigerate for several hours, until cold and set.

5. Remove from the springform pan and place on a serving platter or cake plate.

To make the brandied cherry topping

6. Combine the brandy and the sugar in a medium saucepan and simmer uncovered until reduced by half. Add the cherries and simmer for 10 minutes or until the cherries have softened. Set aside for 15 to 20 minutes. Drain, then scatter the brandied cherries over the pie.

VARIATIONS

For a lower-calorie pie   Use skim-milk ricotta and 3 eggs instead of 4.

For a nut crust   Pour $1^{1}/2$ cups nuts (I like to use a combination of walnuts and hazelnuts) into a food processor or blender, and process until finely chopped. Transfer the nuts to a bowl and mix with 1 egg white. Spread this mixture on the bottom of the buttered springform pan, then top with the ricotta batter. Bake, cool, chill, and garnish as the recipe directs.

For a chocolate topping   Omit the Brandied Cherry Topping and top the cooled pie with $^{1}/2$ cup finely shaved semisweet chocolate (page 221).

Pizza Gran

Wheat Berry, Citrus, and Ricotta Pie

Serves 8 to 10

My mother always made this pie at Easter and I continue the tradition and make it for my own family and friends for a true southern Italian treat. The traditional recipe goes back hundreds of years; every Neapolitan, and many other Italians, makes this pie—along with Pizza Rustica (page 215) and Sweet Lemon-Ricotta Pie with Brandied Cherries (page 232)—to celebrate Easter. This dessert is essentially a lightly sweetened ricotta cheesecake with cooked wheat grains for added texture, fresh orange juice and zest, as well as candied citron.

FOR THE FILLING

One 15-ounce can of cooked wheat berries (see page 235)

½ cup whole milk

1 cup granulated sugar

3 large egg yolks

Grated zest of 1 orange

¼ cup fresh orange juice

1 tablespoon orange extract

½ cup fresh citron, processed in a blender or food processor until finely chopped (see page 8), or ½ cup candied citron

One ½-gram package imported vanilla powder (see page 14) or 1 teaspoon vanilla extract

1½ pounds fresh or processed whole-milk ricotta cheese (drained overnight if using processed ricotta, see page 45)

2 tablespoons lemon or orange flavored liqueur, such as homemade Limoncello (page 248), Grand Marnier, Cointreau, or Triple Sec

FOR THE CRUST

3 large eggs

1 tablespoon olive oil

1 tablespoon unsalted butter

½ teaspoon baking powder

⅓ cup whole milk

One ½-gram package imported vanilla powder (see page 14) or 1 teaspoon pure vanilla extract

½ cup granulated sugar

3 cups bread flour or all-purpose flour, sifted, plus additional flour for kneading and rolling

To make the filling

1. Mash the wheat berries in a large bowl with a fork. Add the milk, sugar, egg yolks, orange zest, orange juice, orange extract, citron, vanilla, ricotta, and orange or lemon liqueur, and mix well with a fork or wooden spoon until all is incorporated. Set aside.

To make the crust

2. Beat the eggs in a bowl with a fork or with the whisk attachment of an electric mixer. Add the olive oil, butter, baking powder, milk, vanilla, and sugar, and beat until well incorporated. If you're using an electric mixer, remove the whisk attachment and replace it with the paddle attachment or dough hook. Add the flour gradually while beating slowly until well incorporated.

WHEAT BERRIES

Canned, cooked wheat berries (sold as "cooked wheat grains") can be purchased at good Italian delis, specialty foods stores, or by mail order from Teitel Brothers (see Mail-Order Sources, page 283). Before canned, cooked wheat berries were available, the home cook had to soak dried wheat berries overnight in water, then cook them slowly for an hour until tender. Canned wheat berries taste just as good and save time.

3. Remove the dough with a floured spatula to a lightly floured work surface. Knead the dough for 5 minutes or until smooth and elastic. Divide the dough into 2 equal pieces. Wrap each piece of dough in wax paper and let rest at room temperature for 15 to 20 minutes.

4. Preheat the oven to 350°F. Grease the bottom and sides of an 8-inch-round, $2\frac{1}{2}$-inch-deep cake pan or springform pan. Set aside.

5. Unwrap the dough and place it on a lightly floured work surface. Roll out one piece of the dough into a circle that is about 16 inches in diameter. Roll the dough onto the rolling pin and place it over the prepared pan. Lightly press the dough so that it fits the bottom and sides of the pan, letting the excess dough hang over the sides.

6. Pour in the ricotta-wheat filling. Smooth the top with a spatula. Bring the excess dough over the filling.

7. On a lightly floured work surface, roll out the second piece of dough into a circle that is about 12 inches in diameter. Cut six 1-inch strips from the middle of the circle (so that you have strips that are as long as possible.) Lay these strips over the top of the pie to form a lattice topping.

8. Bake for 1 hour and 10 minutes, or until the crust is golden brown. Let the pie cool at room temperature for 2 to 4 hours. Refrigerate for 6 to 8 hours, then cut into wedges and serve cold.

Tiramisù

Tirami sù means "pick me up" in Italian and the luscious dessert called tiramisù is aptly named: It's sure to lift your spirits.

Some cooks soak the ladyfingers in espresso and Marsala, but I prefer to use Pergoné liqueur, which adds an intriguing flavor to the dish. Tiramisù is easy to assemble and keeps up to five days in the refrigerator. This version is lighter than most, because rather than beating whole eggs together, I beat the egg whites separately, then fold them into the egg yolk mixture.

½ cup sliced almonds or ½ cup hazelnuts, coarsely chopped in a food processor

1¼ cups brewed espresso

2 tablespoons Pergoné liqueur (see page 12) or Grand Marnier

4 large eggs

1 cup granulated sugar

2 tablespoons grated orange zest

1 pound (2 cups) mascarpone

One 7- to 8-ounce package of ladyfingers

2 tablespoons unsweetened cocoa powder

2 ounces semisweet chocolate, shaved (see page 221)

1. Preheat the oven to 350°F.

2. Spread the nuts over a baking pan and roast in the oven for 2 to 3 minutes, until very lightly brown. Set aside to cool.

3. Mix the espresso with the liqueur in a small bowl and set aside.

4. Beat the egg yolks, ½ cup of the sugar, and the orange zest in a large bowl with an electric mixer until thickened. Add the mascarpone and beat until smooth.

5. In a separate bowl, beat 2 egg whites constantly while slowly adding ¼ cup of the sugar. Continue to beat until stiff peaks form. Fold this mixture into the mascarpone mixture.

6. Dip half of the ladyfingers quickly into the espresso mixture and fit them side by side in the bottom of an 8 X 10-inch baking dish that is 2 to 2½ inches deep. (Note: Do not leave the ladyfingers in the espresso mixture too long or they will be too soft to work with.)

7. Use a spatula to spread about half the mascarpone mixture in a thin layer on top of the ladyfingers.

8. Mix the cocoa with the remaining ¼ cup sugar and sprinkle this mixture on top of the mascarpone. Sprinkle on half of the chocolate shavings.

9. Repeat for a second layer: Dip the ladyfingers in the espresso mixture and place on top of the shaved chocolate. Spread the remaining mascarpone mixture on top of the ladyfingers. Sprinkle with the remaining cocoa-sugar mixture, then top with shaved chocolate and toasted almonds. Cover with foil or plastic and refrigerate for at least 6 to 8 hours.

Zeppole di Ferrara

Makes about 3 dozen zeppole

Just about anyone who has ever been to an Italian street festival knows about zeppole. These sweet, fried dough treats are a specialty of my hometown, and are always made for local celebrations held outside in the beautiful Piazza di Ferrara. I've always loved zeppole, but I've taken the classic recipe a step further by adding fragrant Strega liqueur. Traditionally, zeppole are made for the feast of San Gennaro, a former bishop of Benevento, near my hometown of Cervinara, and the patron saint of Naples. Residents of Naples prayed to San Gennaro when Mount Vesuvius erupted in the 1300s. The eruption stopped. San Gennaro is believed to still watch over the city. The Feast of San Gennaro is also celebrated in Little Italy in New York City. The street festival includes wonderful things to eat, with the featured treat being zeppole.

1 ounce fresh compressed yeast or 1 package active dry yeast
2 teaspoons salt
1 cup warm (105 to 115°F) whole milk
1 large egg
8 cups plus 1 teaspoon light olive oil or vegetable oil
1 cup granulated sugar
1 tablespoon Strega liqueur (see page 13) or homemade Limoncello (page 248)
1/4 cup grated lemon zest, optional
10 cups bread flour
Confectioners' sugar or granulated sugar

1. Combine the yeast and the salt in a small bowl. Add 2 cups warm (105 to 115°F) water and stir. Set aside at room temperature until the yeast and salt have dissolved, about 10 minutes.

2. Transfer the yeast mixture to a large bowl. Add the milk, egg, 1 teaspoon of the olive oil, the sugar, Strega, and lemon zest, and whisk by hand or with an electric mixer. Gradually add the flour, whisking by hand or with an electric mixer fit with the dough hook attachment.

3. Use a rubber spatula to turn the dough out onto a large, floured work surface. Knead until smooth and elastic, 10 to 15 minutes.

4. Transfer to a large, floured bowl. Cover with plastic wrap, stretching the wrap over the rim of the bowl to seal it tightly. Cover with a clean kitchen towel and set aside in a warm spot until doubled in bulk, 3 to 4 hours.

5. Heat the remaining olive oil in a large pot or deep-fat fryer until hot but not smoking, about 375°F.

6. Use your hands to tear off 1/4-pound pieces of dough (about 1/2 cup to 3/4 cup) and add them to the hot oil. Cook, turning frequently, until golden, 2 to 3 minutes. Use a slotted spoon to remove them and drain on paper towels. Dust with confectioners' sugar or roll in granulated sugar to coat before serving.

(continued)

VARIATION

Round Zeppole Filled with Vanilla Cream Prepare the Vanilla Pastry Cream (page 241) as the recipe instructs through step 6. Cover and chill for 6 hours. Prepare the Zeppole dough, above, as the recipe directs through step 4. Roll the dough out to a thickness of $3/4$ to 1 inch. Use a drinking glass or cookie cutter with a diameter of $1^{1}/2$ inches to cut the dough into rounds. Add the zeppole to the hot oil one at a time. Do not add more than 12 zeppole at a time. Cook, turning frequently, until golden, 2 to 3 minutes. Use a slotted spoon to remove them from the oil. Drain on paper towels and let them cool for 10 to 12 minutes. While the first batch is cooling, fry the remaining zeppole. When the zeppole are cool, you can split the rounds in half horizontally and fill with about $1^{1}/2$ tablespoons of the cream. Dust with confectioners' sugar or roll in granulated sugar to coat before serving. Cooled, filled zeppole will keep in the refrigerator for 3 to 5 days.

Italian Cream Puffs

In Italian we call cream puffs *"bocconcini con crema"* (little mouthfuls of pastry with cream). We make them at Easter, for birthdays, first communions, and confirmation celebrations. I like to make some éclairs when I make cream puffs since the ingredients—except for the topping—are the same. (Éclairs are simply longer cream puffs.) I serve them together on a doily-lined tray with after-dinner espresso.

1 recipe Vanilla Pastry Cream (recipe follows) or Chocolate Pastry Cream (see page 242)

1 cup (2 sticks) margarine

½ teaspoon salt

2 cups all-purpose flour

7 large eggs

1 tablespoon grated orange zest

1 recipe Chocolate Icing (recipe follows), for éclairs only

Confectioners' sugar, to garnish, for puffs only

1. Prepare the Vanilla Pastry Cream or Chocolate Pastry Cream as the recipe directs and chill for at least 6 hours or overnight.

2. Preheat the oven to 350°F.

3. Place 1 cup of water, the margarine, and the salt in a large saucepan and bring to a boil. Add the flour while stirring constantly with a wooden spoon, until the mixture is well combined and has come together.

4. Place the dough in a large bowl. Add the eggs one at a time, mixing well with a fork or a wooden spoon after each egg. (Note: The dough should have a firm but smooth texture.) Add the orange zest and continue to beat until well blended. Set aside.

5. Scoop the mixture by one heaping tablespoon and place about 2 inches apart on an ungreased baking sheet. (For larger puffs, use 2 tablespoons of the pastry mixture for each puff. For éclairs, use 3 tablespoons of the pastry mixture to make an elongated shape about 3 inches long.) The dough will rise and expand as it bakes.

6. Place the baking sheets in the upper half of the oven and bake for 40 to 45 minutes or until puffy and golden brown.

7. Let the puffs and éclairs cool to room temperature on the baking sheet.

8. To fill the puffs and éclairs, cut each almost in half—as if you were going to make a sandwich. Fill the cavity in the bottom half with some of the pastry cream, then place the top half of the puff on top. (Use about 2 tablespoons of pastry cream for the small puffs, about 3 tablespoons of the pastry cream for larger puffs, and 3 heaping tablespoons for the éclairs.) May be made 1 day in advance up to this point. If making them in advance, do not fill them; cover and refrigerate the puffs and cream separately until ready to fill.

(continued)

9. To finish the éclairs and the puffs: For the éclairs, make the Chocolate Icing as the recipe directs. Use a flat metal spatula or a teaspoon to spread the icing on the top of each éclair. For the puffs, omit the Chocolate Icing and sprinkle with confectioners' sugar just before serving.

Chocolate Icing

Makes ½ cup

This icing is spread just on éclairs. I don't use the chocolate icing for puffs.

1 teaspoon unsweetened powdered cocoa
1 ¼ cups confectioners' sugar
1 teaspoon orange extract
1 teaspoon orange-flavored liqueur, such as Grand
    Marnier, Cointreau, or Triple Sec

Place the cocoa, sugar, orange extract, orange liqueur, and 2 tablespoons of water in a small bowl. Mix well with a fork, a spoon, a small whisk, or an electric mixer, and beat until smooth and creamy. Use a metal spatula or a spoon to spread icing on top of éclairs that have already been filled with pastry cream.

Vanilla Pastry Cream

Makes 2 cups

½ cup granulated sugar

2 tablespoons all-purpose flour

6 egg yolks

2 cups whole milk or 2 cups light cream

Two ½-gram packages imported vanilla powder (see page 14) or

   1 tablespoon pure vanilla extract

1 lemon

1. Mix the sugar and the flour in a small bowl and set aside.

2. Put the egg yolks in the top part of a double boiler or in a non-aluminum bowl. Beat the egg yolks with an electric mixer on high speed until the yolks are light and fluffy. (Note: Do not use an aluminum bowl or pan; aluminum can cause uncooked egg yolks to discolor.) Gradually add the flour-sugar mixture while beating at a low speed until the mixture is blended and smooth.

3. Add the milk and vanilla and stir.

4. Place the bowl with the egg-milk mixture on top of a double boiler or a saucepan with several inches of water. Bring the water to a boil while stirring the egg-milk mixture constantly with a wooden spoon.

5. Use a sharp paring knife to remove the entire peel of the lemon. The peel will be in one piece and will resemble a spiral or a necklace when you're finished.

6. Add the lemon peel and cook, stirring constantly with a wooden spoon—it will keep the mixture from sticking to the bottom of the pan— for 15 to 20 minutes or until thick and creamy. Set aside to cool to room temperature. Discard the lemon peel. (Note: If the mixture is lumpy, pour it through a fine mesh strainer into another bowl to cool to room temperature.) The mixture can be used at this point for Zeppole di Ferrara (page 237), or cover and refrigerate for at least 6 hours or up to 1 week, then proceed as the recipe directs.

Chocolate Pastry Cream

Makes 2 cups

7 tablespoons granulated sugar

2 tablespoons all-purpose flour

1 tablespoon unsweetened powdered cocoa

6 egg yolks

2 cups milk or light cream

1 orange

1. Mix the sugar, flour, and cocoa in a small bowl and set aside.

2. Place the egg yolks in the top part of a double boiler or in a non-aluminum bowl. Beat the egg yolks with an electric mixer on high speed until the yolks are light and fluffy. (Note: Do not use an aluminum bowl or pan; aluminum can cause uncooked egg yolks to discolor.) Gradually add the flour-sugar-cocoa mixture while beating at low speed until the mixture is blended and smooth.

3. Add the milk and stir.

4. Place the bowl with the egg-milk mixture on top of a double boiler or a sancepan with several inches of water. Bring the water to a boil while stirring the egg-milk mixture constantly with a wooden spoon.

5. Use a vegetable peeler or a sharp paring knife to remove the entire peel of the orange. The peel will be in one piece and will resemble a spiral or a necklace when you're finished.

6. Add the orange peel and cook, stirring constantly with a wooden spoon—it will keep the mixture from sticking to the bottom of the pan—for 15 to 20 minutes or until thick and creamy. Set aside to cool to room temperature. Discard the orange peel. (Note: If the mixture is lumpy, pour it through a fine mesh strainer into another bowl to cool to room temperature.) The mixture can be used at this point, or cover and refrigerate for at least 6 hours or up to 1 week, then proceed as the recipe directs.

Eleanora's Tips

When making pastry cream, be sure to keep the water in the double boiler at a constant temperature. It should be at a steady boil. If the heat is too high, the egg mixture may burn or may become too thick. The water level is important, too. If there is too much water in the double boiler, the top part can "pop" off; if there's not enough, the egg mixture may burn. Also, be sure to stir the mixture constantly as it cooks.

Struffoli

Serves 10 to 12

Every family in the region of Campania—and just about everyone of southern Italian descent—makes struffoli at Christmastime. These little fried balls of dough coated with honey are mounded on a platter or formed into a cone, a pyramid, or a wreath shape, so it's an eye-catching centerpiece as well as a festive sweet.

Homemade struffoli is somewhat time-consuming to make, but the effort is worth it. I've added nuts, chocolate, and citrus zest to my mother's recipe, so my version is even more opulent and delicious than the classic dish. I find that sprinkling the struffoli with freshly grated citrus zest adds a wonderful fresh aroma and flavor. Omit the nuts and chocolate and the result will be the original version—it's delicious, too.

In our house, we enjoy struffoli all through the holidays, with tea, coffee, and on Christmas morning. Struffoli makes a lovely gift for special neighbors and friends. I even make it at Easter with pastel-colored candy sprinkles.

3¾ cups all-purpose flour, plus extra for dusting

6 large eggs

1 teaspoon baking powder

1 tablespoon olive oil

1 teaspoon Strega liqueur (see page 13) or lemon or orange-flavored liqueur, such as homemade Limoncello (page 248), Grand Marnier, or Triple Sec

Grated zest of 1 orange (Note: Do not grate the zest of the entire orange and lemon ahead of time or it will lose its aroma; grate half for the dough and half for the topping)

Grated zest of 1 lemon

6 cups light olive oil or vegetable oil

Roasted Nuts (recipe follows)

Wine-Flavored Honey Syrup (recipe follows)

½ cup semisweet chocolate mini-morsels

¼ cup multicolored candy sprinkles

To make the dough by hand

1. Mound the flour on a large work surface. Make a well in the center and crack the eggs into the well. Beat the eggs gently with a fork. Add the baking powder, olive oil, and Strega. Add half the orange zest and half the lemon zest and mix it into the egg mixture with a fork. Gradually draw in the flour from the sides of the well until all the ingredients are combined and the dough is smooth but not sticky. Knead the dough for 15 minutes or until smooth and elastic.

To make the dough with an electric mixer

2. Combine the eggs, baking powder, olive oil, Strega, half the orange zest, and half the lemon zest, and beat until blended. Slowly add the flour while beating constantly until a dough ball forms. Transfer the dough with a spatula to a clean work surface and knead for 5 minutes.

3. Wrap the dough in wax paper and let it rest for 15 minutes. Place a sheet of parchment paper on two baking sheets, then sprinkle with flour. Set aside.

244   ELEANORA'S KITCHEN

4. Cut the dough into 12 equal pieces that are approximately 2-inch cubes. Working with one piece of dough at a time, roll out logs that are about 12 inches long and $1/4$ inch thick.

5. Dip a sharp knife into flour and cut each log into $1/2$-inch pieces; they will look like little pillows. Place the "pillows" of dough onto the parchment-lined baking sheets.

6. In a pot over medium heat, heat the light olive oil until it reaches 350°F; this will take about 5 minutes.

7. Working in batches, add about 2 cups of the dough "pillows" to the oil and cook until golden, 2 to $2^{1}/2$ minutes. (Note: Do not add more than 2 cups of the dough at a time and do not overcook.) Use a slotted spoon to transfer the fried dough to a large bowl. Repeat with the remaining dough pillows.

8. Prepare the Roasted Nuts as the recipe directs and let them cool to room temperature while you make the Wine-Flavored Honey Syrup.

9. Make the Wine-Flavored Honey Syrup as the recipe directs. Immediately after the syrup reaches the soft-ball stage, add the Roasted Nuts, then add the struffoli while stirring gently with a wooden spoon. Continue to stir until all the struffoli are coated with the honey mixture; some of the honey will also be absorbed into the struffoli. (Note: Do not stir too vigorously or the struffoli may break.)

10. Moisten 2 large serving platters lightly with water. Use a large serving spoon or a large wooden spoon to transfer the struffoli from the pot to the platters, letting the excess honey drip back into the pot. When you have mounded all the struffoli onto the platters, pour any honey that remains in the pot over the mounds of struffoli. Immediately sprinkle the mounds evenly with chocolate morsels and candy sprinkles, and finish with the remaining orange zest and lemon zest. Let the struffoli settle for at least 15 minutes before serving. Can be made up to 1 week in advance. Struffoli is eaten by picking off individual balls and eating them one at a time.

(continued)

Roasted Nuts

I prefer slicing the hazelnuts to chopping them for this recipe. Older children—those who can safely use a small, sharp knife—can help with this job. With my kids helping, slicing the nuts takes about 10 minutes.

$1/2$ **pound shelled hazelnuts, sliced in half crosswise**
$1/2$ **pound shelled almonds, sliced in half crosswise**
$1/4$ **pound shelled walnut halves, sliced in half crosswise**

1. Preheat the oven to 350°F.

2. Spread the hazelnuts, almonds, and walnuts in one layer on a baking pan. Roast for 15 to 18 minutes or until golden brown. Remove from the oven and cool to room temperature.

Eleanora's Tips

For a more-citrus flavor, sprinkle some orange and lemon zest over the nuts when roasting.

Wine-Flavored Honey Syrup

3 tablespoons granulated sugar

¼ cup dry white wine or dry red wine

¼ cup orange-flavored liqueur, such as Grand Marnier, Cointreau,
or Triple Sec

2 cups honey

1. Combine the sugar, wine, and orange liqueur in a large pot over medium heat. Bring to a boil and cook uncovered, stirring constantly, for 3 to 4 minutes, until only about 2 tablespoons of liquid remain. The liquid should look foamy.

2. Add the honey and boil uncovered, stirring constantly, for 5 to 7 minutes, until the mixture has reached the soft-ball stage (234° to 240°F on a candy thermometer). Immediately remove the pot from the heat to stop the cooking. It is very important not to overcook the mixture or the honey will overcaramelize and harden. Immediately proceed to step 9 of the main recipe.

Limoncello

Makes about 2½ liters

"Wow!" That's the usual response I get after someone tastes this refreshing drink. The explosion of citrus awakens the palate. Limoncello is one of southern Italy's best-known drinks. It's served both as an aperitivo and as an after-dinner drink. When I was growing up, I recall my mother bringing gallons of grain alcohol into our apartment in the Bronx. Purchased from my uncle Antonio, this alcohol was used to make a variety of homemade drinks, including crema di menta, crema di cocoa, anisette, and more. These homemade flavored liqueurs were proudly displayed and were always presented to guests.

1 liter 95% pure grain alcohol, preferably imported (I use Desire brand, from Italy)

Peels of 3 to 4 large lemons, white pith included

3 cups (1½ pounds) granulated sugar

1. Pour the alcohol into a large glass jar. Add the lemon peels. Seal and set aside for 3 days.

2. After 3 days, fill a large saucepan with 1 quart plus 1½ cups of water. Add the sugar and bring to a boil, stirring frequently. Cook uncovered at a low boil for 4 to 5 minutes. Remove from the heat and let cool to room temperature. Add the alcohol and lemon peels and set aside for 1 hour.

3. Discard the lemon peels. Use a funnel to pour the lemon-flavored alcohol into 1-liter bottles and seal tightly. Place in a freezer for 6 to 8 hours to chill completely. Store in the freezer, so that the drink is cold whenever you're ready to serve.

Eleanora's Tips

If grain alcohol is not available in your area, 1 liter of 100-proof vodka can be substituted. Soak the lemon peels in the vodka for 5 days. Reduce the amount of water to 1½ cups and the sugar to 2 cups, and proceed as above. This makes 1 liter plus 1½ cups limoncello.

VARIATIONS

Arancello (Orange Liqueur) Proceed as the recipe directs, substituting the peels of 3 to 4 oranges, tangerines, clementines, or mandarins.

Crema di Limoncello Proceed as the recipe directs in step 1. Substitute 1% milk for the water in step 2. When the milk has cooked, add two ½-gram packages of imported vanilla powder (see page 14; vanilla extract will discolor the liquid) and stir to mix. Proceed as the recipe directs. Crema di Aranciata (Cream of Orange Liqueur) can be made by substituting oranges for the lemons.

CANNING AND PRESERVING

Canning and preserving are time-honored traditions that are dear to my heart. I enjoy the process—a true labor of love—as well as the result: An abundance of home-preserved food in the pantry is rewarding and comforting. To me, each jar is a treasure; there's nothing more satisfying than giving delicious home-preserved food as gifts to family and friends.

In this chapter, you'll find recipes for classics such as Marinated Eggplant (*Melanzane sott'Olio*, page 259) and Caponatina Spread (page 270), as well as my recipes for tomatoes and tomato puree, which are tried-and-true methods that I have perfected over time.

Years ago in Italy, my mother canned tomatoes just as my grandmother had done; she packed tomato slices with their skins into clean, empty wine bottles. They were sealed, and then processed in a traditional hot-water bath. (Some of my relatives in Italy still do it this way.) When Mamma came to America, she changed her method slightly; she blanched the tomatoes to remove the skins before packing them whole into Mason jars.

I'm in love with the whole concept of canning, especially canning tomatoes. The method I devised—one that involves leaving the skins on the tomatoes—is not only much easier than my mother's method but results in better texture, deeper color, and a more enhanced flavor. These qualities in turn result in canned tomatoes that are more versatile in the kitchen.

Preserving isn't just for the experienced cook. There are methods—such as drying herbs, for example, and for packing peppers in olive oil or oil and vinegar (such as Preserved Sweet Italian Peppers Vinaigrette, page 263)—that are relatively easy and don't require any special equipment. But I also believe wholeheartedly in the old-timey process using sterilized jars and a hot-water bath. Depending on how much you want to make, the process can take two weeks or two days. Whether you make a little or a lot, canning is worth the effort since having a full pantry actually *saves* you time all year round. On-hand foods like Caponatina Spread (page 270), Preserved Artichoke Hearts (page 254), Cured Green Olives (page 272), and Roasted Red Peppers (page 267) can be enjoyed in numerous ways; they're lifesavers when you want to transform a simple meat or poultry dish into something more elaborate.

Whatever method you use—drying, preserving in oil, or canning—make sure you start with the best possible ingredients; they should be unblemished and at their peak of freshness. Canning and preserving capture the authentic taste of Italy and bring it to the table. Given all the benefits—better taste, better texture, and a full pantry—I say, let canning and preserving be a pleasure, not a chore.

Homemade Dried Herbs

PARSLEY, BASIL, MINT, AND CELERY LEAVES

Once you've dried your own herbs, you'll find it difficult to go back to the store-bought kind. Homemade dried herbs are more fragrant and more flavorful than anything that has been sitting on a grocery store shelf. If you have a garden, drying your own herbs makes use of excess harvest. But even if you don't grow your own, you can purchase fresh herbs to dry and they'll still be better than store-bought dried herbs. Homemade dried herbs keep for months, and they are right on the pantry shelf, ready when you are. They're indispensable for seasoning vegetables, stuffings, soups, broths, and more. I use the oven to dry herbs, but you can use the microwave oven if you prefer (see page 253).

Serving Suggestions
- Add to marinades for flavoring fish and vegetables
- Season stuffings
- Add to soups and broths
- Season homemade bread crumbs
- Add to pasta dishes
- Season homemade breads and bruschette
- Season oils for preserving and canning, such as for olives, peppers vinaigrette, eggplant, artichoke hearts, sun-dried zucchini and pickled tomatoes

Makes about ⅔ cup dried herbs
6 ounces fresh herbs

1. Rinse and drain the herbs, then thoroughly spin-dry or air-dry. Remove the herb leaves from the stems, and discard the stems or save them for soups and stews. For basil, mint, and celery leaves—which are larger than parsley— tear the leaves with your hands. *(continued)*

2. Lay the herb leaves in one layer on a large baking sheet and let the herbs air-dry for at least 8 hours or overnight. (Note: The herbs must be completely dry before proceeding to the next step.)

3. Preheat the oven to 350°F. Bake the herbs until the leaves are dry and crumbly, but not brown, 7 to 10 minutes. Remove from the oven and cool completely.

4. Crumble the leaves with your fingers. For a finer texture, press them through a sieve. Store in an airtight container or small Mason jar in a cool, dry place.

VARIATION

To Microwave Herbs Spread clean, dry herbs on the glass tray in the microwave oven. Microwave on high for $2^1/_2$ to 3 minutes or until dry, but not brown. Remove from the microwave and crumble with your fingers. For a finer texture, press the herbs through a sieve. (Note: Microwave ovens vary in power, so exact timing will vary, too.)

STORING FRESH BASIL LEAVES IN THE REFRIGERATOR OR FREEZER

To store fresh basil, rinse the leaves on the stem and drain thoroughly to remove all moisture. Remove the leaves and place them in an airtight plastic container; store in the refrigerator for up to one week. To freeze, wrap the clean, dry leaves gently with plastic wrap, then place in a Ziploc freezer bag in the freezer.

Preserved Artichoke Hearts

No matter how they're prepared—stuffed, baked, fried, or marinated—artichokes are one of my favorite vegetables. Marinated artichokes are a delight to have on hand in the pantry for antipasto platters or to use in cooking. But I find that purchased canned artichoke hearts lack flavor and texture; in fact, they're rather bland and mushy. That's why I prefer to can them myself. It's totally worth the effort: My homemade canned artichokes are treasured in my home and enjoyed tremendously by my guests.

Serving Suggestions

- Serve with soppressata, prosciutto, and assorted cheeses on an antipasto platter
- Add to mixed green salads or potato salad
- Serve with barbecued meats, grilled fish, braised pork chops, and veal chops
- Pan-fry, broil, or bake alongside meat, fish, or poultry
- Use the flavored oil from the Preserved Artichoke Hearts to marinate or to flavor meats and poultry

Makes twelve to fourteen 16-ounce jars

(Note: The exact yield will depend on the artichokes; some have lots of choke, others do not. Quantities will also depend on how tightly you pack the jars.)

One 20-pound box of baby artichokes

1 to 1$\frac{1}{2}$ cups coarse salt

4 lemons

1 gallon distilled white vinegar per 10 pounds of artichokes

7 cups light olive oil ($\frac{1}{2}$ cup per jar)

3$\frac{1}{2}$ cups extra virgin olive oil ($\frac{1}{4}$ cup per jar)

1¾ cups red wine vinegar or white balsamic vinegar
(see Mail-Order Sources, page 283), 2 tablespoons
per jar

⅓ cup dried celery leaves, preferably homemade (page
251), about 1 teaspoon per jar

⅓ cup finely chopped garlic (about 1 teaspoon per jar)

⅓ cup dried oregano, preferably imported Italian (about
1 teaspoon per jar)

⅓ cup crushed dried hot red peppers or red pepper
flakes (about 1 teaspoon per jar)

2 tablespoons plus 1 teaspoon dried basil, preferably
homemade (page 251, ½ teaspoon per jar)

2 tablespoons plus 1 teaspoon dried parsley, preferably
homemade (page 251, ½ teaspoon per jar)

1. To prepare the artichokes, bend back and discard the outer leaves. Remove the third and fourth layer of leaves, and reserve them to make Seasoned Artichoke Leaves (page 258). You will be left with the pale green inner cores, or hearts. Slice off about ½ inch from the tops to remove the pointed heads, cut off ¼ inch from the stem end, and trim the bottoms.

2. Cut the hearts in half and put enough in a large bowl to cover the bottom. Sprinkle with a generous amount of salt and squeeze on some lemon juice. Continue filling the bowl, layering the hearts with salt and lemon juice. (Note: The lemon juice will lighten the artichokes, giving them visual appeal, and will also add a slight tang to the flavor.) When the bowl is filled, place a plate on top and use a heavy can or similar object to weigh down and compress the artichokes. Set aside overnight at room temperature.

3. Pour off and discard the juices that have gathered in the bowl. Bring the white vinegar to a boil in a large non-aluminum pot over medium-high heat. Add the artichoke hearts, return to a boil, and cook for 4 to 5 minutes.

(continued)

Remove from the heat and cool to room temperature, or set aside 8 hours or overnight.

4. Wash, rinse, and thoroughly dry the jars, lids, and rims. (You can use a dishwasher to do this.)

5. Into each jar, place $1/2$ cup of the light olive oil, $1/4$ cup of the extra virgin olive oil, 2 tablespoons of the white balsamic or 2 tablespoons of the red wine vinegar, a scant teaspoon of celery, a scant teaspoon of chopped garlic, a scant teaspoon of oregano, a scant teaspoon of red pepper, $1/2$ teaspoon basil, and $1/2$ teaspoon parsley.

6. Add enough artichoke hearts to fill the jars halfway. Seal the jars with new lids and rims, and shake them vigorously to distribute the seasonings. Open the jars and fill them with the rest of the artichoke hearts, pressing down with a wooden spoon to make sure the hearts are completely submerged in oil. Seal the jars, wipe with a clean cloth, and store on shelves in a cool area or in the refrigerator for up to 1 year, possibly longer. Once opened, store the artichoke hearts in the refrigerator.

SEASONED ARTICHOKE LEAVES

Use the third and fourth layers of leaves removed from artichokes you are going to can for this recipe. Bring water to a boil in a large saucepan. Add the soft, inner leaves (you should have about 1 pound of leaves from 20 pounds of antichokes) and boil for 2 minutes; drain. Return the artichoke leaves to the saucepan, add $1/4$ cup extra virgin olive oil; 1 teaspoon salt; 4 sliced garlic cloves; 1 tablespoon dried oregano, preferably imported Italian; and 4 to 6 diced, seeded ripe plum tomatoes. Cover and cook, turning occasionally, over low heat for 40 to 45 minutes, until tender. Serve warm or at room temperature as a side dish or an appetizer.

Marinated Eggplant

Canned, marinated eggplant is something that we Italians can't live without. *Melanzane sott'olio* was always in my mother's pantry; my sisters and I snacked on it when we came home from school. I continue the tradition for my own children and relatives. In fact, one of my great-nephews, Anthony, is particularly fond of my preserved eggplant, and I always make sure I give him a jar along with his Christmas present. Baby eggplants are preferable for canning since they have fewer seeds than mature eggplants and are firmer in texture. To make a smaller amount, simply halve the ingredients.

Serving Suggestions
Robust and tangy, canned eggplant is delicious on sandwiches or added to salads or to an antipasto platter.

Makes fourteen 16-ounce jars
- 1 bushel baby Italian eggplants (25 to 30 pounds)
- 1 cup salt
- 1 gallon distilled white vinegar per 12 pounds eggplant
- 7 cups light olive oil ($\frac{1}{2}$ cup per jar)
- $3\frac{1}{2}$ cups extra virgin olive oil ($\frac{1}{4}$ cup per jar)
- $1\frac{3}{4}$ cups red wine vinegar (2 tablespoons per jar)
- $1\frac{3}{4}$ cups white wine vinegar (2 tablespoons per jar)
- $\frac{1}{3}$ cup finely chopped garlic (about 1 teaspoon per jar)
- $\frac{1}{3}$ cup finely chopped fresh red and green hot peppers (about 1 teaspoon per jar)
- 2 tablespoons plus 1 teaspoon dried parsley, preferably homemade (page 251) ($\frac{1}{2}$ teaspoon per jar)
- 2 tablespoons plus 1 teaspoon dried basil, preferably homemade (page 251, $\frac{1}{2}$ teaspoon per jar)
- 2 tablespoons plus 1 teaspoon dried oregano, preferably imported Italian ($\frac{1}{2}$ teaspoon per jar)

1. Wash and peel the eggplants. Cut lengthwise into $1/4$-inch-thick slices, then cut those slices lengthwise into $1/4$-inch-wide strips. (Note: You can also slice the smaller eggplants into $1/8$-inch slices from stem end to blossom end and leave the slices whole or slice with skins.) Place the eggplant slices in a large bowl, sprinkle with the salt, and place a plate on top. Use a heavy can or similar object to weigh down and compress the eggplant. Let stand overnight at room temperature.

2. Bring the white vinegar to a boil in a large non-aluminum pot. Squeeze out the excess juices from the eggplant, add it to the boiling vinegar, and cook for 1 minute, stirring occasionally. Turn off the heat and let the eggplant soak in the vinegar for 45 minutes or until vinegar has cooled. Meanwhile, wash, rinse, and thoroughly dry the jars. (You can use a dishwasher to do this.)

3. Drain the eggplant and set aside until cool enough to handle. Squeeze the eggplant again to release excess liquid. Place the eggplant in a large bowl and set aside.

4. In each jar, place $1/2$ cup of the light olive oil, $1/4$ cup of the extra virgin olive oil, 2 tablespoons of the red wine vinegar, 2 tablespoons of the white wine vinegar, a scant teaspoon of garlic, a scant teaspoon of red and green hot peppers, $1/2$ teaspoon of the parsley, $1/2$ teaspoon of the basil, and $1/2$ teaspoon of the oregano.

5. Place enough eggplant into each jar to fill about three-quarters full. Seal with new lids and rims, and shake to distribute the seasonings. Open the jars and continue to add eggplant, packing it down with a wooden spoon as you work, until the jar is filled to within 1 inch of the top. Make sure the eggplant is completely submerged in oil. Seal tightly, and store in a cool, dry place for at least 2 weeks before consuming. Canned Marinated Eggplant will keep for up to 1 year, possibly more. Once opened, store the eggplant in the refrigerator.

(continued)

VARIATION

Many cooks who preserve and can are very proud of the color of their eggplant. While I like its natural color, some cooks prefer that the eggplant be very light in color—almost white. For "bianco" eggplant, add 4 cups distilled white vinegar to the eggplant when you add the salt in step 1.

Preserved Sweet Italian Peppers Vinaigrette

For preserving, I use the long red and green Italian peppers known as cubanelle. Packed in oil, vinegar, and herbs, these peppers are not only beautiful but versatile, too. As a variation, try my "cheese" peppers canned in vinegar (page 266). Cheese peppers are short, colorful round peppers (see photo, page 36) with thicker skins than cubanelles. Cheese peppers are sold in Italian markets and in some supermarkets—fresh, canned (vinaigrette style), or stuffed. However, I prefer to preserve them myself.

Serving Suggestions

Serve preserved peppers with antipasto, on sandwiches, in green leaf salads, cold potato salads, or alongside grilled steak, pork chops, or poultry. Also, try pan-frying these peppers with meats, or use the vinaigrette to marinate meats and poultry.

Makes two 32-ounce jars or four 16-ounce jars

   4 pounds green and red Italian peppers, preferably cubanelle

   1 gallon distilled white vinegar

   $3/4$ cup salt

   2 cups sugar

   1 cup light olive oil

   2 teaspoons dried oregano, preferably imported Italian

   2 garlic cloves, finely chopped

   $1/2$ cup red wine vinegar (for a less tangy flavor, use only $1/4$ cup red wine vinegar)

   $1/2$ cup extra virgin olive oil (for a less tangy flavor, use 1 cup total extra virgin olive oil and decrease red wine vinegar)

1. Rinse and dry the peppers. Remove the stems, cores, and seeds and discard. Rinse the insides of the peppers and drain. Slice the peppers into lengthwise strips that are $1/2$ inch wide and 2 to 3 inches long.

2. In a large pot, bring the distilled vinegar, salt, and sugar to a boil. Add the peppers and cook for 1 minute. Turn off the heat and let the peppers soak in the vinegar mixture for at least 2 hours, or until they reach room temperature. Drain and set aside. Wash, rinse, and thoroughly dry the jars. (You can use a dishwasher to do this.)

3. If making one 32-ounce jar, proceed as follows: Add the light olive oil, 1 teaspoon of the oregano, and half the garlic. Add the peppers, pressing gently with a wooden spoon, until the jar is three-quarters full. Add the red wine vinegar and seal tightly with a new lid and rim. Turn the jar upside down and shake until the seasonings have blended. Unseal the jar and add the extra virgin olive oil, the remaining garlic, and the remaining oregano. The peppers should be completely submerged under the oil and vinegar; if they aren't, add more olive oil. (Note: If using two 16-ounce jars, proceed as the recipe directs, dividing the ingredients equally between the two jars.) Seal tightly and, for more flavor, set aside for at least 1 week before consuming. After opening, store in the refrigerator until ready to use.   *(continued)*

VARIATION

Preserved Red and Green Cheese Peppers
Marinated in Vinegar

Makes three 32-ounce jars

Bring 12 cups distilled white vinegar to a boil in a large non-aluminum pot. Add 24 to 26 whole cheese peppers and cook for 3 to 5 minutes. Turn off the heat and allow the mixture to cool to room temperature. Discard the vinegar mixture. Pour 1 cup of water and $1^{1}/2$ cups of fresh distilled white vinegar into each jar. Add 1 finely chopped garlic clove and 1 tablespoon dried oregano, preferably imported Italian, per jar. Add the cheese peppers, packing them lightly until they reach just below the rim of the jar. Seal tightly with a new lid and rim. Store in the refrigerator and use as needed.

Canned Roasted Red Peppers

Having roasted red peppers on hand is a joy and a convenience, especially in the dead of winter when really fresh red peppers are hard to find. First I roast them, and then I can them in their natural state. For the freshest flavor, I season them with garlic, salt, and olive oil just before serving (about 2 tablespoons oil, 2 finely chopped garlic cloves, and $1/2$ teaspoon salt per 16-ounce jar). I use them in salads, pastas, and sandwiches; they're especially delicious with prosciutto and fresh mozzarella.

Serving Suggestions

- Add to a cold antipasto platter or an antipasto platter with prosciutto and mozzarella
- Serve with grilled eggplant as an appetizer
- Use as a sandwich filling or topping
- Puree in a blender or food processor to make quick roasted pepper sauce for pasta
- Spread on toasted bread for a quick roasted pepper bruschetta

Makes ten 16-ounce jars

20 to 25 pounds red bell peppers

1. Preheat a gas or charcoal grill. Thoroughly wash and dry the peppers and place them in a flat layer on the grill. Roast the peppers, turning them every 15 to 20 minutes, until completely charred on all sides, 40 to 45 minutes total cooking time. Transfer to a brown paper bag and place on a large tray. (The tray will catch any excess juices from the peppers.) Set aside until cool enough to handle.

2. Peel or carefully scrape off the blackened skins without using water, which would dilute the flavor of the peppers. Cut the peppers in half and gently remove the seeds and remove any inner membranes. Place the pepper halves in a large colander and let them drain for 1 to 2 hours before packing into jars. (Note: This allows the juices from the peppers to drain more completely. This is advisable, since it will eliminate excess liquid and prevent the peppers from floating in the jar after processing.)

3. Wash, rinse, and thoroughly dry the jars. (You can use a dishwasher to do this.) Use a wooden spoon to place the peppers in the jars, pressing gently but firmly, without crushing or tearing the peppers. Fill the jars to the top. Seal the jars tightly with new lids and rings.

4. Place a kitchen towel on the bottom of a canning pot large enough to hold the jars in one layer. (The towel keeps the glass from being in direct contact with the metal pot, which can cause breakage.) Pack the jars tightly into the bottom of the pot to prevent them from rattling against one another; you can also wrap kitchen towels around individual jars to secure them even more.

5. Fill the pot with enough water to cover the jars by at least 5 inches. Cover the pot and place a brick or slab of stone on top to keep the lid in place. Bring the water to a boil and cook for 15 to 20 minutes, boiling continuously. (Note: If some of the water spills over, lower the heat, but keep the water at a boil.) Turn off the heat, and then let the jars sit in the water until it has cooled to room temperature.

6. Remove the jars one at a time, drying each thoroughly and, most important, sealing the jars very tightly again. (The jar rims sometimes become loosened during the boiling process). Store in a cool, dry place.

Canned Caponatina Spread

In winter—when really good fresh tomatoes and eggplants are hard to find—this spread provides a taste of summer. When caponatina is spread on *panella* or Italian bread, it becomes an easy, quick hors d'oeuvre, or a tasty addition to an antipasto platter. Caponatina is great on bruschetta, or add a jar of caponatina to marinara sauce to toss with pasta. Caponatina is also delicious with grilled chicken, pork chops, halibut, swordfish, or striped bass. Caponatina, by the way, has the same ingredients as caponata, but since the ingredients are diced more finely, caponatina is more spreadable.

Makes ten 8-ounce jars or twenty 4-ounce jars

- 3 baby Italian eggplants with skin (about 1 pound), trimmed and cut into ¼-inch dice
- 3 tablespoons plus 2 teaspoons salt
- ½ cup extra virgin olive oil
- 6 garlic cloves, finely chopped
- Two 32-ounce jars homemade canned plum tomatoes (page 275), or two 35-ounce cans whole plum tomatoes with juice, or 3 pounds very ripe, fresh plum tomatoes, crushed in a blender or food processor for 2 to 3 seconds to eliminate large pieces of skin
- 3 tablespoons dried oregano, preferably imported Italian
- 1 cup finely chopped celery with leaves
- ¼ cup finely chopped fresh basil
- 1 cup drained oil-packed capers
- 1½ cups Cured Green Olives (page 272) or green Sicilian olives, pitted and finely chopped

1. Place the eggplant in a bowl and sprinkle with 3 tablespoons of the salt. Place a dish on top of the eggplant and weight the plate with a heavy object, such as a can of tomatoes. Set aside for 1 hour to release juices. Discard the eggplant juices and squeeze the eggplant with your hands. Set aside.

2. Warm the olive oil in a large saucepan over medium heat. Add the garlic, tomatoes, the remaining 2 teaspoons salt, the oregano, celery, and half the basil. Cook, partially covered, for 25 to 30 minutes, stirring occasionally. Add the capers, eggplant, and olives, cover, and cook for 15 to 20 minutes more, until the sauce has condensed. Add the remaining basil, stir to mix, and set aside for 1 hour to cool to room temperature.

3. Wash, rinse, and thoroughly dry the jars, lids, and rims. (You can use a dishwasher to do this.) Use a small wooden spoon to place the mixture in the jars, leaving $1/2$ inch of space at the top of the jars. Seal with new lids and rims.

4. Place the filled jars in a large pot. Place a kitchen towel around the jars to keep them from rattling. Add enough water to cover the tops of the jars by at least 4 inches. Bring the water to a boil, lower the heat to medium or medium-low, and boil for 20 minutes. Turn off the heat and let the jars sit in the water until it has cooled, 8 hours or overnight.

5. Remove the jars from the water, dry them, then tighten the rims. Store in a cool, dry place for up to 1 year. Refrigerate caponatina up to 1 week once it has been opened.

VARIATION

Caponata Proceed as the recipe directs, but do not cut the eggplant, celery, onions, and olives as finely as for caponatina.

Cured Green Olives

Some old-fashioned curing methods will have you wait one full year to enjoy the olives, but my method has them on your table in just two weeks. I use a hammer to crack open the olives, which allows the brine to saturate the olives more quickly.

Serving Suggestions

- Add to antipasto platter
- Pit, puree, and spread on toast to make a quick olive bruschetta
- Toss into green leaf salads or cold potato salads
- Pit, puree, or crush, and make Green Olive Pesto (page 92) to toss with pasta
- Add olives—whole or pitted—to pasta sauces
- Knead into homemade breads
- Crush olives, then combine with roasted garlic and oil and use as a topping for grilled meats or fish
- Add to cooked chicken, rabbit, veal, or pork
- Use the flavored oil from the olives to marinate meat, fish, or poultry or use to season salads or to flavor cooked greens

Makes ten 32-ounce jars

One 18-pound box or crate of uncured green Sicilian or green Cerignola olives

Approximately 10 to 12 cups salt (¾ cup salt per day per 4-liter bottle of olives)

2 cups extra virgin olive oil, preferably Bariani (see Mail-Order Sources, page 283), to season olives (see step 4), plus 15 cups to fill the jars (1½ cups per jar)

6 to 8 small dried hot red peppers, or 4 teaspoons red pepper flakes

½ cup finely diced celery with leaves

3 tablespoons dried oregano, preferably imported Italian

(continued)

10 garlic cloves, finely chopped

5 teaspoons dried celery leaves, preferably homemade
(page 251)

1. Working with one olive at a time, place the olives on a large wooden cutting board and hit with a hammer until the olive cracks open but is not smashed. Place the olives into an empty 4-liter bottle. When the bottle is full, add $^3/_4$ cup salt per liter of olives. Add enough water to reach 2 inches from the top of the bottle. (Note: For the last bottle, which is filled only halfway with olives, add 4 cups water and $^1/_2$ cup salt.)

2. Set the bottles aside for 24 hours. Pour out the water, reserving the olives in the bottle. Add another $^3/_4$ cup of salt to the olives, and again, add enough water to reach 2 inches from the top of the bottle. Repeat this process every day for 9 days total. During the curing process, always keep the olives submerged under the brine; this will keep them from darkening or wilting, which may cause spoilage.

3. After 9 days, taste the olives. If they are still bitter, continue to cure them with salt and water for 2 to 3 more days, until they no longer taste bitter. (Note: Curing time will depend on the size and type of olives. Smaller olives may be ready in 9 days; larger olives—such as Sicilian—require about 2 weeks' curing time.)

4. Drain the olives, then place them into 2 large bowls. Add 2 cups of the olive oil, the red pepper, celery, oregano, garlic, and dried celery leaves. Toss to mix, then set aside for 24 hours.

5. Wash, rinse, and thoroughly dry the jars. (You can use a dishwasher to do this.) Begin to fill the jars with the olives (about $1^1/_2$ pounds olives per 32-ounce jar), pressing them down gently with the end of a wooden spoon. Fill to the rim line and add enough of the remaining olive oil to submerge the olives, about $1^1/_2$ cups per jar. Seal tightly, then store in a cool, dry place for up to 1 year. After the olives have been opened, store them in the refrigerator.

Canning Plum Tomato Halves and Puree

Every year, I'm inspired by the abundance of beautiful red tomatoes at the market. They seem to be begging to be enjoyed in endless ways: in innumerable pasta dishes, to enhance meats and fish, to bring a blush (and flavor) to soups and stews, and most of all, to make the best tomato sauce ever.

To enjoy the flavor of tomatoes at their peak, I have developed a canning method—which I have practiced for almost twenty years—that locks in color, texture, and flavor. My method turns the simple fruit into perhaps the best-preserved puree and tomato halves you'll ever taste.

Although my mother always preserved her tomatoes by parboiling them to remove the skins, I prefer to leave the skin intact. Preserving the tomato with its skin allows for greater options in cooking: If your recipe calls for tomatoes with skin, *eccola*. If the recipe calls for crushed tomatoes, simply process the tomato halves in a blender or food processor for 2 to 3 seconds. If the recipe calls for torn, chopped, or diced tomatoes, my canned tomatoes are good for that, too. And it goes without saying that homemade canned tomatoes are more delicious, more beautiful, and have better texture than anything you can buy at the supermarket.

Canning is an old tradition, one that many cooks still enjoy. I find that it is an incredibly satisfying household chore—a true labor of love—one that takes some time and energy, but is well worth the effort. Imagine having the taste of summer tomatoes all year round! Your family, friends, and guests will be impressed, I promise you that.

Serving Suggestions
- Add to just about any pasta dish
- Use to make a variety of sauces, including traditional meat sauces, Traditional Sunday Sauce alla Russo (page 109), any kind of marinara sauce, or any other sauce—for meat, fish, poultry, or vegetables—calling for tomatoes or tomato puree

- Make homemade Pizza Sauce (page 205)
- Make homemade Tomato Soup with Fresh Basil (page 64)
- Add to soups, stews, or broths for color and flavor
- Make a quick tomato bruschetta
- Add to cooked vegetables and greens
- Add to stuffings
- Use to make Tomato Focaccia (page 202)

How to Select Tomatoes: The Importance of Quality

- Choose plum tomatoes that are plum-shaped, very ripe, heavy in weight, with minimal seeds. They should also be meaty and as blemish-free as possible.

- Buy tomatoes in boxes holding 25 to 30 pounds of tomatoes instead of larger bushels of 55 to 60 pounds. The larger amount inevitably results in damaged tomatoes at the bottom of the bushel.

Basic Tips: Jars and Lids

- Never use lids twice. Used lids can cause air to escape, which will result in spoilage. Purchase them new every year.

- Rims that have been damaged or bent, or are rusted cannot be reused.

- Jars can be reused year after year. Make sure you wash, rinse, and dry them thoroughly before canning.

- Never take jars out of water that is still boiling. Always let the water come to room temperature before removing the jars.

- ˜Tightening the rims to make them absolutely airtight after the jars have been boiled is extremely important, to make sure that no air can escape or enter.

- Opening jars with a round rubber jar sealer will prevent damage to the rim, making it possible to reuse the rim the following year.

Basic Tips: Canning Tomatoes

■ Always use a wooden spoon—not a metal one—to pack the tomatoes into jars. Metal can rust, and can give off a metallic taste, too.

■ Each tomato should be carefully inspected; it only takes one tomato to spoil an entire batch.

■ Always clean the processing machine thoroughly after each use. It should be completely disassembled and each part washed and dried to prevent any dirt, dust, rust, or bacteria from getting into the tomatoes.

■ It is extremely important that all canned (jarred) tomatoes be stored in a cool, dry place (such as a basement) for proper preservation.

Ten to twelve 32-ounce jars

INGREDIENTS

One 25-pound box Roma (plum) tomatoes

20 to 30 fresh basil leaves, washed and dried

Coarse salt

EQUIPMENT

1 sharp knife, with a blade 4 to 5 inches long

A rubber sealer (this gadget, sold in hardware stores, is
    used to grip the jars when sealing them, which helps
    tighten the rims)

2 large stainless-steel bowls

1 large slotted draining spoon

1 extra-large wooden spoon

Ten to twelve 32-ounce Mason jars with rims in good
    condition, washed, rinsed, and dried, or twenty to
    twenty-two 16-ounce Mason jars, washed, rinsed, and
    dried

New lids for the Mason jars (Note: Rust-free, unbent
rims can be reused, but all lids must be purchased
new every year; make sure you have plenty on hand)

2 wooden spoons

2 white cotton or linen tablecloths (Note: These can be
reused for canning year after year.)

3 to 4 prewashed and well-rinsed 38 x 32-inch all-cotton
kitchen towels, for draining

1 enamel canning pot (bath canner), large enough to
hold eight 32-ounce Mason jars (for beginners), or 1
aluminum canning pot (bath canner) large enough to
hold nineteen 32-ounce Mason jars (for the
experienced canner)

1 large stainless-steel pot for making tomato puree

Brick or slab of stone to weigh down lid

Apron

2 to 3 large colanders or wicker baskets that can be
used as colanders

2 to 3 large cooking pots, for drainage

Potholders

Ladle

2 or 3 large plastic bins (for experienced canners canning a large amount of tomatoes, the bins are used
to rinse or clean the tomatoes before draining)

Funnel with a mouth wide enough to fit the Mason jar
when pouring the puree

Tomato processor, manual or electric, clean and completely free of dust particles or rust (see Mail-Order
Sources, page 283)

1 or 2 outdoor burners—used for large pots (see Mail-
Order Sources, page 283)

Setting Up the Kitchen: Let's Start Canning!

Decide where you want to can the tomatoes. For small quantities or for beginners (eight 32-ounce Mason jars per bath canner or pot), you can use your kitchen countertops and stovetop. If you are canning on a larger scale, find a clean workspace—such as a garage or the backyard—with enough room to work. You should also have enough table space to accommodate the tomatoes and some of the equipment (jars, bowls, pots, etc.).

1. Remove the tomatoes from each box and inspect them by discarding any tomato that is damaged or looks spoiled. Rinse the tomatoes well and drain in a colander. As you cut the tomatoes, select which ones are best for canning as halves and which ones are more suitable for puree. (Note: Any tomatoes that are not completely ripe should be used for puree. Any imperfect tomatoes that are marked, blemished, unripened, spotted, or discolored can be salvaged and used for making puree by cutting out the marked or spotted area. When a tomato shows no sign of spoilage and you are still uncertain of its perfection, the best way to check is by its scent. A good tomato will smell sweet; a bad tomato will smell slightly acidic. Any tomatoes that are spoiled should be discarded.)

2. Cut off the tops, and halve each tomato lengthwise. Remove and reserve the core and seeds. Put the halves in a large bowl and set aside. Put the tops, cores, and seeds in a separate large cooking pot for making the tomato puree. (Note: If the tops are marked, spotted, or unclean, discard them.) Add all tomatoes that have not yet matured, or are not in perfect condition, to the pot for puree. Wash, rinse, and thoroughly dry the canning jars, lids, and rims. (You can use a dishwasher to do this.)

For tomato halves

3. Place a basil leaf into each jar. Start packing the jars about three-quarters full with the halved tomatoes. Press down gently but firmly with a wooden spoon (do not crush) to fill any gaps or pockets of air. Add 1 to 2 basil leaves

to each jar, and continue filling with tomatoes to $\frac{1}{2}$ inch from the top of the jar. Do not fill above the rim. Sprinkle a pinch of salt over the tops of the tomatoes to prevent the top layer from drying out.

4. Seal the jars tightly with lids and rims. Place a kitchen towel on the bottom of the canning pot to avoid direct contact between glass and metal. Lay a large cotton tablecloth in the pot, fitting it with ends overlapping the edge of the pot. Pack the jars tightly into the bottom of the pot to prevent them from rattling against one another. If the jars do not fit, you can turn them upside down to allow for extra room. For a more secure fit, you can wrap a kitchen towel around some of the jars to prevent them from rattling or breaking. When you have placed all the jars securely into the pot, bring in the overlap of the tablecloth to cover them. Fill the pot with enough water to cover the jars by at least 4 to 5 inches.

5. Place a slab of stone or clean bricks on top of the cloth, and cover with the lid. Place another stone slab on top of the lid. Bring the water to a boil and cook for about 1 hour, boiling continuously. Turn off the heat, and leave the jars in the pot until the water has completely cooled. Remove the jars one at a time, drying each thoroughly, and most important, tightening the rims very securely again (the rims sometimes become loose in the boiling process). Store in a dry, cool place.

For tomato puree

6. Add salt (about 2 tablespoons per 8 quarts puree) to the pot containing the tops, cores, seeds, and imperfect tomatoes. Before the tomatoes come to a boil, stir occasionally with a large wooden spoon. Bring to a boil and cook until you see that the tomatoes are bubbling; they will be foamy and frothy. Turn off the heat.

7. Line a large colander with a large cotton cloth (I use a 38 X 32-inch pre-washed, well-rinsed, all-cotton, lint-free white kitchen towel). Set the lined colander over a large bowl, letting the cloth hang over the rim of the colander. Ladle the cooked tomatoes into the colander with a large, slotted spoon, and cover the cooked tomatoes with the excess cloth hanging over the rim of the colander). Once the tomatoes have drained and cooled, you can squeeze with your hands over the cloth to release more water from the tomatoes. (Note: The more you drain the tomatoes, the thicker, more condensed, redder in color, and richer in flavor your puree will be.)

8. Using a large slotted spoon, scoop the tomatoes into the funnel bowl of your tomato-processing machine (also known as a hopper). Use the compressor tool to push the tomatoes down through the funnel. The tomato processor will separate the seeds and skins, which will go into a separate pot. The tomato that is released into a clean stainless-steel pot is the puree, which will be preserved. You can run the processed tomatoes through the funnel to extract more juice one or two more times. Then discard the tomato skins and seeds that have been through the processor twice. Begin again by refilling with a new batch of drained tomatoes, and process through the hopper one to three times. Continue until you have processed all the drained tomatoes.

9. Ladle the puree into a wide-mouth funnel set over the prewashed jars. Add basil, seal, and process as for the halved tomatoes (from step 3, above), boiling for only 30 minutes instead of a full hour since the puree has been precooked.

VARIATION

Flavoring the Puree with Celery Proceed as the recipe directs through step 8. Place 2 to 3 fresh celery leaves into the jars, then proceed as the recipe directs in step 9. This celery-flavored puree is ideal for soups and stews.

MAIL-ORDER SOURCES

BARIANI OLIVE OIL
Emanuele Bariani
301 Eleventh Street #3A
San Francisco, California
94103
T: (415) 864-1917
F: (415) 864-1908
www.barianioliveoil.com
Extra virgin olive oil

BIANCARDI'S
2350 Arthur Avenue
Bronx, New York 10458
T: (718) 733-4058
F: (718) 364-0677
www.biancardi.com
Smoked prosciutto, spicy pancetta,
smoked pancetta, soppressata,
traditional Italian sausages, Fiore
di Sardegna

CADET IMPORTERS, LTD.
561 S. Fulton Avenue
Mt. Vernon, New York 10550
T: (914) 961-2763
F: (914) 961-0702
e-mail: pdipaolo@cadetwines.com
Pergoné liqueur

MOUNT CARMEL GOURMET
FOOD SHOP
2344 Arthur Avenue
Bronx, New York 10458
T: (718) 933-2295
Imported Italian oregano, vanilla
powder, panna, Cerignola olives,
Castelvetrano olives

MOZZARELLA COMPANY
2944 Elm Street
Dallas, Texas 75226
T: (214) 741-4072
(800) 798-2954
www.mozzarellacompany.com
Fresh ricotta, basket cheese, dry-
aged mozzarella

QUELER HARDWARE, INC.
610 East 187th Street
Bronx, New York 10458
T: (718) 367-3987
(718) 367-0291
www.quelerhardware.com
Tomato processing machine, large
stainless-steel cooking pots, large
aluminum cooking pots, outdoor
burners

SMITHFIELD
3107 Brassfield Road
Greensboro, North Carolina
27410
www.smithfield.com
Pork loin and other pork products

TEITEL BROS.
2359 Arthur Avenue
Bronx, New York 10458
T: (718) 733-9400
F: (718) 365-1415
www.teitelbros.com
Salted capers, salt-packed anchovies, Gaeta olives, Calabrese
olives, Sicilian olives, sun-dried
tomatoes, fresh citron, candied citron, Bel Paese cheese, canned
cooked wheat berries, cipolline,
white balsamic vinegar

WILLIAMS-SONOMA
www.williamsonoma.com
Flour-sack towels (large white
kitchen-towels)

INDEX

*Note: Page numbers in **bold** indicate photographs.*

lemon, for lemon drop cookies, 225
    for sweet Easter bread, 208
Insalata di mare (seafood salad), 148
Italian beef stew, 82
Italian-style sausage and peppers, 162

J

Jam, biscotti with (biscotti con marmellata),
    222–23

L

Lamb
    baked cavatelli with lamb-tomato sauce, 116–17
    marinated grilled baby lamb chops with fresh
        mint, 163
Lasagna, classic, 24, 128–30
Lemon(s), 9
    homemade limoncello, 248
    lemon drop cookies, 224–25
    orange and lemon sunrise cake, 226–27
    sweet lemon-ricotta pie with brandied cherries,
        34, 232–33
    and white wine sauce, veal Francese, 152–53
Lentil soup with carrots, potatoes, and
        pancetta, 66
Limoncello, homemade, 248
Linguine
    with red clam sauce, 102
    with shrimp, clams, and arugula, 100
    with white clam sauce, 22, 102
Liqueurs
    homemade limoncello or arancello, 248
    Pergoné, 12
    Strega, 13
Littleneck clams, 9–10
    See also Clams
Lobster, in zuppa di pesce, 83–84

M

Mail-order ingredients sources, 283
Manicotti stuffed with ricotta and mozzarella with
        rich marinara sauce, 126–27
Manteca, 10
Marinara sauce
    eggplant Parmigiana, 187–88
    quick Neapolitan, spaghetti with, 90
    rich, manicotti stuffed with ricotta and
        mozzarella with, 126–27
    stuffed chicken breast with mozzarella, 168–69
    veal Sorrentino, 27, 156–57
Marsala
    veal Marsala, 151
Mascarpone, 227
    fig and hazelnut torta, 228–29
    orange and lemon sunrise cake, 226–27
    tiramisù, 236
Meat. See specific types

Meatballs
    for lasagna, 130
    for soups, 81
    tiny, Maria Domenica's chicken and veal soup
        with, 80–81
    traditional Sunday sauce alla Russo, 109–11
Microwaving
    garlic, 67
    herbs, 253
Migliaccio di Cervinara (sweet semolina and ricotta
        pie), 230–31
Minestrone, Nonna's homemade, 21, 62–63
Mint
    fresh, zucchini with, 29, 173
    homemade dried, 251–53
    marinated grilled baby lamb chops with, 163
    old-fashioned roasted artichoke hearts with, 51
Mozzarella, 10
    baked penne with peas, prosciutto, and, 131–32
    manicotti stuffed with ricotta and, with rich
        marinara sauce, 126–27
    mozzarella in carrozza, 56
    panzarotti, 209–10
    ricotta-mozzarella calzone, 212
    smoked: creamy potato gratin with, 186; pork
        and smoked mozzarella patties, 166
    stuffed chicken breast with, 168–69
    veal cutlets with prosciutto, eggplant, and,
        156–57
Mushrooms
    chicken with tomatoes, olives, and, 167
    eggplant alla Scarpetta, 193–94
    fettuccine Alfredo, 89
    fusilli with zucchini, eggplant, and, 98
    grilled eggplant and portobello pizzaiola, 180–81
    pasta with shrimp and, 104
    porcini, spaghetti with cherry tomatoes and, 97
    stuffed, 20, 58–59
    veal cutlets with artichokes, sun-dried tomatoes,
        and, 154–55
    veal Marsala, 151
    wild mushroom pizza, 204
Mussels
    baked, Fra Diavolo, 143
    zuppa di pesce, 83–84

N

Neapolitan spaghetti pie, 133
Nuts
    biscotti con marmellata, 222–23
    roasted, for struffoli, 246
    See also specific nuts

O

Octopus
    seafood salad, 148
    zuppa di pesce, 83–84

Neapolitan spaghetti pie, 133
toma pie, 213–14
See also Calzone; Pizza
Pies, sweet
lemon-ricotta pie with brandied cherries, **34**, 232–33
semolina and ricotta pie (migliaccio di Cervinara), 230–31
wheat berry, citrus, and ricotta pie (pizza gran), 234–35
Pignoli cookies (pine nut cookies with orange liqueur), **32**, 218–19
Pizza
broccoli rabe, 204
cheese, 203–4
eggplant, 204–5
Napoletana, 203
with peppers, 205
pizza gran (wheat berry, citrus, and ricotta pie), 234–35
pizza rustica, **31**, 215–16
ricotta, 205
sauce for, 205
spinach, 204
wild mushroom, 204
See also Calzone
Pizzaiola sauce, 165
eggplant with, 179
grilled eggplant and portobello with, 180–81
grilled steak with, 164
striped bass with, **25**, 139
Polenta noodles, 122
Porcini, spaghetti with cherry tomatoes and, 97
Pork
cavatelli with sausage, spareribs, and pork shoulder in tomato sauce, 114–15
chops: braised, with marinated artichoke hearts and vinegar peppers, **28**, 161; al forno, 160
lasagna meatballs, 130
meatballs, 110–11
pork and smoked mozzarella patties, 166
pork loin roast, 159
See also Pancetta; Prosciutto; Sausage(s)
Potato(es)
croquettes, 184–85
dandelion greens with sun-dried tomatoes and, 175
gnocchi, 118–19
gratin, creamy, with smoked mozzarella, 186
lentil soup with carrots, pancetta, and, 66
split pea soup with, creamy, 72–73
Prawns, in zuppa di pesce, 83–84
Preserving, 249–82
artichoke hearts, 254–58
canned caponatina spread, 270–71
canned plum tomato halves or puree, 275–82
canned roasted red peppers, 267–68

cheese peppers marinated in vinegar, 266
dried herbs, homemade, 251–53
freezing: basil, 253; grilled eggplant, 43; tomatoes, 79
homemade cured green olives, 272–74
hot red peppers, 12
marinated eggplant, 259–62
sweet Italian peppers vinaigrette, 263–65
Prosciutto
baked penne with peas, mozzarella, and, 131–32
cheese and prosciutto pie (pizza rustica), **31**, 215–16
figs, prosciutto, and fennel, 46
prosciutto bread, **21**; with pancetta and basil, **31**, 200–201
Swiss chard with cipolline and, 176
veal cutlets with eggplant, mozzarella, and, 156–57

R
Ravioli, homemade, with ricotta stuffing, 123–25
Rice
rice balls with three cheeses, 54–55
and ricotta pie, savory, 213–14
Ricotta
cheese and prosciutto pie (pizza rustica), **31**, 215–16
fig and hazelnut torta, 228–29
half-moon panzarotti, 210
manicotti stuffed with mozzarella and, with rich marinara sauce, 126–27
orange and lemon sunrise cake, 226–27
and rice pie, savory, 213–14
ricotta balls with Pecorino Romano, 55
ricotta gnocchi, 119
ricotta-mozzarella calzone, 212
ricotta pizza, 205
stuffing, homemade ravioli with, 123–25
sweet lemon-ricotta pie with brandied cherries, **34**, 232–33
sweet semolina and ricotta pie, 230–31
wheat berry, citrus, and ricotta pie (pizza gran), 234–35
Rigatoni
with baby eggplant, tomatoes, and basil, 94
with broccoli rabe, sausage, and spicy tomato sauce, **23**, 105–6
Rollatini, eggplant, **17**, 44–45

S
Salads
baccalà, cold, 146
seafood salad (insalata di mare), 148
See also Antipasti
Salt cod. *See* Baccalà
Salumi. *See* Sausage(s)

Sardines, in frittura di mare, 145
Sauce(s)
    caper, fried flounder with, 137
    pesto: green olive, bruschetta with, 40; green
        olive, fettuccine with, 92; green
        olive-basil, grilled halibut with, 140; Napoletano, gemelli
        with, 96
    white wine and garlic, littlenecks with, 53
    See also Pasta; Tomato sauces
Sausage(s)
    broccoli rabe with, 174
    cavatelli with spareribs, pork shoulder, and, in
        tomato sauce, 114–15
    Italian-style sausage and peppers, 162
    rigatoni with broccoli rabe, spicy tomato sauce,
        and, 23, 105–6
    soppressata, 12–13; pizza rustica, 31, 215–16;
        spaghetti carbonara with pancetta and, 107–8
Scallops, in frittura di mare, 145
Scungilli
    frittura di mare, 145
    seafood salad, 148
Seafood, 135–48
    frittura di mare, 145
    insalata di mare (seafood salad), 148
    zuppa di pesce, 83–84
    See also Fish; specific types
Semolina and ricotta pie, sweet, 230–31
Shallots, dandelion greens with fresh tomatoes and,
    175
Shellfish. See specific types
Shrimp
    frittura di mare, 145
    linguine with clams, arugula, and, 100
    pasta with mushrooms and, 104
    seafood salad, 148
    shrimp Marachiara, 26, 142
    zuppa di pesce, 83–84
Soppressata
    pizza rustica, 31, 215–16
    spaghetti carbonara with pancetta and, 107–8
Soups and stews, 61–84
    cauliflower soup with green beans, zucchini, and
        basil, 65
    chicken and veal soup with tiny meatballs, Maria
        Domenica's, 80–81
    escarole and white bean soup, peasant-style,
        70–71
    homemade minestrone, Nonna's, 21, 62–63
    Italian beef stew, 82
    lentil soup with carrots, potatoes, and pancetta,
        66
    pasta and chickpea soup with tomatoes and basil,
        74–75
    pasta e fagioli, 68–69
    pasta with peas, 76–77
    split pea with potatoes, creamy, 72–73

tomato soup with fresh basil, 64
turkey wing soup with winter vegetables,
    78–79
zuppa di pesce, 83–84
Spaghetti
    carbonara, with soppressata and pancetta, 107–8
    with cherry tomatoes and porcini, 97
    with garlic and oil, 86
    Neapolitan spaghetti pie, 133
    puttanesca, 87
    with quick Neapolitan marinara sauce, 90
    alle vongole (with clams), 99
Spaghettini with calamari Fra Diavolo, 103
Spinach, 212
    calzone with anchovies and, 211–12
    spinach pizza, 204
Split pea soup with potatoes, creamy, 72–73
Squid. See Calamari
Stew
    Italian beef, 82
    See also Soups and stews
Strega, 13
Striped bass
    baked, with littlenecks, 138
    oreganata, 138
    alla pizzaiola, 25, 139
Struffoli, 35, 244–47
Sunday sauce alla Russo, traditional, 109–11
Sun-dried tomatoes, 13
    dandelion greens with potatoes and, 175
    fava beans al pomodoro, 177
    stuffed escarole with capers and, 29, 192
    sun-dried tomato bread, 31, 201
    sun-dried tomato sauce, 120
    veal cutlets with artichokes, mushrooms, and,
        154–55
Swiss chard with prosciutto and cipolline, 176

T

Tagliatelle, Mamma Rosina's homemade, 121–22
Taralli con finocchietti, 206
Tiramisù, 236
Tomato(es), 13–14
    bruschetta, 16, 40
    canned caponatina spread, 270–71
    canned plum tomato halves or puree, 275–82
    chicken with mushrooms, olives, and, 167
    fava beans al pomodoro, 177
    focaccia, 31, 202
    freezing, 79
    fresh: dandelion greens with shallots and, 175;
        substituting for canned, 63
    pasta and chickpea soup with basil and, 74–75
    pizza with oregano, anchovies, and, 203
    soup, with fresh basil, 64
    spaghetti with cherry tomatoes and porcini, 97
    See also Sun-dried tomatoes

Tomato puree, 14
    home-canned, 275–82
Tomato sauces
    marinara sauce: eggplant Parmigiana, 187–88;
        quick Neapolitan, 90; rich, 127; stuffed
        chicken breast with mozzarella, 168–69; veal
        Sorrentino, 27, 156–57
    pizzaiola sauce, 165; eggplant with, 179;
        grilled eggplant and portobello with, 180–81;
        grilled steak with, 164; striped bass with,
        25, 139
    pizza sauce, 205
    sun-dried tomato sauce, 120
    traditional Sunday sauce alla Russo, 109–11
    See also Pasta
Tuna
    escarole hearts with white beans and, 57
    fava beans with, 177
    old-fashioned tuna loaf, 141
Turkey wing soup with winter vegetables,
    78–79

V

Vanilla pastry cream, 241
    zeppole filled with, 238
Vanilla powder, 14
Veal
    and chicken soup with tiny meatballs, Maria
        Domenica's, 80–81
    lasagna meatballs, 130
    meatballs, 110–11
    osso buco, 158
    veal Francese, 152–53
    veal Marsala, 151
    veal Scarpetta, 154–55
    veal Sorrentino, **27**, 156–57
Vegetable oil, 14

Vinaigrette
    broccoli rabe vinaigrette, 174
    preserved sweet Italian peppers vinaigrette,
        263–65
Vinegar, preserved red and green cheese peppers
    marinated in, 266
Vinegar peppers, braised pork chops with marinated
    artichoke hearts and, **28**, 161
Vodka, penne alla, 88

W

Walnuts
    biscotti con marmellata, 222–23
    struffoli, **35**, 244–47
Wheat berries, 235
    wheat berry, citrus, and ricotta pie (pizza gran),
        234–35
White beans. *See* Beans
White wine
    and garlic sauce, littlenecks with, 53
    and lemon sauce, veal Francese, 152–53
Wine-flavored honey syrup, for struffoli, 247
Winter vegetables, turkey wing soup with, 78–79

Y

Yeast, 14

Z

Zeppole di Ferrara, 237–38
Zucchini
    blossoms, fried, **18**, 47
    cauliflower soup with green beans, basil, and, 65
    with fresh mint, **29**, 173
    fried, with cheese, 183
    fusilli with eggplant, mushrooms, and, 98
    zucchini carbonara, 107–8
Zuppa di pesce, 83–84